MURDER UNDER GOD'S EYE

MURDER UNDER GOD'S EYE

THE NIGHTMARE KILLING IN STANFORD'S CHURCH

SCOTT HERHOLD

Charleston, SC
www.PalmettoPublishing.com

Murder Under God's Eye

Copyright © 2023 by Scott Herhold

First Edition

Paperback ISBN: 979-8-8229-0774-4

eBook ISBN: 979-8-8229-0775-1

PART ONE

CHAPTER 1

THE SECURITY GUARD

"We got a stiff in here," crackled the voice of Stanford University security guard Steve Crawford over the police radio. Lifted from the slang of a gangster movie, the phrase was meant to describe the half-nude body of the young woman splayed on the floor inside Stanford Memorial Church. It was 5:45 a.m. on Sunday, October 13, 1974, and Crawford was calling for the police to arrive "Code 2," without sirens or lights, a request that discounted an emergency. A stiff? What did he mean? A few seconds later, the security guard told dispatcher Charlie Papp that he thought the young woman had suffered from an overdose. "It's a cold stiff," he said. Papp asked if he wanted an ambulance. "I don't think that will help," Crawford replied.

At the rear of a curved row of pews in the east transept of the ornate, seventy-one-year-old church, the body of nineteen-year-old Arlis Perry lay faceup on the dark-brown cork floor. She wore a brown suede coat, a light-brown sweater, and a beige bra. Nude from the waist down, she was laid out in quasi-ritual fashion, her jeans laid over her in an upside-down pattern. An altar candle had been jammed into her vagina, and a second candle had been pushed under her sweater with enough force to break her bra straps. Her face was a splotchy pink-white color, and she had a split lower lip. The inner parts of her eyelids were red, signaling the bursting blood vessels that come with strangulation. Crawford was correct in judging Arlis beyond rescue. But this was no overdose. It was murder. Whoever ended her life brought fury and passion to the task.

Until that moment, it had seemed like a normal fall weekend on the Stanford campus, a dry, palm-dotted expanse of red tile buildings ambling toward the foothills. The football team, in the middle of a mediocre season, was playing UCLA in Los Angeles. An amnesty rally by the Vietnam Veterans Against the War had taken place at noon on Friday in White Plaza, led by Robert McAfee Brown, a charismatic theology professor. A sprinkling of parties was under way at the fraternity and sorority houses. And everywhere, students were studying, perfecting their Frisbee tosses, and flirting without appearing to try too hard. It wasn't that violent crime was unknown. In the last two years, three young people had been murdered in Stanford's environs, a fact that lent a dull toothache to assumptions of campus safety. Still, no one expected murder in a church, let alone a killing with ritual overtones. At Sunday worship that day, the dean of the chapel, Robert Hamerton-Kelly, was scheduled to preach on the topic of "Glorious Liberty."

At Quillen House, an apartment building that housed married students, one Stanford sophomore was growing deeply worried in those early morning hours. Arlis's nineteen-year-old husband, Bruce Perry, an ambitious premed student with a heavy academic load, wondered where his wife was. The two high-school sweethearts from Bismarck, North Dakota had been married in their hometown less than two months before. After traveling cross-country to California, the two were still learning to live together. Two weeks before, Arlis had taken a clerical job with a Palo Alto law firm. Although they loved each other deeply and shared a strong faith in God, Arlis was lonely, and Bruce was busy with his studies. On a late-night walk to mail letters at the Stanford post office, the couple had a minor spat. Arlis left to walk toward the church. When she didn't return to Quillen, Bruce walked back to the church to try to find his wife. Finally, at 3:00 a.m., he called the police to report Arlis missing. A "be-on-the-lookout" (BOL) was put out for the young woman. But no one checked the church. In the early going, the police assumed it was an ordinary husband-wife tiff that would resolve itself.

The killer's defiance of a house of worship wasn't lost on anyone, although no one could conceive that this case would baffle generations of detectives, launch a theory of satanic crime, and spur the career of one of America's foremost experts on child trauma. Known as "MemChu" on campus, the church had been conceived as a family shrine and an architectural jewel by Jane Stanford, the widow of railroad baron Leland Stanford. Like the European churches that inspired the Stanfords, the sanctuary was built in the shape of a cross, decorated in rich Mediterranean hues of blue and gold, and overseen by a clutch of angels and gorgeous stained-glass windows. Before the earthquake of 1906, the tower of the chapel had featured a huge fresco of an eye, known as "God's Eye" or the "All-Seeing Eye," complete with a tear that seemed ready to fall on worshipers. Viewed from above, Arlis's body was at the edge of the left-hand arm of the cross. She lay about twenty-five yards from a mosaic of the Last Supper behind the altar, a superb artwork that depicted Judas with a winged devil on his shoulder.[1]

It did not take Stanford police officers Debbie Whittemore and Art Nebgen long to grasp that they were confronting a murder with the power to haunt any career. Given the setting, the innocence of the victim, and the layout of the body, the scene bore the unmistakable whiff of evil, as if the devil had stepped from Judas's shoulder to wield havoc. As they tried to bring the situation under control, they waited for help from the Santa Clara County sheriff's department. Only twenty-two, Whittemore showed remarkable poise for a young officer. Hired just a year before, she was reputed to be one of the best shots on the force. She had already had a busy night taking the report of an assault with a wineglass on a walkway at Stern Hall, one of Stanford's residential dorms. Nebgen, thirty-one, a veteran cop but no star, had served a stint with Sunnyvale Public Safety before coming to Stanford. He tried to calm the rattled Crawford over the radio.

"Crawford, back out into the open and stand clear so you can see what's going on around you," Nebgen ordered.

"Yep," Crawford replied. "For information, I just unlocked the three front doors; they're open," he added.

Crawford's report of an overdose confused the reaction to the crime. If it was a murder, an officer would ordinarily call for the full lights-and-siren treatment—"Code 3" in police language. Dispatcher Papp tried to clarify matters, asking Crawford whether he could confirm that he had found a drunk inside the church.

"Negative, a, uh, dead body," the security guard replied.

"Does she have a suede coat on, blue jeans?" asked an unidentified voice, possibly Nebgen, repeating the description put out in the BOL message a few hours before.

"Uh, believe blue jeans present," replied Crawford. "Do not know on the coat."

At 6:05 a.m., the first sheriff's deputies on the scene were Nick Consolo and Ed Nissen, who had been patrolling the affluent West Valley cities of Saratoga, Monte Sereno, and Cupertino, a quiet beat where a burglary counted as a significant event. The sheriff served a huge swath of unincorporated territory, but the department also forged agreements with smaller cities to provide patrols. At Stanford, the sheriff's office handled serious crimes like homicide. Following the playbook for a major crime, the two deputies secured the church, took measurements, and drew a map of the scene. The twenty-eight-year-old Consolo, who had never been assigned to a murder before, took a statement from Crawford, who said he found the body after he opened the church around 5:30 a.m. Spotting an interior door forced open on the west side of the church, Crawford passed in front of the altar and discovered Arlis in the east transept, her body partly hidden by a pew.

Consolo's mission was to hold the scene for the detectives, not to investigate the crime. But the scene struck him as staged, as if an attack had taken place and the body had been arranged afterward. At the time, he thought the most likely suspects were the husband, always under suspicion in the unexplained murder of a spouse, or the security guard who found the body. Years later, Consolo remembered having questions about Crawford's narrative. The deputy did not understand the damage to the interior door, which Crawford said he had locked the night before. "Two and two just didn't add up to four," Consolo recalled.

When the first sheriff's detectives arrived around 6:45 a.m. after racing up Highway 280 from San Jose, they confronted one more mystery. Crawford had left the scene. In a case this serious, his absence was more than irritating. Security guards are expected to know that anyone who discovers a body should remain at the scene. It's one of the tenets of criminal investigation. Any police officer understood it was essential to preserve the evidence and explain what preceded the discovery. The killer could still be lurking around, checking how his work was received. Was the body moved? When was the church last checked? Had he seen the victim before? The smallest detail could matter.

Dispatcher Papp tried to reach the security guard by radio and then by phone in the police annex, a double-wide trailer attached to headquarters at 711 Serra Street, less than a mile away from the church. A few minutes later, as if checking in from exile in a foreign country, Crawford came on the air.

"I'm in the annex," he said. "Did I hear traffic?" Papp told him that he had just tried the telephone in the annex and gotten no answer. Crawford was wanted back at the church. Just how long he was incommunicado is difficult to pin down—it appears to have been at least thirty or thirty-five minutes, though some investigators believe he may have been gone from the scene for an hour.[2] Crawford's colleagues noted he had been upset at finding the body. At Stanford, the not-so-secret truth was that the security guards, who went by the title of community service officer (CSO), possessed only rudimentary training. A number of them, like Crawford, were ex-police officers who were demoted by a new chief who had arrived three years before. What seemed like incompetence could be interpreted as fear.

At 6:55 a.m., not long after Crawford's call, Bruce Perry called the police a second time. It had been almost four hours since he had reported Arlis missing and more than seven since they had parted company near the library. He held out hope that she was locked in the church, a hope that seemed to be vanishing. When he reached Charlie Papp, Bruce asked if there was any news. Papp told him no. For the moment, the young husband did not quibble with the dispatcher.

What investigators were learning from the crime scene could rattle anyone. Arlis's body was splayed behind the rear pew, her left arm flung out to her side, her right arm folded back so that the palm faced down under the small of her back. Her head lay toward the north entrance of the church. Her neck bore two noticeable bruises, one the size of a quarter, the other a dime. There was froth on her lips and beeswax on her inner thigh. Her jeans had been removed and draped over her lower body in a loose V, with the waistband near her feet and the cuff ends extending above her waist, covering her pubic area.

While Arlis still had on her brown suede jacket, the rest of her clothing was in disarray. A thirty-inch altar candle with a 1.5-inch diameter had been pushed up under her bra and lay next to her head. One of the jean legs was draped over the lower part of the candle. The second altar candle, the one jammed into her vagina, had been broken about six inches from the body. Her flower-print panties and clog shoes were found a few inches away from her right foot, on the east side of the body. Although it was not visible immediately, blood stained the cork floor beneath her. The murderer seemed to have nourished an extraordinary hatred for his victim. But Arlis had been in California for only six weeks or so. Who would want to kill her?

At 7:30 a.m., Crawford gave a statement to Sheriff's Sergeant John Johnson at Stanford police headquarters, a red-tiled building that served both police and fire. Despite Crawford's absence from the scene, it was not a hostile talk. A six-footer with a rebellious beard, long sideburns, and a wiseacre manner, the twenty-eight-year-old Crawford traced his routine from the night before much as he had with Consolo. Reporting for his graveyard shift around 10:00 p.m., Crawford went through the sanctuary for the first time around 10:30 or 10:35. He told Johnson he checked the entire church, including the east transept. Making sure that the interior doors were locked, he saw nothing unusual. "He was sure the body was not in the church," Johnson noted in his report. Before he left, Crawford turned up the lights in the sanctuary, which had been dimly illuminated by the altar lights.

When Johnson asked whether he had seen anything suspicious inside Memorial Church, Crawford mentioned that he had seen a young man, about twenty years old, with a Prince Valiant haircut and a dark plaid shirt, sitting not far from where the body was found. Crawford said he had returned around 11:45 p.m.—"give or take"—and announced that the church was closing. He came to the middle of the aisle and found no one inside. After locking up the sanctuary, Crawford walked around the outside of the church, making sure the exterior doors were secured. He said he returned to the Round Room—the church office—around 1:00 a.m. and spent ten or fifteen minutes there checking out the room and the basement.

By his account, Crawford returned to open the front doors of Memorial Church around 5:30 a.m. With Sunday services at 11:00 a.m., worshipers would arrive in a few hours. Crawford reported that the lights in the sanctuary were still on. He had forgotten to turn them off. He noticed that an interior door on the west side of the sanctuary was broken open—investigators determined that it had been damaged—and the door to the outside was closed but unlocked. (On its west side, Memorial Church had a corridor that ran between the interior and the exterior doors.) Then he made the rounds of the church, exploring the corridor behind the broken door and crossing to the eastern transept. Behind the rear row, he found Arlis and pulled her out from under the pew. Crawford told Johnson that he might have touched Arlis's wrist, her waist, and the candle on her body. Unable to revive her, he tried first to reach dispatch from inside the church. Then he went outside through the front door and radioed for help.

Johnson and his partner, Dave Pascual, began assembling the story of how and why Arlis Perry had visited the church the night before. In the first hours after the discovery of the body, the investigators were convinced they had to focus on Bruce Perry. On the radio later that morning, Officer Whittemore teased out the chronology from Papp. Whittemore told Papp that the deputies wanted him to call Doug Williams, the chief dispatcher, and ask him to come down to review and mark the tapes to establish exactly what Bruce had said in his 3:00 a.m. call.

"OK," Papp replied.

"'Cause they're thinking on the husband," Whittemore said.

CHAPTER 2

ARLIS

On a quiet Sunday in Bismarck, Tim Clausnitzer was refereeing a flag football game at Sertoma Park, a popular refuge that sprawled for three miles along the eastern side of the Missouri River. Though the game did not involve tackling, it was no less competitive than a contest with pads. The players were enjoying the brisk fall day. Suddenly, a curly-haired, sixteen-year-old girl named Liz Karlgaard came running across the field.

"Arlis got murdered!" she shouted. "Arlis got murdered!"

Initially, it made no sense. Arlis and Bruce Perry had just settled into their new living quarters in California. Then the story spilled out. Arlis had been found murdered inside the church at Stanford University, where Liz's brother was a student. The authorities were investigating and had arrested no one yet. Clausnitzer felt sick. He knew Arlis and Bruce well, having run with Bruce on Bismarck High School's track team.

"I walked away," he remembered, years later. "I said, *Guys, I'm out of here.*"

Clausnitzer's dismay echoed the thunderclap that hit the city of forty thousand when news of Arlis's murder spread on Sunday afternoon. It was disbelief at first, then a sad quest for facts, and finally, as more details emerged, revulsion that a bright and optimistic young woman should have met such a brutal end. People in Bismarck knew Arlis as an enthusiastic Christian, the daughter of Marv and Jean Dykema. Reliable, practical, and kind, she had graduated from Bismarck High School and gone to the local junior college. Only two months before, she had married Bruce in a ceremony at Bismarck Reformed Church. Now a newlywed who made her faith central to her life had been slain in an ornate house of worship on the campus where her husband studied. The twenty-six-year-old pastor of the Bismarck church, Reverend Don DeKok (pronounced DeCook), got a call from Bruce's father, Duncan Perry, asking him to break the news to the Dykemas. "Just going over to the Dykema household, that was very difficult," he remembered years later. "How do you, in a nice way, tell them what happened?" The news defied any rational explanation.

After the murder, it was easy to cast Arlis as a one-dimensional person, the innocent victim of a horrific crime. The murder inside Memorial Church was so terrible—and affected people so deeply—that the character of the murdered woman was swamped in a tsunami of sorrow. Seeking to cover their bases, deputies inquired about the state of the marriage. Everything they learned was favorable: she was a solid person, someone who loved kids and worked hard. But her personality was not central to their investigation. For the moment, the worst that could be said about Arlis was that she went to pray alone at a church late on a Saturday night. The oddest thing was that she had spoken of feeling that she would die a violent death before she was thirty.

No one in Bismarck doubted that Arlis Dykema and Bruce Perry loved each other. But inside the imposing yellow-brick structure that was Bismarck High School, their classmates had not seen them as a couple destined for each other from the start. Arlis's father worked as a mechanic and ran a service station. Bruce's father was a prominent dentist. Bruce's family lived in one of the most affluent parts of town, Highland Acres. Arlis lived in a plainer house on Twenty-Ninth Street, on a tract that hugged an industrial area on the east side. Bruce wanted to study at an elite university like Stanford or Northwestern. Arlis was tugged more by home and friends and faith. In their religious beliefs, Bruce was more cerebral, Arlis more evangelistic. While Bruce was a track star and Arlis was a cheerleader, their friends didn't foresee the epoxy of romance.

Before they started dating in their senior year, 1972–73, an incident occurred that revealed much about the pair. Despite his superior performance in sports and academics, Bruce was shy and reserved around girls. His friends remember that he wasn't convinced he would swoon over any woman.

"I don't think I'm going to date anyone," they remember him saying. "Whoever I date, I think God is going to have to drop her in my lap." Having heard of this prediction, which disheartened other girls, Arlis approached him one day and plopped into his lap. When Bruce asked Arlis to the Snowball winter dance, their friends were surprised. The tale revealed Arlis's pluck, humor, and boldness in deflating bravado. Bruce admired all three qualities.

Molded by her Midwestern family and community, Arlis was a vibrant woman, amiable yet with her own quirks and foibles. She came from a lineage of farmers. In the late nineteenth century, her Dutch ancestors migrated to Emmons County, southeast of Bismarck. Arlis's great-grandfather, John Millenaar, a full-bearded man sometimes called "Father John," was born in 1862 in Barendrecht, a town just south of Rotterdam. Her family grew wheat and raised animals near a crossroads named Westfield, North Dakota, nicknamed "Dutch Shoe" for the "Hollanders" who settled in the southern part of the county. Westfield had a church, a school, a telephone office, and a blacksmith shop. In those early days, the church played an essential role in immigrant communities—and the Dykemas attended the Hope Reformed Church, a wooden structure with a steeply pitched roof. In a large extended family living off the land, survival demanded hard work. A mid-1920s photo reveals that Arlis looked very much like her grandmother, Wilmina Millenaar Dykema (1903–1998)—the same build, the same cheekbones, the same way of brushing her hair.

Arlis Kay Dykema was born in Emmons County on February 22, 1955, as Marv and Jean's third child. When she was a year old, Marv moved the family to Mandan, the small town across the Missouri

River from Bismarck, where he worked as a mechanic at the Chevrolet dealership. From there, the family moved to Eighteenth Street in Bismarck, and then to Twenty-Ninth Street, where Arlis had a basement bedroom. In the tight-knit town, Marv and Jean paid attention to their kids. During the Vietnam War and the surge of the counterculture, Arlis was shielded from the anger and violence that swept other parts of the country. She was not a rebellious girl—but she was no pious wallflower either. She had dated only one boy seriously before going out with Bruce.

If life wasn't always easy or luxurious, it was upbeat and marked by close friendships. For seventy-five cents an hour, Arlis and a friend would rent a tandem bike, tying a transistor radio to the handlebars, for a tour around town. In music, her tastes were mainstream rather than edgy. She liked pop and rock but not heavy metal—Paul Revere & the Raiders were an early favorite. Endowed with a gentle sense of mischief, she knew how to tease. In ninth grade, when the school day began with the Pledge of Allegiance, one of Arlis's friends drew the task of leading the recitation. Nervous about getting the pledge right, the girl wrote out the words on a sheet of paper. On the appointed day, Arlis grabbed the sheet away, and her friend froze.

"She probably enjoyed every minute," her friend remembered later.

In the memories of her friends, Arlis's sense of humor shines through. When Arlis's very Dutch aunt had trouble pronouncing her friend Peggy's name—she called her "Piggy"—Arlis rolled with laughter.

On the cheerleading squad for the Bismarck High Demons (colors: maroon and white), Arlis thrived. A picture in her senior yearbook showed the cheerleaders gathered around a two-toned mid-'50s sedan, with most of the girls perched atop the vehicle. Arlis sat smiling in the front passenger seat, leaning backward as if she enjoyed the ride. Skilled in sewing clothes, she was always stylish. In junior high school, she once took a final exam with rollers in her hair because she was due to attend her aunt's wedding. Her swept-across blond hair resembled that of the Rolling Stones' Brian Jones, who died the year that Arlis entered ninth grade. The photo of Arlis that ran with the first stories about her murder, a geeky and unfocused shot, did no justice to how attractive she was.

After the murder, some of her acquaintances described her as quiet. But that adjective missed the mark. As a cheerleader, Arlis displayed the instincts of a sorority rush chair. To honor the birthday of a cheerleader or a favorite athlete, she insisted on baking a cake, a project in which her enthusiasm outpaced her skill. A cake project would end with every cupboard open and flour sprinkled around the Dykema kitchen. Arlis once took an upside-down layer cake out of the oven, turned it over, and saw its contents running in every direction.

"I said, *You have to check whether it's done first,*" her sister Karen remembered later.

Dutiful and hardworking rather than brilliant, Arlis was known for marking up textbooks and underlining passages she wanted to remember. Because Bismarck High had to reuse textbooks, the prac-

Arlis as a cheerleader at Bismarck High School.

tice irked teachers. Arlis, however, was too conscientious for them to reproach her. As a teenager, she almost always held a job. She was a popular babysitter, and a coach at Bismarck High School, Rudy Steidl, later told police that she was absolutely trustworthy around children. (In fact, Arlis adored her young niece.) Outside the home, she worked at the Dairy Queen. In the year after she graduated from Bismarck High School, when Bruce was a freshman at Stanford, Arlis had a job as a receptionist at the dental firm of Bruce Perry's father, Duncan Perry.

Like her older brother, Larry, and her sister, Karen, Arlis was steeped in the church. Marv and Jean Dykema had been founding members of the Bismarck Reformed Church, which first met at the Dykema home and later constructed a soaring sanctuary southeast of downtown at 1617 Michigan Avenue. The family attended church on Sunday mornings and, as her friends remember it, usually on Sunday evenings. The Dykemas always prayed before meals. A child who arrived late for grace had to do all the dishes rather than splitting the task with other family members. Arlis was rarely tardy, but the punishment fell more than once on Larry.

All this prepared her for the template of belief that she adopted with four of her friends in her sophomore year at BHS. Calling themselves the "Soul Sisters," the five girls embraced the idea that Jesus was their savior. Their relationship to God was no longer a transaction brokered through the church. It was a personal commitment. With her friends, Arlis was attracted to Young Life, a Christian movement sparked by a charismatic leader named Ron Keller, a former advertising man who urged the students to think about their purpose in life—which, in his vision, was to follow Jesus. Avoiding the hard sell and opting for entertaining skits instead, Keller invited kids to meetings at the American Legion Hall, where it wasn't unusual to find three hundred students from Bismarck High and its Catholic rival, St. Mary's Central High School. Arlis and her friends carried their shared faith further, meeting for Bible study and praying for one another. The five girls even took road trips together, once camping—disastrously—at a pig farm.

Like many of her classmates, Arlis joined the Fellowship of Christian Athletes, the most popular extracurricular group at Bismarck

High. The FCA grew through the encouragement of several influential coaches who believed in Christianity themselves and saw it as useful motivation for athletes. Bruce Perry belonged, as did many of Arlis's friends. A photo in a yearbook from that era shows the members spilling out of the room. Arlis and Bruce helped out with FCA "huddles," small groups centered on devotion and Bible study. Bruce had even taken the weekend before his wedding to teach leadership to kids in junior high school. Rejecting the drugs and rebellion of the 1960s, the FCA and Young Life drew an astonishingly diverse circle. Even nonathletes joined the FCA.

Arlis did not shy away from talking about her faith. It was one of the first things people noticed about her. In a way that seems unusual in a more secular age, her judgments about others turned on their spiritual progress. In her first month at Stanford, she wrote to her friend Jenny Wavrin and mentioned that a mutual acquaintance named Mark had lost his mother to death.

"I had heard that Mark was advancing spiritually so I only pray that this will not be a set back (sic)," she wrote. "I'm glad to know that all of you will help him and encourage him."

Nor was Arlis afraid of confronting others who rejected Jesus. In the early 1970s, high school students in Bismarck often gathered at a large, flat parking lot near a pizza place on the north side of town, a perch with a view of the city. The gatherings were so popular that they attracted a group of cultists who wore red clerical-style collars in imitation of priests. Calling themselves the "Sons of Man," they were clean-cut young men who mingled with the high school students, challenging their embrace of evangelical Christianity. At least one time, according to Bruce's track comrade, Tim Clausnitzer, Arlis and Bruce confronted the red-collared men about their beliefs.

"Bruce and I and Arlis and a couple of other people got into an argument with these guys," Clausnitzer remembered.

All of that, however, fell short of a portrait of Arlis as a proselytizer who so offended cultists that it planted a motive for murder. Though she could be judgmental, Arlis had a sweetness and sense of humor that tempered her approach to evangelism.

"In the connotation of the time, she was just a girl who was learning about her faith," said a friend, Dale Preszler. "If you're talking about religious fundamentalists who were out on the street and waving a flag, that was not her," he said.

In the academic year 1973–74, when Bruce was a freshman at Stanford, Arlis attended Bismarck Junior College, now Bismarck State College. Lonely for her boyfriend, she visited Bruce at Stanford in May 1974, staying in the dorm room of another girl. Eager not to spend another year apart, they agreed to marry three months later. Certainly, physical attraction was a big reason for their decision. In their circles in Bismarck, it was not generally accepted for couples to live together before marriage. Premarital sex was not assumed. Bruce and Arlis were only nineteen—Bruce was two months younger than Arlis—but in many ways, they were more mature than their age. Arlis was solid, kind, and down-to-earth. Bruce was ambitious, smart, and eager to be married to Arlis.

So at 7:00 p.m. on August 17, 1974, they were wed by Rev. De-Kok at Bismarck Reformed Church, the church her parents had helped to found. A photo of the bride and groom that appeared in the *Bismarck Tribune* showed an elated Arlis tightly holding Bruce's arm with a bouquet of flowers in front of her. Bruce had a more sober look, holding his hand at a right angle to his waist as he gazed at the photographer. After the ceremony, the newlyweds headed west in Bruce's car for the 1,610-mile trip to Palo Alto, stopping in Yellowstone National Park on the way. In early September, they settled into married housing: apartment 2-C at Quillen, a twelve-story high-rise that had been completed three years before. Arlis wrote to a friend that the apartment was "really nice," with a small but handy kitchen. The newlyweds bought a tapestry carpet for the living room. It seemed like a hopeful moment—the forging of a new life.

At Stanford, however, Arlis was lonelier than she had ever been. She wrote poignantly about missing her friends. "Friends are hard to find here," she wrote. "Been tempted to knock on doors and ask if anybody needs a friend. That is the only bad thing I have to say about my new life. But I guess we just have to appreciate each other and trust the Lord for new friends too." In an earlier letter, she had told Jenny, "Nobody is very personal at all, and they don't even say hello when you ride up the elevator with them."

With pride, Arlis reported that Bruce was beginning classes in drama, biology, and organic chemistry as well as teaching bonehead math. "Get that, would ya?" she wrote. "Now all we need is a job for the little wife." She told Jenny that she had been going to interviews "right and left." One promising lead was as a receptionist at a law firm. "One other good thing about that one—no uniforms," she wrote. Arlis seemed to have a confidence that reflected the ups and downs of married life. "I've, I mean *We've* really, really learned a lot together lately (since we've been married)," she wrote. "It seems like we've been faced with trial after trial, but we've settled down a lot about worrying and everything, and we're really learning to trust a lot more." At another point in the correspondence, she wrote that Bruce's freshman roommate had joined a fraternity with a number of football players. "So I do have an inside source on available good-looking men," she wrote to Jenny. "However, I'm sure you'll never find one as great as mine!"

Arlis's letters foreshadowed nothing of what would happen to her. But the investigators later learned something unsettling from Arlis's sister, Karen, who was four years older. Arlis told her family that she had a feeling that she would die a violent death before she was thirty. The detectives noted it down without embellishment. It didn't seem to have anything to do with the murder. Years later, I asked Karen about Arlis's statement.

"She said that, yeah," Karen said. "I don't know if it was a dream or just a feeling. I said, You're crazy. You have no way of knowing that. It was almost as if she didn't expect to get older. But you know, sometimes people just say things like that. It wasn't a gloom-or-doom kind of thing. She was probably the most positive person I've ever known."

Arlis never made it to twenty years old, much less thirty. After she was murdered, the public memories of her life centered on her faith rather than her strange hunch. Five days after the murder, on Friday morning, October 18, Rev. Don DeKok presided over Arlis's funeral at Bismarck Reformed Church, the same place he had conducted the wedding two months before. Using Arlis's Bible, DeKok read from the remarks she had written in the margins next to the text. ("Nice," Arlis wrote next to a Psalm she liked.) One of those passages came from Psalm 34, a work attributed to David as he appeared before a Philistine king. "I will bless the Lord at all times. His praise shall continually be in my mouth."

DeKok paused and then said, "It was."

"Somebody's going to say that Arlis didn't have a chance to learn what life's all about," DeKok said. "On the contrary, Arlis knew exactly what life is all about—that it is full of joy and of sorrow, of victory and trials, and *man is like a mere breath, his days like a passing shadow.*"

CHAPTER 3
THE DISPATCHER

For more than four hours early Sunday morning, Stanford police dispatcher Charlie Papp could not get Bruce Perry's name straight. When Bruce called to report his wife missing at 3:00 a.m., Papp asked him to spell his name. "P-E-R-R-Y," Bruce said. Papp heard "Terry" and embraced the mistake with the conviction of a man misreading a compass and leading a scouting party in the wrong direction. Announcing the name of the missing woman on air, he identified her as "Arlis Terry." When Bruce called back at 6:55 a.m., Papp addressed him as "Mr. Terry." This could not have reassured a distraught husband.

In the end, the miscue made little difference, though it confused the first police attempts to obtain the backgrounds of key characters.[1] What mattered was not Arlis's last name—by then, it was no longer something the victim could answer to—but the description: five foot six, 120 pounds, blond, with a brown suede jacket and blue jeans. (Arlis was actually five-five and a half and 125 pounds.) If Papp's mistake hinted at anything, it was the frenzied night that was about to envelop the sixty-year-old dispatcher. Without a local watch commander, and with only a small crew of officers on campus, Papp was left to manage the unfolding tragedy from a C-shaped console in a modest first-floor room at the Stanford police and fire complex. Neither his training nor his temperament had prepared him for the task.

Dispatchers serve as a police department's link to the public and the nerve system for its officers. They do not direct an investigation. Like football assistants who signal plays from the sidelines, they strive to deliver facts and orders as clearly and succinctly as possible. Papp's duties that night, however, went far beyond gridiron semaphore. In football terms, he was asked to strap on pads, run onto the field, and start blocking in a melee he did not understand. For all the adrenaline that coursed through him in those hours, he ended his shift exhausted and chagrined. "He tried to do the best he could with what he had," said a Stanford officer who knew him. "It all fell on him like a ton of bricks."

In the mid-1970s, Stanford's dispatchers did not enjoy an enviable reputation on campus. In his memoir, *War Stories Down on Stanford's Farm*, retired Stanford Police Captain Raoul Niemeyer noted that the dispatchers often mistreated callers.

"The complaints kept streaming in," wrote Niemeyer, who reserved special scorn for two early-evening dispatchers he called "The Bobbsey Twits." "The same old saw: arrogance (primarily from the

Bobsies), smart-mouth talk, hanging up on callers, not answering the radio when the officers in the field called, and even blowing off high-ranking officials." Niemeyer was so upset by the duo that he once took to the microphone himself when the dispatchers walked out in a job action.

Charles Carl Papp, who was left out of Niemeyer's critique, was a rangy, gray-haired veteran who wore badge number two among Stanford's team of five dispatchers. Born in Alton, Illinois, and raised in Youngstown, Ohio, he was an Army Air Corps veteran who had pursued a cavalcade of careers—potato-chip-company employee, steelworker, freight-train conductor, title-company man, insurance salesman, police officer. His wife, Mary, was a well-liked secretary at the university. A fit man at five foot nine and 185 pounds, Papp could flash humor, even at his own expense. In 1968, when student demonstrators took over the Old Union, a three-story building that housed several offices, then-patrolman Papp joked that they had seized control of the television set he used. "I haven't been able to watch TV since you've been keeping me away from it," he lamented.

Unenthusiastic about patrol work, Papp applied for a dispatching position when one came open, even though other dispatchers wondered whether he was well-equipped for the job. He could resist—"get his back up," one colleague noted—if he felt disrespected. "He was the kind of guy who didn't walk away from anything," said his son, Bill Papp. "People never got in his face for very long."

On the night Arlis Perry was killed, Charlie Papp could not avoid having people in his face. They commanded him, they admonished him, they evaded him, they questioned him. He did not handle it well. Papp's nightmare began unfolding when he got the first call from Bruce, who had returned to the married-student apartment at Quillen House.

"Um, I think my wife is missing," Bruce said. "I think she might be locked in MemChu." Odd as the notion sounded, the nineteen-year-old sophomore had a reason for that idea. He later told investigators that in his freshman year at Stanford, a roommate who suffered from obsessive-compulsive disorder had gone to Memorial Church one night and gotten locked in. It wasn't out of the question that the same thing had happened to Arlis.

Bruce did not tell Papp about the nature of his tiff with Arlis except to say it was something he did not want to talk to his wife about—and that Arlis had broken away and headed toward the church. Papp was skeptical.

"You don't really know where she's at, do you?" he asked.

Bruce explained that the last time he had seen her, Arlis was by the Meyer Memorial Library and walking toward the church. "And I went back, and she went, um, she wasn't, I don't think she was too mad at me," he said.

Papp took a description of Arlis, saying, "Well, we'll have someone look around for her. And, uh, if she does come in, give us a call, huh?" The dispatcher then got on the radio with Steve Crawford, the security guard responsible for the Old Quad and Memorial Church. Papp and Crawford had worked together for three years, and the two friends began with a joke. After identifying Crawford, who went by the call signal L-25, Papp said, "Well, what are you selling? Or are you buying?"

The facile Crawford responded in kind: "Whatever you have the price for."

After the two shared a laugh, Papp got down to business:

> PAPP: Well, I just got a call from an unhappy husband. He and his wife had an argument earlier, and they sound like youngsters, and he thinks his wife might have gone into MemChu.
>
> CRAWFORD: Hmm. The church has already been locked up.
>
> DISPATCHER: It's been locked up; there's no one in there at all that you know of?
>
> CRAWFORD: No. It's been locked up at twelve o'clock.
>
> DISPATCHER: Did you see a WFA (white female adult) walking around, blond, shoulder-length hair, glasses?
>
> CRAWFORD: Let's see, there was six or nine people out in front of the church. A white blouse, by chance?
>
> PAPP: No, he says a brown suede coat and blue jeans.
>
> CRAWFORD: Hmm—no, I can't say that I did. Yet there were some dressed couples drifting around, around midnight, when I locked up, and there was

a girl with two guys, two girls with a guy, you can't tell…

PAPP: Two girls with a guy? Two guys with a girl?

CRAWFORD: You can't tell these days.

As the two men joked about the oddities of gender appearance, Crawford promised to keep an eye out for Arlis. "We get the lost and found, uh, calls now?" Crawford said, a remark that prompted more laughter between the two men. He then continued to his lunch at the Jordan Quad, about five blocks away. Papp put out a BOL for Arlis, but no one ever checked the church itself. When a couple of young women were spotted behind Memorial Church a while later, Crawford got on the radio once more to caution that he had already locked the church. Although he did not explicitly warn other officers away, his words suggested no search of MemChu was needed.

That missed check later emerged as a critical point. Had police searched the church after Bruce's 3:00 a.m. call, Arlis's body might have been found a few hours earlier. (The coroner put the time of death between midnight and 1:00 a.m.) Instead, the body wasn't found until after Crawford reopened the church at 5:30 a.m. While an earlier search would not have saved Arlis, it would have spurred a quicker investigation. It was a failure that underscored the lack of weight Stanford police gave to Bruce's report.

When Crawford returned to the air at 5:45 a.m. to announce that he had found a stiff inside Memorial Church, Papp's nightmare started to crest. Officer Nebgen reported that there were "very definite peculiar circumstances" around the body. Then came a series of turf comedies that foreshadowed later disputes. An unnamed sheriff's official ordered Papp not to allow anyone into the crime scene.

"You didn't call the coroner, did you?" the official asked.

"Yeah, we did already," Papp replied.

"OK, the coroner is not to go into the scene whatsoever," ordered the sheriff's man. Nebgen and Officer Debbie Whittemore, who had gone into the church to view the body, were ordered to retrace their steps, touching nothing.

The demands on Papp did not relent. A chorus of law enforcement agencies converged on the church, singing in different keys. A sheriff's car could not find the scene. The sheriff's office ordered Papp to call the dean of the chapel, Robert Hamerton-Kelly, to tell him there could be no services inside the church that morning. At several points in the hubbub, the dispatcher confused MemChu, the nickname for the church, with MemAud, the nickname for the nearby Memorial Auditorium. The sheriff's watch commander in San Jose, Lieutenant Richard Saldivar, wanted to know if it was really a homicide. "They don't know at this time," said Papp, playing it safe.

As if that weren't enough, Papp was then asked to locate Crawford, who had gone missing from the crime scene. Papp understood how ridiculous the situation was: he was trying to find the guard who found the body. When he called the guard's apartment, Crawford's wife, Joyce, answered the phone. Papp identified himself and asked, "Is your husband there?"

"No, he's not," replied Joyce.

"Did he call earlier or something?" Papp asked.

"Uh," replied Joyce.

Papp pushed further. "I know I called your line a little earlier and it was busy," the dispatcher said.

"No, why, what seems to be the problem?" Joyce asked.

"Well, we need him out here," replied Papp. "If he comes home, or if he calls, tell him to call the station. It's urgent, OK?" Joyce said she would. "Thank you," Papp said.

"Um-hmm," replied the twenty-two-year-old waitress.

One of Papp's most trying moments came a few minutes later, at 6:55 a.m., when Bruce Perry called back to find out whether his wife had been found. It was more than an hour after Arlis's body had been discovered in the church and nearly four hours after Bruce had reported his wife missing. Papp had been skeptical when the young man called at 3:00 a.m. Now he fudged the truth.

> PAPP: Stanford fire emergency, Papp.
> BRUCE: This is Bruce Perry.
> PAPP: Yes sir.
> BRUCE: I called before about my wife.
> PAPP: Yes sir.
> BRUCE: Is there any information yet?
> PAPP: Not that I know of as yet, Mr. Terry. If we do get any, we'll give you a call.
> BRUCE: OK.
> PAPP: OK.

It wasn't accurate that Papp had no information, but in a homicide case, a dispatcher can be cashiered for divulging too much. The first allegiance is to the troops in the field. (Any reporter who has spent time on the police beat knows this well. It's not uncommon for a dispatcher to say nothing is happening even when a double homicide has occurred a half hour before.) Moments later, Papp radioed his officers to ask them whether the body in the church was in fact Arlis. "The reason I asked is that I just received a call from the, uh, Mr. Bruce Terry, again, questioning if we had any whereabouts on his ex," he told them.

Officer Debbie Whittemore answered, saying, "The sheriff's office advises, do not give him any information. She's still missing." Then she added for Papp's benefit: "The coroner will contact him when he gets done here."

Later that morning, Whittemore went over events with Papp, seeking details of the call from Bruce. "At three o'clock, can you remember if he said she had left a couple hours earlier or if she had just left?" she asked.

"No, no, no, he said twelve o'clock…that's what I told twenty-five [Crawford]," Papp said.

"OK," Whittemore said. "Because he (Crawford) couldn't remember. He's kind of shaken up."

Knowing that he had not been forthcoming, Papp was still bothered by his conversations with Bruce. He explained to Whittemore that he had told the sophomore at 6:55 a.m. that he had no information.

PAPP: And then the reason I called you people to find out if—if I did know if this is the party. It is the party, isn't it?

WHITTEMORE: Yes, it is.

PAPP: Well, I'll be damned. Well, what happened, overdose or what?

WHITTEMORE: Well, she's laying on the floor with her clothes off. With a bunch of candles.

PAPP: With what?

WHITTEMORE: I'll tell you when I come in.

CHAPTER 4

PASTOR'S SON

When I arrived at the San Jose *Mercury News* as a reporter in November 1977, the Memorial Church murder was still fresh in public memory. Among the stories that circulated at our bureau in Mountain View, it was lumped in with the other young women killed on or near the Stanford campus within a twenty-month period: Leslie Perlov, Janet Taylor, and Arlis Perry, recited as a trinity of lethality. Several reporters had covered parts of the cases—and everyone had a theory, embellished with a journalistic sense of the macabre. Before I knew its strange tendrils, Arlis's murder intrigued me. It felt like a crime that occurred in my front yard.

I am the son of a Lutheran pastor, a good and gregarious man who had a profound influence on my life. In the lore of the church, I am a "P.K.," or preacher's kid, which means I was destined to be one of two things: a virtuous, well-behaved child or an absolute hellion. In my circles, there was no middle ground. Perhaps because of a lack of imagination, I erred on the side of virtue. My worst transgression growing up was to crawl down a manhole with my buddy Jon and smoke cigarettes at the bottom. It said something about my aptitude for crime that we were caught by a utility worker, who warned us—implausibly, I thought—that we had committed a federal offense. Because I was no hellion, I was instead immersed in the church. I knew the liturgy, the imagery, the hymns, and many of my father's anecdotes by heart. In a pinch, I could mimic the giving of the bread and wine in Communion.

In an indirect way, it was my father's six-month departure from his Sunday job that led to my interest in the Arlis Perry case. Partly because my dad, Bob Herhold, was more liberal than his flocks—and defied the boundaries of Lutheran political consensus from the pulpit—we moved often. In the early 1960s, with the hope that a drier climate might ease the asthma of my sisters, the Herhold family trekked westward to Tucson, where there was no Lutheran pulpit immediately available. My father took an interim job as the night police reporter for *The Arizona Daily Star*. I remember visiting him in the offices of *The Star*, a place that reeked of cigarettes and ink and sweat. I was transfixed. I loved the humor of the newsroom. (When the big sign for the nearby Hotel Pioneer lost the lights for the "E" and "L" in its first word, reporters savored the moment.) Later, when I saw my dad challenge speakers at the Tucson Press Club, I came to think of journalism as a meld of crusade and verbal brawl. Assigned to write about the cross-country team on my college daily, I decided then and there that I wanted to be a reporter.

In 1967, just as I was leaving for my first year in college, my parents and younger siblings moved to Palo Alto, where my father came to know many of the preachers on the Stanford campus. Most of the clergy were active in the same social-justice circles, joining in the same anti-Vietnam War protests. A number of them came over to my parents' house in Palo Alto to argue politics. I can remember the great Stanford theologian, the movie-star-handsome Robert McAfee Brown, sitting in a chair in our family house and talking about the disgrace of Vietnam. As it happened, my father had his own odd take on the Perry murder. He thought the cops should not exclude ministers from their radar. Given the strange setting and layout of the body, one of them might have done it. He need not have worried: the detectives gave no clerical discount to ministers. I teased my dad that he lacked faith in his brethren. My father always ministered to doubters. It was the strength of his preaching and writing.

In the *Mercury News* bureau, which operated on the first floor of a forgettable six-story office building at the San Antonio Shopping Center, Stanford offered the most fertile territory for stories. I was assigned to the City of Mountain View and the Whisman School District, but these were muddy detours from the on-ramp of big-time journalism. I'm not sure I ever did a story on the Whisman School District. *The Mercury News* was on the ascent as a newspaper, and by today's standards, we were given lavish space for our stories. I can remember doing a long story about the first day of school for an incoming Stanford freshman, a young man who later became a media executive in Los Angeles. It was hard to find someone dull on the Stanford campus.

Over the years that followed, I covered a clutch of prominent murders. I wrote about a high school teacher who was stabbed to death outside her San Jose classroom, an accountant who was strangled to death in her cottage on Meridian Avenue, and a Los Altos woman who disappeared amid a bitter separation from her husband. All of them were heartbreaking. But the Perry murder stood out. From a journalistic standpoint, it had three elements that lifted it beyond the mundane: its setting in the church, the ritual layout of the body, and the sheer unfairness of the crime. The killing evoked something in my own past. My parents had come from Minneapolis, one of the early stops on my father's nomadic path as a preacher. I *knew* Midwesterners as devout and likable as Arlis. It was like the murder of a second cousin. Although I wended toward skepticism about religion as an adult, the Memorial Church murder left its mark on me too. Everything about the killing insulted belief. It snubbed my father's faith.

One other reason for my interest in murder lingered, though it was more removed and from my mother's side of the family. My great-grandfather, Charles Wilmot Townsend, a doctor on Staten Island, was murdered in a sensational case in 1907. When a woman died in childbirth under his care, her husband held it against my great-grandfather. Breaking into Dr. Townsend's house a year later, he waited in the hallway, checking his watch until the hour and minute his wife had died. Then he shot my great-grandfather as he lay in his bed. Knowing the path of the bullet through his abdomen—he had served as a coroner himself—Dr. Townsend diagnosed it as a mortal wound. "It's all up with me," he said. He died without identifying his killer, saying that it was better that one person died than two. (Capital punishment was still very much alive then.) He left five children, including my grandfather. By the time I came to maturity two generations later, it was not really a sensitive topic in my family. But the story endured, in part because the killer promised revenge on his wife's tombstone. (He was spared the electric chair on grounds of insanity.) Every time I thought of the death of the "poor doctor," as my mother called her grandfather, I was reminded of how far the coils of murder reached for the survivors.

In the public eye, most old murders are forgotten as time passes. There are too many new ones. But the Perry case was a scab that refused to heal, resistant to disinfectant. Every time the bandage of facts was peeled away, the wound was just as raw, maybe rawer. Whenever my newspaper did a story about unsolved murders, the homicide in the church stood at the top of the list. I told myself that if the cops ever solved the case, I was going to quit my day job and try to write a book.

As an amateur investigator, I nourished my own conceit, born of my P.K. past. I thought I knew more about church symbols than the detectives did. If I could just find out what the murderer was trying to say by laying out her jeans in such a manner, I could explain the motive and solve the case. I ordered several books and a CD about Christian symbols. Was the body laid out as a kind of cross? As one of the many symbols in the church? The Alpha and Omega? The Chi Rho? I was assuming that the killer was trying to send a message about religion with the layout of the body. As I got deeper into my research, I learned more humility about my ability to untangle symbols.

Later in my career, I became a local columnist, a challenging and time-consuming job that took me away from the murder in the church. I wrote about development proposals, about local history and politics, about odd figures in the news. Despite all that, I was still curious when I learned that sheriff's detectives had renewed their interest in the Arlis Perry case. When I retired after forty years with *The Mercury News*, in November 2017, I began researching the murder that had intrigued me for so long. After all, I was still a pastor's son—and, for that matter, a pastor's father. A few years before I began my quest, my daughter Becky was ordained as a Lutheran minister.

CHAPTER 5

THE CYCLIST

The phone rang at Sgt. John M. Johnson's home in Campbell at around 6:00 a.m. on Sunday, October 13, piercing the blanket of morning darkness. The thirty-eight-year-old detective, a fit man and committed cyclist, was on call, prepared to catch a big case. On the line was Lt. Richard Saldivar, the sheriff's watch commander, who told Johnson he was needed at Stanford. There wasn't much information, but a young woman had been found slain in the church. In police language, it was a 187, or murder.

"There had been a homicide, and they wanted me to respond," Johnson remembered in his laconic way years later.

Johnson quickly got dressed. A native of the Sunset District of San Francisco, where many of his neighbors were cops, firefighters, or city workers, Johnson was known as a by-the-book man, a detective who knew how to organize a case and follow leads. In his decade in the sheriff's office, Johnson had served on patrol, worked in the jail, and completed an unsatisfying stint in the organized-crime unit before joining the detective bureau to investigate robberies and homicides. Known as "JJ" or "Johnny," Johnson was well-liked by his peers, respected as a straight shooter. His bicycling regimen left him in enviable shape. It wasn't unusual for the sergeant to pedal twenty or twenty-five miles with a friend before heading to work, sometimes following up with an afternoon game of racquetball. A decent and honest supervisor who helped found the Deputy Sheriffs' Association, Johnson could still flash a temper if things were done improperly. On a task force of detectives in another homicide case, he once snapped a pencil in half in disgust when he heard that an investigator had interviewed a witness without preparing himself. "Just do the job," he liked to say.

When Lt. Walt Konar of the Stanford police arrived at Johnson's house for the twenty-one-mile trip up Highway 280 to Stanford Memorial Church, it was still murky outside. In mid-October in California, the sun did not rise until after 7:00 a.m. Konar was the Stanford officer assigned to the Arlis Perry case, which meant he worked in tandem with the sheriff's office, the agency responsible for handling serious crimes on campus. Tall, athletic, and fascinated by sports cars, the twenty-eight-year-old lieutenant was a hardworking investigator who had recently joined the Stanford department after serving in the sheriff's department. With an urgency unknown to Sunday churchgoers, Konar sped up the freeway with Johnson as his passenger. In an irony that stayed with them for years, they were pulled over for speeding by a California Highway Patrol officer, who let them go after learning their mission. ("What the hell," Johnson said later.)

As the case unfolded, it consumed the attention of dozens of law enforcement officers, including investigators from the FBI, the California Department of Justice, the sheriff's department, the district attorney's office, Stanford University, and the San Jose police. It produced a case file of hundreds of pages. It haunted a campus and a sheriff's department for more than forty years, easily eclipsing murders in less exalted settings. Three cops, however, stood out early on. One was Johnson, who tried to impose order on the initial case, assembling whatever scraps of evidence and testimony he could. The second was Sheriff's Sgt. Tom Beck, a dogged investigator who identified a critical missing clue. And the third was Captain Raoul Niemeyer of the Stanford police, an ex-sheriff's deputy who strove to sustain public interest in the case. For all of them, the murder of Arlis Perry stood as an outrage, almost as if one of their own children had been killed. "The old-school cops lived it; they took it home with them," said retired Capt. Kevin Jensen, who joined the department later. "To them, this was personal."

In the mid-1970s, the Santa Clara County sheriff's department counted as an established varsity in county law enforcement, though it was emerging from a checkered past. Just after World War II, a longtime sheriff, Bill Emig, was convicted of running a gaming operation and forced to quit. Under the pipe-smoking Sheriff James Geary, the department was growing but not improving as swiftly as the San Jose police, which had a nonelected chief. An accomplished athlete and skier who had served as undersheriff before defeating ex-Supervisor Sam Della Maggiore for sheriff in 1970, Geary had focused on the operations of the 1958-era jail, which grew overcrowded as the Santa Clara Valley boomed. Some of his deputies grumbled that the sheriff gave less attention to the patrol and detective divisions. In criminal justice circles, the joke was that a murderer was better off dumping a body in unincorporated territory, where sheriff's deputies patrolled, than in the city of San Jose. That was probably unfair. The sheriff's office boasted a number of veteran investigators who were versed in handling big cases. But it spoke to a reputation the department would have preferred to shed.

It was about 6:45 a.m. when Johnson and Konar arrived at the church. Like everyone else who glimpsed the crime scene, Johnson could not forget it. "It happened in a church, that was the biggest thing," he told me. "I'm not that religious a guy, but it just wasn't right. The second thing was that it was gruesome. It was beyond the pale for me."

Putting aside their disgust, the sergeant and his partner, Sgt. Dave Pascual, divided up the work. Pascual and Stanford Capt. Raoul Niemeyer interviewed Arlis's husband, Bruce. Johnson talked to security guard Steve Crawford, who found the body. From that conversation, police developed their first chronology of what had happened the night before. Johnson also took responsibility for the crime scene investigation, which sought to establish how the killer had gotten to Arlis and how he had escaped. Among other duties, Johnson had to keep the media outside the church at bay. Years later, he remembered talking to one aggressive television reporter who wanted to film the scene inside Memorial Church. "Look, you and I both know that's not gonna happen," he warned the newsman.

The detectives were operating in a baffling half-light. They did not yet know what the murder weapon was. Beyond learning that Arlis was married to a Stanford sophomore, Johnson had no background on the victim. And the investigators did not know what was said when dispatcher Charlie Papp sent out a "be-on-the-lookout" for Arlis shortly after 3:00 a.m. Because of the size of the crime scene—the whole church—the dimensions of the job were daunting. The detectives had to interview everyone who was in the church late that night, a group of between ten and twelve people. They obtained a list of the people who had keys to the church. They fingerprinted scores of others and gave lie detector tests to key witnesses, not so much to establish a suspect, but to eliminate potential killers. It was painstaking, time-consuming work. "Just do the job" felt like an order to read the encyclopedia.

In the search for people with elusive names or descriptions, the detectives interviewed a gamut of strange characters who wandered in and out of campus. Johnson ran down a man who lived on the Tresidder Union heating grate. He found a student who had once threatened to make love with a female employee on the floor of the registrar's office. He interviewed a witness known to appear at the Denny's restaurant in San Mateo at 3:00 a.m. The sergeant even assembled a list of all Stanford students from Bismarck. One of them, Jeff Lacher, who worked at the university's telecommunications center, told the detective that he had seen Arlis about a week before, walking by herself in Palo Alto.

"Stanford (police) knew who was on campus," Johnson said later. "You just followed it up. Everybody who was a witness, I found."

With mixed results, Johnson interviewed the Perrys' neighbors in Quillen House. One of them was a thirty-year-old graduate student who lived across the hall in apartment 2-D. In a high-rise like Quillen, she did not have much contact with the young couple. She remembered Arlis as shy, saying that it was hard to have much of a conversation with her. One time, she had to ask the Perrys to turn down their radio, which they did politely. Asked whether anything stood out from the night of murder, the neighbor remembered waking up at about 1:00 a.m. and hearing a "strange noise" in the building. But as Johnson's report later noted, "She did not know what it was and had no idea where it came from."

More intriguing was Johnson's conversation with a husband and wife whose bedroom backed up to the Perrys' bedroom. Constructed in 1971, Quillen lacked soundproof walls. The husband said he had once overheard what appeared to be a ten-minute argument next door, with a female voice repeating "I don't want to do that" over and over. On Monday night, October 14, a day and a half after the murder, the wife overheard what she described as a sound like "laughing" coming from the Perry apartment. Stanford authorities who know of her report say she was mistaken. The sound was Bruce Perry keening in grief.

In October 1975, a year to the day after Arlis was murdered, Johnson and his wife went to Memorial Church. Johnson sat in the balcony, where he could survey the sanctuary. His watch was both an homage to the victim and a long-shot hope that the killer would return to the scene.

"I could see the door next to the chancel," Johnson told me. "I figured that's where he'd come in." Though he was not deeply religious, Johnson offered a prayer. "I just wanted someone to talk to about it," he said.

CHAPTER 6

BRUCE

When Stanford police officer Tony Navarra knocked at Bruce and Arlis's apartment in Quillen House at about 7:15 a.m. on Sunday, the door was answered by a distraught, long-haired young man who still had no idea what had happened to his wife. Under orders not to enlighten him, Navarra was there to bring the husband in for an interview. The thirty-three-year-old officer, known as "Tone" to his colleagues, did not tell Bruce that police had found Arlis or that she was dead. Instead, he talked about the need for a missing persons report. Then he delivered Bruce to Stanford police headquarters, where Sheriff's Sgt. Dave Pascual and Stanford Capt. Raoul Niemeyer interviewed the sophomore in the conference room.

An accident of nerves worsened the plight of the young man from Bismarck. The police noticed there were drops of blood on his shirt. For a husband who had waited three hours to report his wife missing, the blood raised more questions. Bruce explained that the blood came from a nosebleed, which he got in stressful situations. The investigators, however, could not assume his innocence. So during this first session, Pascual and Niemeyer put Bruce through a searching interrogation.

"During that interview, they didn't tell me (at first) that she was dead," Bruce explained to a cold-case investigator many years later. "The first part of that interview, I had no fucking idea what was going on. They were actually trying to suggest to me that she might have been having an affair, that our relationship was rocky. You know, none of that was true. I didn't understand what the hell was going on. I was pretty offended and pretty upset. It was a bad interview."

In a 1992 interview with the *Chicago Reader*, Bruce recalled that he was dazed, terrified, and chilly from the early-morning cold. When he asked repeatedly, "Where's my wife?" he got no response. Bruce said the detectives kept asking him whether he wanted a cigarette, though he told them he did not smoke.

Years later, Niemeyer dismissed the idea that he and Pascual had treated Bruce harshly. "We told him pretty much right away what happened," he recalled. But between the lines, the interview sounded much worse than the bland summary Pascual put in his report.

In the unexplained killing of a wife, the first commandment for police is that the husband is a suspect. It is a rule that can be wholly unfair, as it was in Bruce's case. But Pascual and Niemeyer were starting with scant information. So they parsed the events of Saturday night, probing for discrepancies. Why had Bruce and Arlis left their apartment? Bruce explained that they left Quillen before midnight to mail a couple of letters at the Stanford post office, about fifteen minutes away by foot. As they walked out of their apartment building, he noticed that one of the tires on their car was low. He told Arlis that she ought to inflate the tires the next time she got gasoline. Arlis didn't like that comment. In Bismarck, men took care of such things. She told Bruce it was his job. Plagued by a headache from a night of studying, Bruce said he didn't want to talk about it. In turn, that annoyed Arlis. After mailing the letters, the couple started back, and Bruce paused at the Meyer Library to read a poster. Arlis left to walk toward Memorial Church, a place she often visited for prayer. Bruce returned to their apartment.

When Arlis did not arrive back at Quillen by 12:30 a.m., Bruce walked back to the church and found it locked. He banged on the front doors but was unable to rouse anyone. He told Pascual and Niemeyer that he saw a young man with dark hair sleeping on a bench near the main entrance. Thinking Arlis had taken a different route home, he returned to his apartment to find that she still had not come back. Now worried, Bruce got into his car and drove around campus, searching for his wife. Finally, at 3:00 a.m., he called the dispatcher, Papp, to report Arlis missing. "She was walking around on campus, and she probably went to the church, and she hasn't been back," he told the dispatcher.

Pascual showed Bruce a card that outlined his rights—proof that he was being treated as a suspect. Bruce said he understood and was willing to talk. The investigators then told him that they had found

Bruce when he was interviewed at the Stanford police station.

the body of a young woman in the church, and they were 99 percent sure it was Arlis.

"Bruce Perry denied killing his wife and stated that he loved her and kept asking why we were accusing him of killing her," Pascual wrote later. Because of security guard Steve Crawford's assurances that the church was locked, the search of Memorial Church did not occur until nearly three hours after Bruce reported Arlis missing. In a trifecta of suspicion, the cops had discounted the young husband's story, kept him in the dark about his wife's fate, and then questioned him about his role in her murder. A photo taken of Bruce shows a stunned young man wearing a loosely fitted white pullover shirt, arms at his sides, a look of infinite sadness in his gaze.

Having absorbed the news of his wife's killing, Bruce asked to call his mother, Donna Perry, in North Dakota. When he was done, Pascual and Niemeyer went over the events once more—mailing the letters, the tiff about the tires, Arlis's departure for the church. Bruce's story was consistent. Pascual took the young man's fingerprints, samples of his hair, and scrapings from beneath his fingernails. Then Pascual drove Bruce back to Quillen and collected the clothing he had worn when he took his last walk with Arlis. The sergeant also went through Arlis's mail and purse, finding several letters that revealed her deep faith. Everything Pascual found spoke of a young couple deeply in love.

In hindsight, people who have followed the case have questioned why Bruce waited three hours before reporting Arlis missing. In part, that question reflects post-9/11 standards of fear. Today, it's hard to imagine a young husband waiting that long to report his wife missing. And it raised questions among investigators at the time. In the fall of 1974, Stanford students were aware of the murders in and around the campus over the previous year and a half. Arlis had written to her parents that Bruce did not want her to go out alone at night. But Bruce and Arlis came from Bismarck, where the idea that a walk to the church invited danger seemed far-fetched. A self-sufficient young man, Bruce hoped to find Arlis without involving the police if he could. Adding the time for walking around Memorial Church and exploring the campus by car, the timeline fit the portrait of an anxious husband reluctant to believe the worst.

Many years later, a cold-case investigator asked Bruce how often Arlis had gone to the church. He estimated that she visited it a couple of times a week. "It was a pretty place to go; it was peaceful," Bruce said. Did she ever go to the church at night? "Not that I'm aware of," Bruce said. Then he qualified his answer. In the afternoons and evenings, he tutored math—"math for some people who are afraid of math," he said—and he remembered that Arlis once took a run in the evening. He met her when she was finished. "It's possible that on those nights that I was teaching, she may have gone to the church, but almost every other night, I was home and with her," he said. It was a critical point, because it touched on the issue of whether Arlis's killer had seen her before. In 1974, Bruce told the *Palo Alto Times* that he and Arlis liked to go to the church late at night together. "It's dark in there at night," the *Times* quoted him as saying. "There are only some peripheral lights. Sometimes there would be two or three other persons in there."

One member of the 1974 interview team, Capt. Niemeyer, came away convinced Bruce was not the killer. "I said, Dave, I just don't see him as the guy," Niemeyer remembered. "There was just no way he would have killed his wife."

Pascual agreed—but wanted to see the results of the lie detector test. Like most of the witnesses, Bruce agreed to a polygraph. Throughout the questioning, he cooperated with the investigators.

The investigators' doubts were put to rest on Monday. Around noon, Pascual picked up Bruce and took him to the sheriff's office for a lie detector test. In a session with San Jose Police Sgt. Rex Newburn, the Stanford sophomore was given his constitutional rights and asked a series of benign questions. Then came the four key queries: "Do you know for sure who murdered your wife?" Bruce answered no. "Did you murder your wife?" Again, no. "Did you have some third person to murder your wife?" Newburn asked. No once more. And finally, "Was your wife all right the last time you saw her?" Bruce said yes. Newburn concluded Bruce was telling the truth. To be certain, he asked a series of questions meant to provoke tension in the young husband. It began with an accusatory question: Did you murder your wife with…Newburn filled in the weapon—an ice pick, a club, etc. Bruce again answered no. Again, he passed the test.

To anyone who knew Bruce or Arlis, none of the questions needed asking. Bruce grew up in Bismarck as the second of four children of a well-respected dentist, Duncan Perry, and his wife, Donna Perry (née Henry). Both parents had been fine athletes—his mother had been an all-state basketball player—and Bruce inherited their athletic genes as well as a capacity for hard academic work. Although he described himself as a skinny, asthmatic kid, he grew to be six foot two, with a big build, a quick brain, and the gift of leading others—the kind of player football coaches covet. Though he went out for football early in his high school career, Bruce settled on running track. "He was very quick to let me know that he wasn't going to waste his brain on athletics," said his English teacher, Tom Hesford. "I assumed he was going to play football. No, no, no, he ran track. He wasn't gonna let big guys jump on him."

Bruce didn't simply run track. He excelled at it, sharing a state record in the 100-yard dash and setting new ones in the 220-yard and 440-yard races.[1] He also ran on championship relay teams, running a key leg in the mile relay. Bruce later told a writer that he got into Stanford on the basis of his track prowess, not his grades. In a bit of gamesmanship, Bruce often ran the third leg of the four-part mile relay, fooling opponents who assumed the Bismarck High team would have their best runner anchor the final leg. By the end of the first three legs, the Demons would have a lead that deflated opposing teams. A film of a May 1973 state track meet shows Bruce as a big, powerful runner who pumped his arms furiously and seemed to have a canny sense of when to make his move from the pack. While Bruce reveled in the competition, two oddities set him apart. First, his asthma was serious enough that he had to control it with medication. Second, he sometimes got nosebleeds at big track meets. It was the same thing that afflicted him at Quillen House.

In the classroom, Bruce shone equally brightly. Arlis's friends remember that he once dashed off a paper between the races of a track meet, getting an "A" on the effort. He was particularly talented at math and used it to measure his workouts. His English teacher, Hesford, remembers that Bruce and a friend dropped by to see him after they graduated. "They said they were working on a novel together," Hesford said. "I said I'd look forward to it." Another time, Hesford remembers asking Bruce what he wanted to do in life. "He said "I want to go into pharma psychology," the teacher remembered him saying—the use of drugs to help people with mental afflictions.

When Hesford asked Arlis the same question, she responded, "I want to go with Bruce where he goes."

While Bruce had dated a girl before Arlis, he preferred athletic competition to a busy social life. In an echo of his statement that God would have to drop a girl in his lap, his friends remember that he once said, "The only thing worse than a girl is a canceled track meet." One of his classmates remembers that Bruce went to Christian meetings and asked questions—not hostile, but thoughtful. In his police report, Sgt. Pascual said Bruce had described himself as a "liberal Christian" and his wife as a "fundamentalist." That probably overstated the difference between them. They shared an understanding of their faith, an important anchor of their relationship. Bruce, however, was less evangelistic than Arlis. He had a time-consuming medical career ahead of him.

The couple's friends remember that Bruce's family, particularly his mother, was less than enthusiastic about his choice of Arlis. But in many ways, the two young people were a good match. Arlis provided a solidity that Bruce craved. Bruce was the smart, athletic prince she adored. Her enthusiasm served as a counterpoint to his reserve.

"They were so terribly in love," said Jenny Wavrin Leet, one of Arlis's friends. "His family had some reservations; he was on a path to become a doctor, and they were only nineteen. I think her parents genuinely loved Bruce. Had it been anyone else, there may have been some hesitation. I mean, it *was* young. But I don't think there was any way to stop it."

At the start of his sophomore year at Stanford, Bruce embraced an ambitious academic agenda. He took biology, organic chemistry, a chemistry lab, and a math course that he helped tutor, earning the princely sum of $5 an hour (more than $25 in today's money). He also took a drama course, a break from the demands of his other work. But his interests lay broadly in how the mind worked. In his freshman year, one of his advisers had been Dr. Seymour "Gig" Levine, who used rats to study neuroscience, a field that was the foundation of Bruce's later career.

Arlis's murder threatened to upend his life. If being treated like a suspect while his wife lay dead was agony for Bruce, the days that followed offered no respite. His father, Duncan Perry, flew out to California, as did his uncle, Gordon Henry, the associate dean of students at the University of North Dakota. But the mystery of who killed Arlis would not go away. The media attention to the crime made it worse. In one of his few public statements, Bruce said he did not understand why the church had not been checked when he called at 3:00 a.m. "Whoever did this has to be insane," he told the *Palo Alto Times*.

Then, on Tuesday evening, October 15, Bruce attended a memorial service for Arlis in the place where she had been murdered. It had to have seared the young man. At home in Bismarck, the grief continued to crest. Arlis's friends say that before the young couple left for California, Bruce had assured Marvin Dykema that he would take care of Arlis. The murder did more than destroy a life and end a marriage. For wholly unfair reasons, it seemed to betray a promise.

CHAPTER 7
THE ARBITER OF DEATH

In most homicide cases, investigators nourish an idea of what caused the death, a theory that demands refinement in an autopsy. In the language of industrial disaster, they know a speeding train caused the crash. They want to learn how fast the engineer was driving, whether a cell phone was involved, or if the track was defective. When Arlis's body arrived at 11:02 a.m. Sunday at the Santa Clara County morgue, located in the basement of Valley Medical Center in San Jose, detectives assumed she had died of strangulation. The coroner's investigator at Memorial Church, John Semple, who went by the memorable nickname of "Dudley Doom," had noted that the front of Arlis's neck had two deep bruises, one bigger than the other. The inside of her eyelids was red, a condition known as "petechiae," a bursting of blood capillaries that occurs in strangulation. Very little about this case, however, unfolded neatly.

The autopsy fell to Santa Clara County's veteran coroner-medical examiner, John Hauser, a forty-six-year-old physician who savored the macabre the way someone else might nurture a passion for crossword puzzles. A man of precise habits and quirky interests, Hauser always wore a white shirt and bow tie, never leaving his house without donning his jacket, even in the hottest weather. As a hobby, he collected and repaired antique pocket watches. Driving a black 1959 Mercedes, he took only a flashlight, rubber gloves, and a few slides when he visited crime scenes. When he left an autopsy, he checked his shoes for blood spatters. In a shoebox on a shelf in his lab, he stored the skull of an unidentified woman found in a dumpster on San Jose's East Side. Prizing frugality, the coroner reused cheap surgical gowns from autopsy to autopsy, despite the stains. The dead did not complain.

In the back alleys of Santa Clara County's bureaucracy, the bow-tied doctor was known as an engaging storyteller and a fierce street fighter, a man unafraid to battle for his budget and his beliefs. In the late 1960s, not long after he became coroner, Hauser engaged in an epic struggle with Stanford doctors who sought transplant organs from bodies before the coroner had completed an autopsy. He accused the Stanford physicians of running a "Pick-Your-Part" operation, as if harvesting organs were a matter of pawing through stray parts at a junkyard. Although Hauser had attended Stanford himself, the charge won him few friends. Occasionally, too, the coroner offended homicide investigators by releasing what they saw as too much detail about a crime. While this practice helped reporters—

coroner's reports were among the few sources of information about big cases—it earned him foes among police. Three decades later, after Hauser left, the coroner-medical examiner's team was assigned to the sheriff's office, which regarded transparency about the dead as a form of communicable disease.

In a big case, it wasn't unusual for Hauser to go to the scene of a homicide himself. He liked to absorb the setting before examining the victim. In this case, however, he awaited the body in San Jose. When the four-hour autopsy began at 11:45 a.m. on Sunday, Hauser was accompanied by Sheriff's Sgt. John Johnson, county photographer George Halverson, and morgue attendant William Stanley. The coroner noted the basics first: Arlis was five feet, five and a half inches tall and weighed 125 pounds, with six-inch-long blond hair. Her nails bore a pinkish lacquer, and her ears were pierced. Rigor mortis had already set in fully. The blood in her body had pooled toward her back, no surprise given that she was found lying with her face up. The coroner noted both bra straps were torn in front, with the hooks on the back unfastened. A yellow wedding ring was on her left-hand ring finger, an opal ring on her right hand. Whatever this was, robbery did not seem to be the motive.

Not long into his examination, Hauser turned the body over and noted a one-eighth-inch puncture wound below the left ear, about an inch and a quarter to the left of the midline of the neck. An oblong scrape about a half inch long bracketed the entry wound. "Mass palpable," the doctor wrote in his notes. Then, as the autopsy proceeded, he found the surprise. A 5.5-inch tapered ice pick shaft had been jammed into Arlis's skull at a forty-five-degree angle upward and to the right. The blade had gone through the dura, a thick protective membrane, before piercing the brain stem, or pons, and ending in the right-frontal lobe of the brain. Though he noted evi-

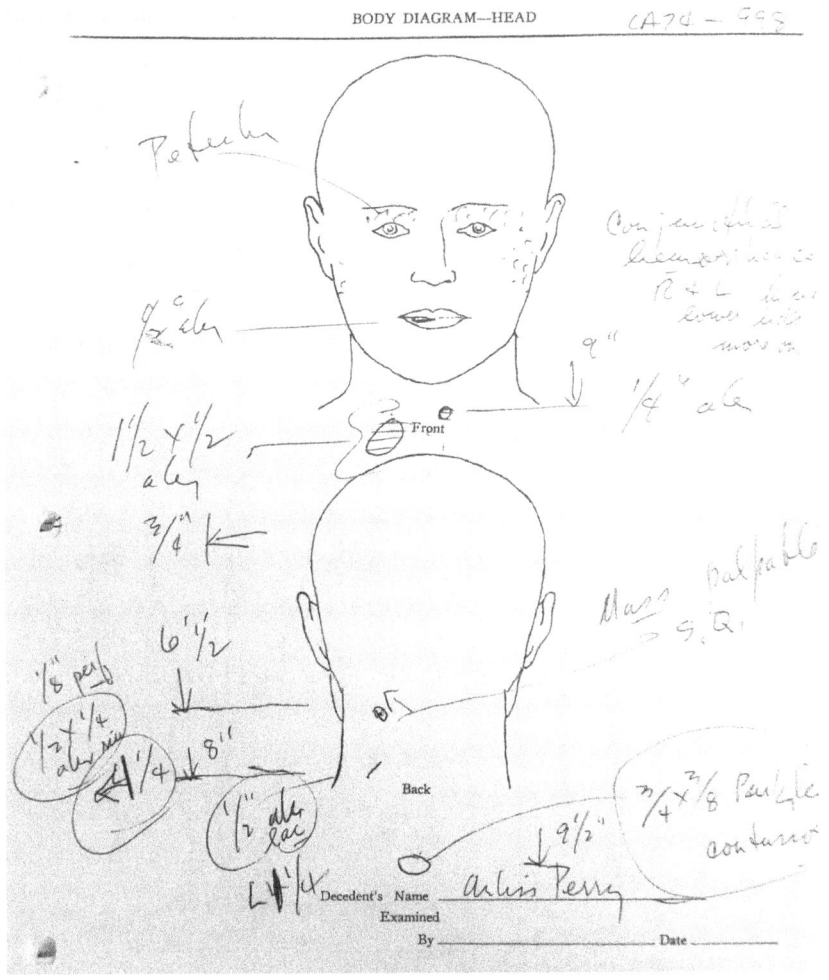

A coroner's sketch of the wounds inflicted upon Arlis Perry.

dence of strangling as well, reinforcing Semple's observation about the bloody eyelids, Hauser concluded that the ice pick was the murder weapon. The handle was nowhere in sight.

It would have taken a serious but not impossible blow to kill Arlis. The ice pick had pierced the base of the skull near the point where the spinal cord passes through. A killer would have felt resistance at first—but once in the brain, little would have impeded the thrust. Years later, when I asked how much force was needed, Hauser said, "Enough." While that was no detailed answer, it conveyed the rough idea. It did not take a specialist to kill Arlis. But the killer was determined and savage. He may also have had a rudimentary knowledge of anatomy. Sheriff's Capt. Frank Mosunic described it as either a "lucky thrust" or the work of someone "like a premed student who knew exactly where to do it." When Hauser extracted the ice pick from the body, he left a piece of bone attached, a fragile, curved section that did not look like it would stop a determined killer. As macabre as that seemed, the bone graphically illustrated the crime. "Homicide," Hauser wrote on his request for a toxicology exam. "Stab of Head."

The find stunned the investigators, upending the strangulation theories at the scene. At the church, there had been no way of guessing that an ice pick had been embedded in her brain. The entry wound was scarcely visible.

"It looked like a classic strangulation," said Sgt. Ken Kahn, one of the investigators. "Then the bomb dropped with the ice pick." The coroner's finding was widely accepted, although investigators continued to believe Arlis had been choked into submission manually first. Hauser did not dispute this, but his report noted that there had been no fracture of the hyoid bone, a horseshoe-shaped bone that is often—but not always—broken in strangulation.

Hauser recorded several other wounds that filled out the story. First, petechiae, or burst blood vessels, were more extensive than Semple had noted. The condition affected not just the eyelids but also the left side of the face, near the front of the ear. The coroner also found bleeding in the layer of muscle near the neck as well as in the larynx. All of this was consistent with strangulation. On the right-lower lip, the coroner measured a half-inch-long scrape. Hauser noted a "bloody, frothy" fluid in the mouth. The right wrist bore several bruises that suggested she had been bound or restrained.

On the back of Arlis's neck, about an inch and a half below the fatal entry wound, Hauser found a superficial half-inch scrape that ran diagonally up and to the right. Though it was hard to know with certainty, it suggested her killer had measured his mark before adjusting his aim upward. (When I mentioned this to a prosecutor acquaintance of mine, he immediately suggested that the killer had almost certainly practiced on an animal. It's an intriguing theory, but one that we have no way of proving.) On her lower-right-front neck, the coroner found a large, reddish bruise, about one and a half inches by one half inch. Near the middle of the neck was a smaller, quarter-inch bruise that could have been its cousin. Because they were so raw and red—they looked like wine stains on the skin—these two bruises were the ones spotted first by deputies at the scene. Hauser also recorded bruises on her back, elbow, and right shin.

On the front of the body, just above each hip, were a pair of purple-blue bruises, each about two inches in diameter, as if the damage was done symmetrically. In the vagina, the coroner found that the candle had penetrated about three inches into Arlis's body, its yellow metal cap measuring 1.75 inches in length. The coroner found a small amount of bleeding in the tissues there. The detectives concluded that Arlis had not been raped, but her body had been sexually violated. It was hard to avoid the comparison between the candle and the ice pick. Both had been broken off. Both revealed a killer who wanted to defile a woman.

The coroner's exam seemed to allay the worst fears at the beginning—that Arlis had been tortured. The investigators came to believe that Arlis's killer surprised her from behind, choked her with both hands, and stabbed her with his left hand, measuring his mark before he did. Though that was the most logical narrative, it did not explain all the evidence. The symmetrical bruises just above her hips suggested a killer who held her down while choking her. If the murder happened that way, Arlis was probably unconscious when the killer thrust the ice pick into her brain.

The discovery of the ice pick narrowed the probe but unearthed a litany of questions. First, it suggested that the killer was left-handed, like some famous killers in history (Jack the Ripper, for example, is believed to have been a lefty). An assailant stabbing a victim from behind would almost certainly use the left hand to inflict a wound with an upward trajectory into the right brain. A backhanded stab could be delivered with the right hand, but it would demand the precision of a tennis pro.

The next questions were practical and logistical: Who would carry an ice pick in a church? The lethal weapon felt like an anachronism, a 1920s tool employed for a 1970s murder. Where could such an instrument be found in an age of refrigeration? What kind of planning was involved? How much force was needed to detach the handle? And what had become of that handle? Old-timers around Memorial Church suggested that the ice pick could have come from a cabinet that contained a potpourri of things in the small room between the church office and the sanctuary. A pick might have been left over from the days when it was used to chip ice for soft drinks at parties. But it seemed clear that an assailant would not have come across the ice pick by accident. He would need to have an idea of what he was looking for. While ice picks were available in hardware stores and still are, it was hard to conceive of a killer carrying one in preparation for murder. After all, no one knew that Arlis was headed to the church late that night.

A couple of days later, deputies scoured the details of a chat between Stanford night security guard James J. Golden and one of the campus's characters, a tall, thin, unkempt man named Noel Rogers, a onetime tennis player who had never attended Stanford. Shortly after midnight on Tuesday morning, October 15, almost exactly forty-eight hours after the murder, Golden and Rogers met outside Tresidder Union. Like everyone else at Stanford, they talked of the murder. Rogers asked how Arlis had died. Golden said he didn't know—he was careful in doling out facts—but that the news media had called it a stabbing. Rogers then asked a question that ensured he would be hauled in for questioning.

"Was it an ice pick?" he said.

CHAPTER 8
POWDER THROWERS

When they were summoned to Memorial Church to gather evidence, Wes Bowling and Tom Sing were climbing the middle ranks of the sheriff's hierarchy, a slippery pole more than a sturdy ladder. As partners midway through a seven-year stint together, they were good friends as well as colleagues. One of the force's first African American deputies, the thirty-one-year-old Bowling was a stylish man in the early stages of a career that would take him through tours of the homicide bureau, a countywide narcotics force, and the main jail. Sing, a thirty-three-year-old Hawaii native, was equally ambitious, a genial officer whose mustache curved upward in a smile. Years later, after he became head of the Deputy Sheriffs' Association and delved into electoral politics, Sing liked to say that his ability to communicate was his strong trait.

Sing and Bowling formed an undercover team known as H-4, a plainclothes unit devoted to crime suppression and surveillance in high-crime areas. If a rash of burglaries or other crimes erupted in an unincorporated neighborhood, the H units were dispatched. In large part, this kind of policing has been replaced today by electronic scrutiny. But before cell phones, computers, and omnipresent video, the H units formed an elite in the sheriff's department. On a day of rest—not even criminals did much work on Sunday—the murder demanded the top talent in the sheriff's force. "It would have been surprising if we *weren't* called out," said Bob Pulling, another H unit member sent to the church.

The workmanlike ritual of the investigators mimicked the Sunday ceremony they were displacing. Instead of worshippers bending forward in prayer, deputies wandered the pews in search of scraps of paper or bits of wax. In place of a minister delivering a homily, a sergeant barked commands. Rather than acolytes lighting altar candles, investigators dusted them for fingerprints. In place of a hymn board with the numbers of songs, numbered placards announced each clue. (Arlis's sandals, for example, were given the number twelve.) Everyone understood the stakes. This case had to be handled by the book. The man in charge of the crime scene, Sgt. John Johnson, would not have it any other way.

The assignments reflected the department's emphasis on having all deputies versed in the nitty-gritty of gathering evidence. "When you arrived at a crime scene, you were expected to try to get fingerprints," said Stanford Police Capt. Raoul Niemeyer, who had been a sergeant in the sheriff's department. "If you didn't throw some powder around, you would hear about it at briefing." Usually applied with a brush, powder adheres to the residue and oils left by a fingerprint. An investigator can then lift the print with tape and transfer it to another surface. It is the origin of the phrase "dusting for prints." A picture in the *Stanford Daily* on Monday, October 14, showed Bowling hunched over an outer door of the church, trying to obtain prints. Wearing a leather jacket and nice slacks, he looked overdressed for the job.

When Bowling and Sing arrived at 9:10 a.m., a cadre of deputies were busy in the east transept, the main crime scene. A sergeant quickly snapped several rolls of film. Other deputies cataloged evidence found near Arlis's body. The two partners began work on the west side of the church—on the right side as a visitor approached the altar—where an interior door had been found broken open. If this seemed like a secondary theater, it became critical, a major front in the attempt to understand the murder. The H-4 team focused on the vestibule, or chamber, on the west side of the church, between the sanctuary and the outside door. (Memorial Church had two sets of doors. The inner wooden doors, which led from the nave into the vestibule, could be locked, meaning a visitor could be trapped inside the sanctuary. It was like a box, or a partial box, in a larger container, akin to the nested boxes given as joke presents.)

From the start, Bowling noted that neither the inner nor the outer doors were locked. While Bowling dusted the doors leading to the outside, Sing examined the inner set of double doors leading from the sanctuary to the vestibule. The left-hand door was open, while the right-hand door, the one closest to the main church entry, bore a fresh crack that ran about eighteen inches from the top downward, perhaps half a foot from the inner edge. Three inches from the bottom of the door, directly over the door latch, the deputies found a half-moon-shaped crack. Bowling wrote that it appeared "as if great force was applied from the nave side of the door."

In other words, it looked as though someone had kicked out the door, hard enough to partially separate the boards that made up the thick barrier. Eight inches above the doorknob, Sing found a full handprint on the nave side of the door. The deputies located splinters of wood that landed nearby. In the corridor near the exit door, Bowling also found six smaller "cabinet doors" that appeared to have been forced open, suggesting that someone had searched furiously for something they concealed. It looked like the route the killer had used.

On the other side of the church, next to Arlis's body, deputies cataloged several key pieces of evidence. On the lower part of the candle stuffed into Arlis's body, investigators spotted a partial palm print believed to have come from the web of the right thumb. This was a significant discovery, though palm prints were not as useful as fingerprints—they were harder to compare and less codified. On a pew just north of Arlis's hand, deputies found a clump of burnt candle wax on the arm of a pew. The candles used on her body had come from large brass holders on each side of the altar. Backup sexton Bill Aaron told deputies he remembered installing the candles on Friday, October 11, the day before the murder. On the floor between the altar and the east transept, deputies found candle drippings, suggesting that the killer had carried lit candles from the altar toward Arlis's body.

Near a column in the west nave, about seventy feet from the body, deputies found a set of burnt matches. Next to the wall of the east transept, they recovered a Wrigley's Spearmint gum wrapper. Neither find was necessarily linked to the crime. A lot of strange things happened inside Memorial Church. Gum-chewing and match-lighting were the least of them. Nonetheless, they were noted and filed away. So was a small, yellow metal cross found on the west side of the sanctuary.

In a Dempsey dumpster to the west of the church, deputies labored through Monday to find anything related to the murder. Deputy Bob Pulling retrieved two *Bismarck Tribune* newspapers addressed to a Stanford student as well as a book entitled *Satan's Controversy and Destruction*. (Many years later, when I did a Library of Congress search, I did not find a book with precisely that title, though Ellen Gould White, a founder of the Seventh-Day Adventist Church, wrote a much-reprinted 1884 book entitled *The Great Controversy Between Christ and Satan*, which begins with the subtitle "The Destruction of Jerusalem.") While it was unclear whether the book had any relevance to the murder, its presence fed ideas that the crime had satanic links.

In retrospect, the most intriguing discovery in the dumpster was a cluster of three bloodstained green rags. The deputies put the rags into an evidence bag—but they ordered no tests of the blood. These were the days before DNA. Even if investigators had been able to establish the blood type on the rags, it would not have led them to the killer. It was a missed opportunity, not a clue that would have solved the case in 1974.

With such a haul of evidence, the Santa Clara County task force determined that it needed help from the FBI's crime lab. Late on October 16, the Wednesday after the murder, investigator Ken Kahn boarded a red-eye flight to Washington, D.C., with an army duffel bag stuffed full of evidence, including the candles, the kneeling pillow, and Arlis's clothing.

"I got to the airport, showed them my ID, and told the flight attendant, *This bag doesn't get out of my sight*," Kahn remembered years later. "I took a middle seat and put the duffel bag by the window. And that's where it stayed. I don't think I even dozed off." The next morning, Kahn handed the bag over to the FBI's crime lab, which operated on the sixth floor of the Justice Department headquarters on Pennsylvania Avenue.

From the scene in the church and the findings of the coroner, the detectives had a preliminary scenario about how the crime unfolded. Arlis habitually prayed near the front of the church, in a center pew, not in the far reaches of the sanctuary. It was likely that the killer had approached Arlis from behind and strangled her manually, not giving her a chance to resist. She may have been bound: one wrist showed signs of a ligature. She was held against a hard surface—possibly the floor, or perhaps a pew—which accounted for the symmetrical bruises just above the hips. Though she struggled, she was unable to scratch her killer: the FBI found no remnants of skin tissue beneath her fingernails. She was almost certainly rendered unconscious fairly quickly. At some point, the killer then thrust the ice pick into her brain, probably with his left hand. Less certain was how Arlis was moved from her place of prayer to the rear of the east transept. The FBI discovered no marks on her shoes that suggested she was dragged.

After she was dead, the murderer would have had to construct his scene, retrieving the candles from the altar, using them on Arlis's body, and lighting one of them for his ceremony. He removed her jeans and laid them upside down on the body, placing her panties to the side. This was a killer who took his time, a neat murderer, a lethal Tony Randall. He seemed confident that no one would interrupt him. In the first analysis, the damage to the doors suggested that he kicked his way out of the church.

The "who" of the crime puzzled deputies more than the "how." Initially, the logic of the case dictated that two men could be suspects: Arlis's husband and the man who found the body, security guard Steve Crawford. But that was based on surmise more than hard evidence. While deputies scoured the church for clues, Bruce Perry was denying that he had anything to do with killing Arlis. And while Crawford had thrown up a red flag by going missing after reporting the crime, he was still part of the law enforcement fraternity, a former Stanford cop. At first glance, the kicked-out doors suggested that Arlis was killed by an outsider, someone unfamiliar with the church. In the following week, deputies tried to identify everyone who had been in Memorial Church that night.

A last piece of evidence offered the faint promise of identifying the killer. Between the first and second pew in the east transept, about thirty-five feet from the body in a line to the altar, deputies found a red kneeling pillow, or "hassock," that bore a semen stain. That prompted detectives to ask whether the killer had masturbated after killing Arlis. In the years before DNA, the deputies were unable to pinpoint the source of the semen other than to say that it came from someone with an "O" blood type, the most common. The distance between Arlis's body and the hassock, however, diminished the significance of the find. In Crawford's words, "ding-a-lings" often visited the church. Could one of them have been responsible?

Whatever its source, the semen stain could not be ignored. If it was connected to the killing of Arlis, it made the murder a more understandable sex crime. In the years that followed, the cloth on the hassock was cut up, examined repeatedly, and submitted for testing. The comparisons to law enforcement's DNA database produced nothing usable. Then, stunningly, investigators found a match forty-four years later. And it did not point to Bruce Perry or Steve Crawford.

CHAPTER 9

THE WITNESSES

As a freshman from rural Oregon, eighteen-year-old Brent Davis explored Stanford Memorial Church on Saturday night with fresh awe for its architectural wonders. Having finished his studies about 10:00 p.m., he walked to the church from his room at Branner Hall, one of Stanford's older dorms. The sanctuary reminded Davis of why he had come to Stanford. He loved music, a mainstay of the church. His music teacher in Oregon had recommended Stanford as a place to study. And Davis was developing a lifelong interest in archeology. Many years later, after a career in the high-tech industry, he earned a PhD in archeology in Australia. For him, the church was a feast of art, history, and design.

"I thought it was beautiful," he recalled forty-four years later. "Those Italian mosaics were extraordinary. I had never seen anything like that before."

Something else he saw at the church that night, however, lodged in his memory as vividly as the decor. Aside from the killer, Brent Davis was one of the last two people to see Arlis alive.

In his tour of the sanctuary, Davis lingered over the inscriptions on the walls, particularly in the west transept, the right arm of the cross as the church was viewed from above. He told investigators he was in the church for close to an hour and a half. He saw a young man sitting next to a pillar in the eastern transept, sniffling as if he had a cold. "He was not visible except for his head; his clothes could barely be seen," Davis told police. As Davis turned to leave by the central aisle, he paused to rest in a pew near the front for about five minutes, absorbing the splendor Jane Stanford had commanded. He remembered hearing the door to the sanctuary open and close. Ten or twelve rows from the front on the left-hand side of the main aisle, he saw a light-haired young woman learning forward, her arms propped on the pew in front. "She was obviously praying," Davis remembered. Bruce Perry was right. Arlis had gone to Memorial Church to commune with God.

After finishing his tour of the church—he turned one last time to take it in as he left—Davis saw a security guard matching Steve Crawford's description on the top outdoor step of the church, just to the right of the door.

"He said, *It's time to go, I'm closing up*," Davis remembered. "I said, *No problem, I'm going now*, and I left." He remembers that Crawford was jiggling his keys and wearing a satiny jacket or blazer with an insignia. Asked about the security guard's attitude, Davis told me,

"It may have been a bit gruff. My memory was that he was a bit impatient to close it up." The student marked the time at around 11:45 p.m. On his way back to the dorm, he passed by the Meyer Memorial Library—since demolished—and saw its lights go off, which suggested to him that it was midnight.[1] Davis got back to Branner about five minutes after midnight. The next day, realizing that what he had seen might be important, he got in touch with police.

One of a handful of visitors to Memorial Church on the night of the murder, Davis did much to convey the texture and feeling of the scene that night—at once inspiring and unsettling. To investigators, the significant piece was that the freshman placed Arlis in the church around 11:45 p.m., in a pew not far from the front. Davis did not recall Crawford coming halfway down the aisle to announce the closing, as the security guard had told Sgt. Johnson. Nor did anyone else interviewed in the next few days. Neither the report filed by Sgt. Dave Pascual nor the handwritten statement from Davis recorded that the freshman had seen Crawford standing outside the church, jiggling his keys.

The Stanford campus was hardly quiet that Saturday night. At Memorial Auditorium, a few blocks away from Memorial Church (in campus shorthand, it was MemAud to the church's MemChu), John Pasqualetti's Pacific Ballet was putting on an 8:30 p.m. performance that included Stravinsky's *Song of the Nightingale*. At Cubberley Auditorium, a few hundred yards from the church, the Law School Film Society had scheduled showings of *Casablanca* at 7:00, 9:00, and 11:00 p.m. Although the weekend football game against

UCLA had been played in Los Angeles, there was the standard smattering of fraternity parties. In the middle of this, a dozen or so people found their way to the church, which ordinarily stayed open until midnight. Though none of them saw the murder, they were important witnesses to its prelude.

The trickle of significant visitors to the church began at about 10:50 p.m., when two singers from San Jose State University, David Simi and Kathleen Nolan, arrived to test the acoustics inside. As they entered, they spotted a young man leaving—Simi remembered that he may have had a goatee. "He had his hands up by his face," Simi told me many years later. Members of a vaunted choral program at SJSU, Simi and Nolan sang to each other across the sanctuary. Despite Memorial Church's cavernous space, they found the sound welcoming. With the exception of a dark-haired man with long sideburns on the western side of the sanctuary, they saw no one. Nolan remembered that they left the church at about 11:15 p.m. without seeing Arlis.

Not long after Simi and Nolan visited the church, and likely overlapping with their visit, a twenty-year-old San Jose woman, Ann Marie Chapatte, arrived at the church with a friend, Tim Warner. The two had gone to dinner and remembered getting to the church around 11:00 p.m., though they did not enter the sanctuary right away. A year before, they had visited Memorial Church, and this trip was meant as a remembrance. Chapatte recalled seeing a young man in a blue short-sleeved shirt with his face to the western wall, examining the inscriptions in a way that she found "weird." Investigators later identified him as Brent Davis. Chapatte left the church after about twenty minutes. Like Simi and Nolan, she did not see Arlis.

Aside from Brent Davis, three other witnesses played a critical role in the timeline that detectives assembled for the hours leading up to Arlis's death. The first two were a couple, Betty Banks and Stuart Cain, who had attended a class at Foothill College before visiting Memorial Church. Once inside, they sat in the first pew in the east transept, admiring the beauty of the sanctuary. What Banks and Cain saw when they left the church made a critical contribution to the probe. The twenty-three-year-old Cain remembered seeing a man with dark, medium-length hair standing outside—a man who could have been Crawford. Behind him, Cain and Banks saw a young woman approaching the front door. Banks recalled her as being five foot five to five foot seven, with medium-length blond hair, wearing a dark jacket and faded blue jeans. That was a clear description of Arlis.

Banks and Cain put the time they left Memorial Church between 11:30 and 11:40 p.m. At the midpoint, that suggested Arlis entered the church around 11:35. Bruce Perry may have been a bit off in his recollection. According to the deputies, he had placed the time Arlis left for the church at close to midnight. At the time of his interview at the Stanford police station, however, Bruce was under pressure from his interrogators, who were quizzing him about his marriage. If he got the time wrong by fifteen minutes or so, it might have been understandable. In the days before video cameras, when the best investigators could hope for were estimates, the recollections of Banks and Cain stood out for their clarity.

That left one significant witness, possibly the last person to leave the church before Crawford locked up: Mark Kral, a twenty-three-year-old Menlo Park resident. Kral told deputies that he had left his apartment around 10:30 p.m. to go to the church, a place he liked to visit every five weeks or so. This time, he went to study a prayer book, read a business magazine, and enjoy the solitude. He drove his car and parked near the School of Business, just west of Hoover Tower, a walk of a couple of minutes from the church. Carrying the magazine and wearing a red-and-black Pendleton and sandals, Kral remembered thinking he wasn't dressed correctly for the cool October night. When he got to the church, he found that one iron door to the outside was partially shut and the two inner doors from the vestibule into the sanctuary were completely shut. He remembered closing the wooden doors behind him, thinking it would keep the cold away.

Kral's account backed up Brent Davis's observations about where Arlis was praying—and validated the memory of other witnesses. Kral told investigators that he spent a few minutes wandering through the east transept and the chancel, reading the inscriptions. Then he sat down near a pillar in the east transept and began reading. He remembered seeing Stuart Cain and Betty Banks as well as Davis. After half an hour to forty minutes, he walked across the central nave of the church to read inscriptions in the west transept. He saw a blond and petite young woman, presumably Arlis, to his right.

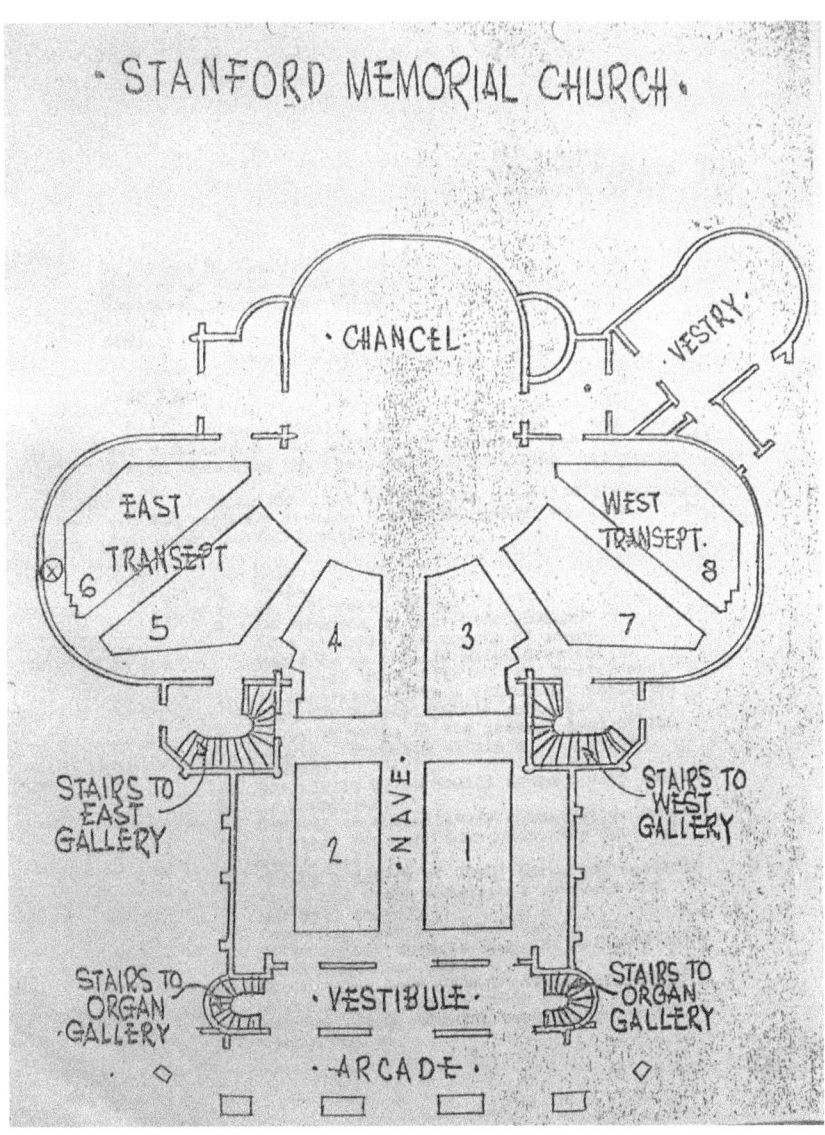

Map of the interior of Stanford Memorial Church.
Arlis' body was found in the east transept.

Kral recalled that the church was quiet and his sandals were noisy, making a leathery, squeaking sound. He tried to tiptoe past. He did not remember seeing a security guard or anyone else in the church. Kral was vague about when he left, though he put his time arriving home after 11:30 p.m. Back at his apartment on Sharon Drive, he made a salad and watched Channel 44, a nonnetwork station, before going to bed.

The story from the Menlo Park man contained one humorous aside. When his roommate arrived at the apartment after midnight, he noticed Kral was sleeping naked. The roommate later told deputies it "was a strange bed dress for Mark." That evoked the interest of detectives, who had to entertain the possibility that Kral had shed clothes that might incriminate him. Kral, however, had a believable explanation. Having not done his laundry, he had no clean clothes left. When detectives interviewed him, he handed over the outfit he had worn to the church that night. Kral also passed a lie detector test. A state Department of Justice polygrapher asked him, "Did you yourself cause the fatal injuries to the woman in that church?" Kral answered no.

Two other people spoke to investigators about arriving at Memorial Church *after* it was closed—and their stories offered a coda to the recollections of the visitors inside the church. A young Stanford student, Robert Firth, said he passed by the church around 11:45 p.m. One of the few witnesses who wore a watch, Firth spotted a woman and two men on a bench to the east of the church's entrance.

As he walked by, the woman called out to him, "Are you Mark?" Firth said no and kept going. Then, around 1:30 or 1:45 a.m., a seventeen-year-old Stern Hall resident named Jorge Garcia arrived at the church with a female companion. Garcia reported seeing a young white man with black hair, blue cutoff pants, a striped pull-over T-shirt on a bench near the church doors. As he walked away, Garcia heard a "shuffling sound" from the choir loft, a sound that repeated itself once as he listened.

Pulling the strands together, the sheriff's deputies could recon-struct what happened before the church closed. Brent Davis and Mark Kral were the last two people to see Arlis praying near the front of the church. Davis saw an impatient Steve Crawford at the church's front door. No witness remembered the security guard coming down halfway and announcing that the church was closing. Arlis had al-most certainly arrived at Memorial Church around 11:35 p.m. That left Crawford and Arlis as the last people in the church unless a killer had entered earlier and hidden. But what exactly did that mean? The deputies had no immediate answers.

CHAPTER 10

THE DEAN

No murder in a church, particularly not one as sensational as the one at Stanford Memorial Church, could stand without response from the clergy. As an insult to a place of worship, a rebuke to the idea of God's grace, the killing demanded not just solace for survivors but a vow to defeat evil. Hours after Arlis's body was found on Sunday morning, that job fell to the dean of the chapel, Robert Hamerton-Kelly, a South Africa native who had been in his post for only a year and a half. When police told him that the congregation could not hold its usual 11:00 a.m. service in the sanctuary, the dean presided over a makeshift service outside the church that drew about 150 worshipers, a conclave of the stunned. As the day progressed, Hamerton-Kelly emerged as the face of Stanford's reaction. His story illustrated how anyone could be a suspect in Arlis's murder, even a prominent clergyman trying to summon hope for his parishioners.

At thirty-five, Hamerton-Kelly boasted a lustrous resume. Born in Cape Town, he graduated from Rhodes University before obtaining two more degrees from Cambridge University. At Cambridge, Hamerton-Kelly ran with the Cambridge Hare & Hounds, the university's venerable running club. After obtaining a doctorate from Union Theological Seminary in New York and teaching at Scripps College and McCormick Theological Seminary in Chicago, he came to Stanford in the spring of 1973. In the theological constellation of the day, Hamerton-Kelly was a bright star, a philosopher in sunglasses. Good-looking, deeply learned, an aficionado of fine wine and dark chocolate, he taught New Testament Greek and Western Civilization as well as preaching at Memorial Church. The dean told friends he was sometimes mistaken for the actor David McCallum from the television series *The Man from U.N.C.L.E.*

For all his academic gifts, however, the dean possessed a naive instinct about how to deal with the media and the police. In the hours after the murder was discovered, deputies brought Hamerton-Kelly into the sanctuary to view the body. After all, it was his church, and there was a chance Hamerton-Kelly could identify the victim. Later, the investigators came to regret that move. While detectives typically withhold details of a crime scene—compared to homicide investigators, World Series of Poker finalists are emotive firebrands—Hamerton-Kelly felt no such inhibition. In talking with reporters, he gave out details of the way Arlis was laid out, including the news that a three-foot candle was jammed into her vagina while another was pushed up between her breasts.

The Stanford Daily quoted Hamerton-Kelly as saying he could draw no conclusions about whether the killing had been "ritualistic." Once the notion had been floated publicly, however, it was hard to call it back. Other news outlets, relying on a loosely sourced wire story, attributed the words "ritualistic and satanic" to the dean. In a story without a byline, the San Jose *Mercury News* quoted the dean as saying it appeared that she had been tortured by her killer, perhaps the most inflammatory idea of all. To make matters worse, the sheriff's office said it was looking at all possibilities, including the idea that the murder had been part of a Black Mass, a parody of a religious ceremony. An attempt to assure the public of investigative thoroughness incited ugly speculation.

The next day, Hamerton-Kelly sought to clarify the situation. The dean said there was "no disarray or desecration" that one "normally finds in a Black Mass ritual." Inevitably, that raised the question of how a dean of the chapel at a prestigious university knew the norms of a Black Mass ritual. In fact, a Black Mass was staged inside the church on Halloween in 1972, about six months before Hamerton-Kelly arrived at Stanford. Many years later, Hamerton-Kelly's widow, Rosemary, acknowledged to me that her husband was no expert in messaging. "He was quite distressed that reporters who had been given the straight scoop spread it about," she told me. In truth, there *was* something ritual-looking about the way the Arlis was laid out with the jeans draped upside down over her body. Hamerton-Kelly was not wrong in his observations. In that moment on the Stanford campus, however, the suggestion of diabolical or cult-like evil deeply unsettled students and faculty.

Believing that Hamerton-Kelly had complicated an already baffling murder inquiry, the detectives seethed. Even more irksome for the preacher, he appeared on their list of suspects for a brief time. The dean was one of the three dozen people who had master keys to the church. Certainly, no one would question his coming or going. When dispatcher Charlie Papp called the dean early on Sunday to tell him about the discovery of the body, the conversation had a clipped quality that betrayed Hamerton-Kelly's unfamiliarity with police practice. It may have been the early hour, or the dean may not have registered the seriousness of events, but Hamerton-Kelly did not ask questions about how a dead body came to be in his church. From the conversation, it seems evident he was not thinking of a murder:

PAPP: Uh, Dean Kelly.

HAMERTON-KELLY: Speaking.

PAPP: This is Stanford Police Communications.

HAMERTON-KELLY: Uh-huh.

PAPP: Uh, you are in charge of Memorial Church, aren't you, sir?

HAMERTON-KELLY: Yes.

PAPP: We, we've had a, found a dead body there.

HAMERTON-KELLY: Yes.

PAPP: And the sheriff's office has requested that you don't open the church this morning.

HAMERTON-KELLY: That we don't open the church this morning?

PAPP: That's right. They've got, they've got some cleaning up to do over there.

HAMERTON-KELLY: Not even by eleven o'clock?

PAPP: This I don't know, sir. The only thing I can tell you is that I've got instructions from the sheriff's office not to—to call you and, uh, not to open the church, as of now, and any further information, if I get any, I can give you a call or you can drop down to the church and see for yourself.

HAMERTON-KELLY: Are the sheriffs there now?

PAPP: Yes sir.

HAMERTON-KELLY: Thank you.

With their distrust of the dean cemented by his statements to the media, the investigators quizzed Hamerton-Kelly twice about where he had been on the weekend. He explained that he had left the campus at about 11:30 a.m. on Friday for a retreat, returning to Stanford around 6:00 p.m. on Saturday. After coming into the church office, known as the Round Room, to check his mail, he went home for the evening. He told Sgt. John Johnson that he did not know Arlis or her husband. Although he was the top official of the church, Hammerton-Kelly seemed able to offer only limited context to the crime scene. Asked about a Bible missing from the altar, the dean said he had no idea how long it had been gone. A set of matches found near the west transept door were probably left there by ordinary services—but Hamerton-Kelly said there was no sanctioned practice of candlelight services in the east transept.

Had the dean seen any strange characters in the church? Hamerton-Kelly told Johnson he had seen a long-haired, stoop-shouldered man "fooling around" with wiring near the Round Room door three or four months before—and asked him to leave. The deputies identified him as a twenty-seven-year-old named Jonathan who often wandered around shirtless, wearing only jeans. Known for bellowing his discontent in the quad when he was excluded from the church, Jonathan boasted to a church sexton that he had died and was resurrected. Eventually, the investigators were able to eliminate him from consideration. Finally, Hamerton-Kelly mentioned one enduring mystery. A year before the murder, he discovered that his stoles, religious vestments used in services, had been taken from his office. Draped around the pastor's neck like large, unknotted ties, stoles are changed to denote seasons in the church calendar. (The word "stole" comes from the Latin *stola*, meaning garment or equipment.) Hamerton-Kelly said he had acquired replacements and locked them away since the theft. Nevertheless, the report of the stolen stoles added a strange footnote and a questionable pun to a case bristling with odd clues.

With the investigators' suspicions of Hamerton-Kelly lingering, the dean faced the delicate task of arranging the memorial service for Arlis. It was held at Memorial Church at 7:30 p.m. on Tuesday, October 15, less than three days after she was killed. It had already been a big day at Stanford. In the morning, news broke that a Stanford professor, Paul Flory, had won the Nobel Prize in chemistry. The evening drama at the church was darker and more striking than the morning triumph. In effect, a religious leader who remained a suspect was called upon to knit together the scar of murder in the place Arlis was killed. (It was not the first attempt at reclamation. On Sunday, in a ceremony meant to cleanse the site of evil, members of the Catholic community at Stanford had sprinkled holy water on the spot where the body was found.)

Among those attending the memorial service were Bruce Perry and his father, Duncan Perry. "A powerful organ hymn flowed through the ornate stone church, seeming to bring with it the full impact of the brutal murder," San Jose *Mercury News* reporter Chuck Buxton wrote. The newspaper noted that Bruce broke into muffled sobs. The mourners sang, 'Abide With Me,' written by Scottish Anglican Henry Francis Lyte several weeks before his death of tuberculosis in 1847. ("Abide with me, fast falls the eventide/The darkness deepens, Lord, with me abide.") At the direction of Arlis's law firm, a Stanford student who worked with Arlis, Ken Newman, ordered chrysanthemums from a local florist. Newman made a mistake of a decimal point in his order, which meant ten times as many flowers were delivered than planned. It was a mistake the mourners forgave.

While some people on campus wondered whether it was insensitive to Arlis's family to hold the memorial in the same place where she was murdered, Hamerton-Kelly's words reflected his determination to proclaim the triumph of good over evil—and to redeem the reputation of the church. In a different setting, the dean once described Memorial Church as an "ambiguous presence," saying that its "physical grandeur belies the humility of its message." Now, in a sermon that he said he wrote "right on top of the murder scene,"[1] the dean sought to inspire his listeners in the face of tragedy. "Arlis is now part of us," he said. "She fills the church with her glorious presence." Looking directly at Bruce Perry, the dean told him that he was "part of a cloud of unseen witnesses" whose triumphs would "drive out every malign force and every lurking hound." Acknowledging that the chapel had been infected with evil and that a battle was taking place, the minister urged his listeners to stop the swing of belief from "freedom to fear" and "from openness to suspicion."

Given Hamerton-Kelly's uneasy relationship with police, the choice of that last word—and the reference to "lurking hounds"— seemed more than coincidental. Despite the dean's warning, suspicion thrived inside Memorial Church. A sheriff's detective and five Stanford officers attended the memorial, mingling with the mourners on the chance that the murderer would attend. Lt. Walt Konar ordered a videotape made of the grievers entering and leaving the services as well as still photographs. The police recorded the numbers of twenty-two license plates near the church. None of that seemed to daunt the dean, who told reporters that he hoped to continue keeping the church open until midnight. A photo in the newspaper the next day showed the minister hugging a young mourner.

A week after the murder, Hamerton-Kelly submitted his finger-prints to Konar. The deputies eventually eliminated the dean as a suspect, though not without more questioning. When detective Johnson interviewed Hamerton-Kelly for a second time on Monday, October 21, he asked the dean if he had any further information about the case, the kind of open-ended question police sometimes use with suspects. Hamerton-Kelly said he did not. But even the hint that Hamerton-Kelly was briefly considered a suspect was sensitive on campus. As I did my reporting, I learned that a Stanford police officer was cashiered after he leaked that fact to a friend in the News and Publication Office. (It was never published.)

Five days after the dean's homily, the associate dean of the chapel, Ernlé Young, delivered a Sunday sermon entitled "Murder in the Cathedral," a reference to the T.S. Eliot verse drama about the murder of Thomas Becket in Canterbury Cathedral in 1170. A for-ty-one-year-old Methodist who had known Hamerton-Kelly as a fellow runner in South Africa—and who escaped apartheid after being warned he was about to be subjected to house arrest—Young was a charismatic preacher, better at connecting with an audience than the dean. Quoting Eliot's words about a martyr's blood being given for Christ, he cast the murder in moral and political terms. Stanford students, he proclaimed, would someday be in positions of power in the boardrooms of big corporations, "where evil often has its head-quarters." Only when their policies were challenged, he said, would there be "some real expectation that what happened to both Arlis Perry and to her murderer will happen no more in our midst."

It was a bold sermon, one that reached beyond the mourning and shock to assail the injustices of the broader society. But in a laudable appeal to correct economic wrongs, Young departed from the context of the crime. There was no sign that bad corporate practices had anything to do with Arlis's death. None of the cops shared Young's implied compassion for her murderer ("What happened to both Arlis Perry and to her murderer"). Finally, his audience was unaware that the evocation of blood on holy ground was more current than most people thought. Several days after the murder, investigators found a softball-sized stain of blood near a heating grate not far from where her body lay in the east transept. Although one theory was that Arlis's blood had leaked underneath the cork floor, the stain was never convincingly explained.

CHAPTER 11
THE REPORTERS

On Sunday evening, a dozen hours after the body of Arlis Perry was found, KGO-TV Channel 7 aired its report on the murder at Memorial Church with a single word superimposed behind the newscaster: "Torture." The local newspapers followed suit the next day. "Torture Slaying in Campus Chapel," read the Monday headline in the *Palo Alto Times*. The first paragraph of the story in the San Jose *Mercury News* said Arlis was "the apparent victim of a vicious sex torture-style slaying." On that first day, the media found torture too arresting an idea to ignore. It made a terrible murder unthinkable. The salacious details combined with the understanding that this was the fourth murder at Stanford in the last two years launched the story into the stratosphere of sensationalism. And while deputies concluded the torture element was not true—that while Arlis was strangled, the lethal blow came from an ice pick—the specter of cult-like punishment lingered with the public. That exaggeration was driven by sloppy sourcing by the media, an inconsistent message from the sheriff's department, and the way gruesome specifics dribbled out.

In the mid-1970s, before the internet and social media, Bay Area newspapers wielded far more clout than they do today. The San Jose *Mercury News* and the afternoon *Palo Alto Times* boasted healthy circulations. *The Stanford Daily*, staffed by student journalists, had a trove of talent. But electronic news media had a more visceral grasp than the printed word. Television drove home the visual aspects of murder. The video from Channel 7, with the camera whirring in the background, lingered on the stained-glass windows, the inscriptions on the walls, and the chalk outline of Arlis's body. A picture might be worth a thousand words, but *footage* was worth ten photos. Grabbing viewers by their emotional collars, the electronic media dared them to change the channel.

To a degree that would not happen today, details of the crime emerged from the start. From the dean of the chapel, Robert Hamerton-Kelly, reporters learned that one candle had been inserted into Arlis's vagina and another thrust between her breasts. To many journalists, the concept of church candles being used so gruesomely defined torture. And there seemed to be no acceptable explanation for the crime. A story in *The Stanford Daily* described the mood: "The scenario was becoming tragically, frighteningly familiar. For the fourth time in less than two years, police were faced with a murder at Stanford."

The sensational nature of the news had a huge impact on Stanford and the Bay Area, heightening the pressure on the university and the sheriff's department to find the killer. Stanford put up a reward of $10,000, the equivalent of more than $50,000 today. The sheriff's department formed a task force to investigate the killing. A flood of tips came in to the investigators—some that seemed credible, others marked as far-fetched, and others that were downright ludicrous. In the media world, it was a running story. Even if their efforts added little to the narrative, reporters competed to find new angles.

It was no surprise that the coverage ratcheted up the fear on campus, which was already on edge after the murders of Leslie Perlov, David Levine, and Janet Taylor. With a constant churn in population—a quarter of undergraduates were replaced every fall—it was hard under normal conditions to sustain the alarm. But these were not normal conditions. Even before Arlis Perry was killed, police had begun courses in self-defense for women at Escondido Village. (One of the teachers was Officer Debbie Whittemore, who was called to the scene inside Memorial Church.) Now efforts to reinforce safety were redoubled. The newspaper stories quoted women as saying they would think twice about walking around Stanford freely. The television coverage had a breathless, spooky quality that emphasized heartbreak. Covering Arlis's memorial service, KPIX reporter Norm Woodruff stood before a painting of a child with an outstretched hand. "The relatives and friends gathered at Stanford chapel to re-member nineteen-year-old Arlis Perry, who was murdered here in a gruesome manner," Woodruff reported in a stage whisper.

In the first telling, the accepted belief was that the murder was committed by an outsider, a theory that became part of the lore of the case. A piece of that theory reflected a Stanford-centric view of the world. It was hard to fathom that someone at Stanford—staff member, student, or teacher—could commit such a heinous crime. The murder tested the belief that universities offered an umbrella of shelter to its members. "I used to look on this whole place as a haven where you don't have to worry about people coming in from the outside and disrupting the established order," said a female student quoted in *The Stanford Daily*. The initial reports from the cops, who speculated that the killer might have hidden in the church before closing time, deepened the fear. If you couldn't find refuge in a church, where could you find it?

In the mid-seventies, the case added to a litany of ugly crimes in California. The Memorial Church killing occurred only five years after the Charles Manson gang murdered actress Sharon Tate and the LaBianca couple in Southern California, murders with a memorably satanic cast. A series of killings linked to an unidentified man who went by the codename "Zodiac" convulsed the Bay Area in the late sixties and early seventies. In San Francisco, fifteen people were murdered between October 1973 and April 1974 in a series of racially motivated killings known as the Zebra killings, a spree that was linked to one of the Stanford murders. In February 1974, Patty Hearst was kidnapped from her Berkeley apartment by the Symbionese Liberation Army, an abduction that was followed by a bank shootout two months later. All this produced a dimension of anxiety unseen before. It also produced insatiable curiosity: Could the fresh outrage top the last? For the media, it was a moveable feast.

At Stanford, an immediate backlash arose to the way details of the crime were printed in the first *Stanford Daily* story. To many who sympathized with Arlis, printing the specifics about the candles seemed worse than insensitive. In an unusual letter to the editor, a *Daily* staffer, Gordon Firestein, wrote, " I believe such a description is a disservice to its readers. It could only aggravate the grief of the friends and relatives of Arlis Perry, and the rest of the Stanford community, already thoroughly shocked by the crime itself. Although a newspaper enjoys the right to disseminate information freely, it should not ignore its concomitant responsibility to use intelligent discretion." The editors responded by saying it was better to print all the facts to defuse the speculation from vaguer reports. But on campus, there was little consensus on this point. In the hysteria of the moment, intelligent discretion sounded abstract.

By Sunday afternoon, detectives learned that coroner John Hauser had discovered an ice pick thrust into Arlis's brain. Because the weapon was so unusual, the detectives withheld the detail from the public. Instead, they talked in vague terms about a stab to the head. The fact that the killer had used an ice pick and had broken off the handle was critical to their probe. It was something only the murderer would know, a piece investigators could use in questioning a suspect. A key fact that might have stifled the speculation about torture—an ice pick was at least swift—was thus concealed from the public.

By Monday, in damage-control mode, sheriff's authorities sought to dismiss the reports of ritual murder tied to the church. "The murder seems to fit the typical pattern of a sexual psychopath," said Undersheriff Tom Rosa. "It has no cult-like overtones. It just happened to occur in a church." Rosa's statement hardly reassured the fearful. It was true that the murder had a sexual component. But it was difficult to describe the typical pattern of a sexual psychopath. And there were enough strange things about the way the body was laid out to suggest that the killer mocked a ritual linked to the church.

In their public explanations, sheriff's officials followed the template of the story that was provided by security guard Steve Crawford, who said he locked the church at 11:45 p.m. on Saturday after walking halfway down the aisle and announcing that the church was closing. Crawford insisted he did not see Arlis. On Tuesday, both Stanford Police Chief Marv Herrington and Sheriff's Capt. Frank Mosunic attempted to clarify the chronology and defuse talk about torture. Mosunic said Arlis was strangled, probably lost consciousness, and was stabbed in the back of the neck with a "stabbing instrument." Pressed to describe the weapon, Mosunic said, "We have to keep some of these things quiet."

Herrington, meanwhile, speculated that Arlis was *already* dead when Crawford locked up at 11:45 p.m. Quoted in the San Jose *Mercury News*, the chief underscored the loose security around the church. "There are lots of keys floating around and almost anybody can get into the church if he wants to," the chief said. The night after Arlis's killing, he noted, the police assigned two security guards to search and lock up the church. Nonetheless, they found a door unlocked a couple of hours later. Herrington also insisted that a security guard had checked the doors of the church after Bruce Perry called to report his wife missing at 3:00 a.m., a point not supported by the radio transcript. Although Bruce told the Stanford dispatcher that his wife might be locked inside Memorial Church, Crawford never looked. No one ordered him to check.

In Bismarck, the coverage had a more subdued cast. On Monday morning, *The Bismarck Tribune* ran a front-page story headlined "Ex-Bismarck Woman Is Murdered" with an appealing photo of Arlis wearing her glasses. Drawn largely from wire-service sources, the story noted that "large candles found on the body prompted speculation by church and law officials that the murder could have been ritualistic." On the next day, Tuesday, the *Tribune* followed with a lengthy story that talked about Arlis's deep religious faith. "God was very real to the former Bismarck girl; her religious faith was deep and strong," the story read. "That was one of the things she shared with Bruce, her husband of less than two months. Both were used to going to church to pray, taking it to the Lord in prayer, as the old sacred song says."

Over the next few months, virtually any crime in the Bay Area that sounded similar to the Memorial Church murder received extra attention from the media. Eight days after Arlis was murdered, a man jumped into the car of a woman on the Stanford campus, making her drive around and forcing her to disrobe before he left her near Page Mill Road without assaulting her sexually. (The woman suffered a serious case of poison oak and was treated with cortisone.) Noting the different mode of the crime, sheriff's deputies said it was not linked to the Arlis Perry case. Then, on October 28, just two weeks after the murder in the church, a twenty-seven-year-old woman from Milpitas, Josephine DeCaso, was found dead at the stables near her home after being seen hitchhiking early in the day. This time, the cops arrested the man who found the body.

Meanwhile, sheriff's deputies announced that they were sending more evidence to the FBI in the hope that its advanced fingerprint analysis would produce something new. The media noted that Bruce Perry had taken a polygraph test and passed it. In Bismarck, the *Tribune* gave extensive coverage to Arlis's funeral, which was held on the morning of Friday, October 18, in the same church in which she and Bruce had been married two months earlier. Gradually, the case faded from prominent coverage. The investigators acknowledged that they had no firm leads.

The story of the ice pick was uncovered by a mix of shoe leather and serendipity. A savvy young reporter for the San Jose *Mercury News*, Maline Hazle, developed her own hunch after learning that it was likely a puncture wound. Married to a Sunnyvale public-safety officer, Hazle was well-connected in police circles and had covered breaking news for years. The inspiration, however, came from something her mother told her. As a kid growing up in Montana, Hazle's mother thought of writing a story in which murder was committed with a sharpened icicle that would melt away. A strange idea, the stuff of noir fiction, but not inconceivable in the cold of Montana. Crime aficionados who have explored the idea say it would take a lucky thrust to succeed. But an icicle, at least in the mind's image, is not that different from an ice pick. So Hazle called one of her best law enforcement sources and asked whether Arlis was killed with an ice pick. Having known Hazle for too long to lie, the source answered yes. Hazle did not use the revelation immediately in print. When she did a retrospective on the murder in 1980, she referred to the weapon as a "rod-like instrument." But word began to leak out. While detectives were still trying to hold back their most important clue, the task was getting harder.

CHAPTER 12

THE HUSKY YOUNG MAN

It was about noon on Friday, October 11, 1974, when attorney Guy Blase peered out of his office to ask the new receptionist to pull a file for him. At the law firm of Spaeth, Blase, Valentine and Klein, a few blocks from Palo Alto's downtown, almost everyone had gone to lunch or was preparing for the weekend. In the greeting area for visitors, Blase spotted the receptionist, Arlis Perry, having a conversation with a husky, casually dressed young man with blond, curly hair, about five foot ten. From the intensity of their talk, Blase figured the visitor was her husband. Employed at the law firm for only a couple of weeks—her first day was Monday, September 30—the young Bismarck woman did not have a wide circle of friends in California. Later, Blase remembered thinking the conversation was unusual. Arlis had told people in the office that she didn't want her husband to visit her. She was still too new to the job. It wasn't until four days later that the forty-five-year-old Blase realized how wrong his assumptions were. By then, Arlis was dead.

Although her evangelistic Midwestern background differed from that of the jockish West Coast attorneys who gave the firm its character, Arlis seemed to be settling into the work. As a new employee, she was not assigned to a particular lawyer. She greeted visitors, answered phones, and did paperwork, preparing documents for filing in court. It did not seem like a stretch for Arlis, a conscientious worker who had been a receptionist at Duncan Perry's dental offices in Bismarck.

"She was an absolutely lovely person," said Ken Newman, then a Stanford undergraduate with a part-time job at the firm. "She was very pretty. She had an ebullient personality but wasn't high-profile. She was very well-spoken. She was also very much in love with her husband."

Founded in 1965 by Blase and two fellow Stanford Law School alumni, Grant Spaeth and Dick Farman, the firm practiced general business law at a time when the Santa Clara Valley's legal trade was burgeoning. Located in a converted house at 400 Channing Avenue, it was a small operation, with eight lawyers and as many secretaries. Spaeth, the son of former Stanford Law School dean Carl Spaeth, had been a member of the 1953 NCAA golf title team at Stanford. Farman had been a high school basketball star, and Blase was a passionate tennis player. The athletic flavor of the firm came with a commitment to public service. Over his career, Blase worked for a variety of causes, including the Children's Health Council and an opportunity center for the homeless. A gregarious man with a quick wit, he nourished doubts about the warlike side of the law. Blase joked that he made his living by "writing letters."

On Tuesday evening, October 15, along with a cadre of people from the firm, Blase attended the service for Arlis at Memorial Church, a sad ceremony presided over by the dean of the chapel, Robert Hamerton-Kelly. For the attorney, the moment of revelation came when he understood that the sobbing Bruce Perry was not the husky young man he had seen talking to Arlis on the previous Friday. With dark hair and a large, angular frame, Bruce looked very different from the law-firm visitor. In turn, that raised the question of just who the husky blond man was and why he had visited Arlis. Blase let the investigators know of his discovery, and on Thursday afternoon, October 17, Sgt. Neal Pate was dispatched to the law firm.

Pate had little difficulty finding people who knew Arlis. He noted that one law firm employee, Jeanine Goodman, had a few conversations with the young Bismarck woman. Arlis had told her that she was proud to be working to put her husband through school. All the same, she was eager to return to college and sorry she had not started that semester. Goodman described Arlis as sweet, naive, and not the kind of young woman likely to have an affair. Ken Newman, who shared administrative tasks with Arlis, remembered one other thing about the murdered woman. She was devout. She readily talked about her faith in Jesus.

About 6:00 p.m. on Friday, October 11, the day before the murder, Newman and a female friend had a conversation with Arlis as the work week ended. Relaxing outside the office of Larry Klein, a young attorney who later became mayor of Palo Alto, they talked about what it was like to be married so young. Arlis was a wife at an age when many Stanford undergraduates were still searching for an opening line with the opposite sex. Her faith in her marriage seemed as strong as her belief in Jesus. "I remember her saying that she knew it was an unusual choice, but they were very happy; they had a life plan; they were the type of people who could make that set of decisions," Newman told me.

What puzzled detectives about Blase's sighting at noon was that Arlis apparently did not tell her husband of the visit. By their account, Bruce had no idea who the husky young man was. Everyone who knew Arlis dismissed the idea of an affair. Aside from her upbringing and love for her husband, she had been in California for only a few weeks and married for less than two months. A lover would be unlikely to pick her workplace for a confrontation. That left questions: Who was the visitor? Why not tell Bruce?

Some followers of the case have suggested that Arlis could have been withholding news that would upset Bruce during his bouts of heavy study. This explanation is plausible, although Arlis's friends say she would have been more inclined to tell her husband of an intense conversation. Without a clear idea of the husky man's identity, the focus turned to someone who might have followed Arlis to California from Bismarck, someone she knew from an earlier period of her life. The sheriff's investigators had already asked for help from William J. Doherty, an agent of the North Dakota Bureau of Criminal Identification, who did a background check that concluded that Arlis and Bruce were trustworthy young people.

Could the husky man have been a classmate from Bismarck High School or Bismarck Junior College, where Arlis studied in 1973–74? The evidence is fleeting, though investigators apparently weighed the idea. Bruce's friend from the BHS track team, Tim Clausnitzer, who is blond but lean, remembers talking to a similarly built classmate about the quest at the time. The friend told Clausnitzer that detectives were trying to establish the whereabouts of various young men, including Clausnitzer, when the murder occurred. Clearly, the investigators were probing a Bismarck link.

One possibility was that the visitor came from a religious group Arlis was involved with—perhaps Young Life, which focused on evangelizing high school students. But why would a young man cross the country to talk with Arlis at a Palo Alto law firm? On the other hand, if the theory was true, it might explain why Arlis would not tell Bruce about the visitor. Arlis was more evangelistic than her husband, and bringing up a Bismarck religious connection might have been something she preferred to do when the time was right. The last possibility was that Guy Blase was mistaken in judging the talk as intense. But that seems difficult to accept without knowing more. Blase was too shrewd a judge of humanity to be so wrong.

All this left the larger issue: Could the law-firm visitor be the killer? Plainly, he was not Bruce Perry or Steve Crawford. Plainly, too, he knew enough to find Arlis at her workplace. One theory put forward by aficionados of the case was that he might have agreed with

Arlis to meet her at the church late Saturday night. Then, after she arrived and settled into a pew to pray, he slipped into the sanctuary and killed her. But that defies logic. Arlis would have had to find a way of leaving her husband, an unlikely possibility. The young wife had not planned her walk to the post office in advance. She had not planned the spat with Bruce. If the law-firm visitor had stalked Arlis, he would have had to follow her for thirty-six hours, waiting outside Quillen House for the couple to depart. Aside from the tedium of the task and the low chance of success, it ran the risk of alerting the victim. On the night Arlis was killed, Quillen House had at least a couple of vigilant observers of the neighborhood. Two women, including a neighbor of the Perrys, reported seeing a red-bearded man parked near the apartments between 7:00 and 10:00 p.m. Saturday in a white Volkswagen van. Police determined he had nothing to do with the murder.

I came to think the husky young man was not a random visitor, though what his visit meant is open to question. While investigators have generally dismissed the significance of the incident, the visit so close to Arlis's death has formed the backbone of various conspiracy theories. In the weeks before she died, Arlis noted a strange coincidence. In a letter to her high school friend Jenny, she revealed that there was another Bruce D. Perry at Stanford. His middle name was Duncan, the same as her husband's, and he had just gotten married the previous summer—though his wife's name was not Arlis. Arlis had discovered this when a friend called Stanford and got the wrong Bruce Perry. "So I'm sending you the right number, and you'll know that you have the right Bruce Perry," she said. Was there a chance that the law firm visitor was the second Bruce Perry? Was someone shadowing Bruce and Arlis?

CHAPTER 13

THE ALIBI GIVER

To his Stanford colleagues who had served in the military, Jim Cobb was known as a "club sergeant." Unless you admired a man who cut corners, it fell short of a compliment. It meant he supplied drinks and food to the noncommissioned officers' club in the army, a job that offered rich chances for petty graft—skimming, deception, theft. It was a reputation that later dogged Cobb at Stanford. But early on October 13, 1974, his problems at the university lay well in the future. Driving his three-wheel Cushman motor scooter around Beat 10, the Old Quad, Cobb was performing the job of a Stanford community service officer, a "door shaker" in police slang. In the Arlis Perry story, he appeared at a critical juncture, likely a few minutes after she was killed.

With duties at the center of the Stanford campus, Cobb worked a 5:00 p.m. to 1:00 a.m. shift, a stint that overlapped with Steve Crawford's 10:00 p.m. to 6:00 a.m. shift. The two men shared duty for the Old Quad—checking doors, patrolling courtyards, trying to stave off boredom. Fifty-three years old, five foot nine, a Texan who was hired at Stanford in 1970, Cobb shared a military past with Crawford. Despite the twenty-five-year gap in their ages, the two got along. They were kinsmen in discontent.

Assigned earlier in his shift to what police dubbed "a kitchen detail" at Wilbur Hall, a large residential complex a half mile to the east of the church, Cobb checked in at the police annex about ten-thirty on Saturday night to get the ring of keys to lock up his portion of the Old Quad. He learned Crawford had taken them out, not unusual in the relaxed protocol of the security guards. A short while afterward, Cobb retrieved a set of keys from Crawford in the quad—he remembered they met near President Richard Lyman's office—and began locking up. Memorial Church was so generous in handing out keys that the locks were almost a formality, a nod to the pretense of security. Among the three dozen people who had master keys to the church were the organist, the wedding hostess, the sexton, the church secretary, and the church's California Avenue florist, Mock's Flowers. A list prepared for investigators said the police had one or two and the fire department had one. After meeting Cobb, Crawford retained a set to lock the church.

Around 12:05 a.m., "give or take a few minutes," by his account, Cobb met Crawford again at the west end of the quad. Seated on his scooter, Cobb chatted with his colleague for about fifteen minutes about school, the job, their union, and the buildings on campus. Crawford owned a sense of gab that made conversation easy. By the accounts of both men, Crawford said, "You may as well give me the keys." It made sense. Cobb was going off work shortly, and Crawford would return them to the police annex when he finished his shift. Glancing at his watch, Cobb marked the time as 12:20 a.m. Cobb said he saw nothing unusual about his colleague. Crawford wasn't breathing hard or looking harried. From passing through the arcade outside the church a few minutes after midnight, Cobb had the feeling that MemChu might have been open. Vague as his observation sounded, it could have reflected something unusual. Crawford had neglected to turn off the lights.

The time of their talk mattered because of what investigators learned from witnesses at the church. The best estimate was that Arlis arrived at the church between 11:30 and 11:40 p.m. Steve Crawford said he closed up the church around 11:45. If he was the murderer—a possibility the detectives had to consider—that meant he had only twenty minutes to kill Arlis, stow her body in a place where it would not be found, and emerge into the quad to talk with Cobb. That demanded not just swift conception but speedy action, a decision to commit murder on the spot. Crawford had no advance warning that Arlis would arrive. If he committed the crime, the timing suggested he killed Arlis minutes before he chatted amiably with his counterpart. It seemed hard to fathom.

If, on the other hand, an intruder had hidden in the church and killed Arlis after closing time, it begged the question of why neither security guard heard or sensed anything untoward. Neither was a sterling character—within a few years, Stanford would learn how untrustworthy each man was—but an outsider orchestrating an attack and then staging the body would risk being overheard or interrupted. Although the quad was a big place, and not every noise from the church penetrated the courtyard, a killer from the outside would not know the rhythms of patrol. Whatever theory of the murder emerged as prevalent, it was likely that Arlis was dead by the time Cobb and Crawford talked.

Interviewed for the second time on Monday night, October 14, Crawford gave a babbling and unclear account of his conversation with Cobb. It seemed to verify Cobb's account, but the stops and starts of Crawford's words made it confusing. The detectives strove to write down his words verbatim, adding punctuation:

> CRAWFORD: "That at approximately one o'clock, this guy who has this half of the beat went home. I picked up the keys. I met him in the middle of the quad. I picked up the keys from him at about; just after I closed the church between; but it about one o'clock, picked up the keys from him at twelve o'clock, I'm sure I picked up the keys from him and just drifted around the area."

Given what investigators later learned about Crawford and Cobb, the two men could have colluded on an alibi. But it would have demanded more coordination than their accounts seemed to reflect. Crawford's statement was confusing. Cobb's narrative, however, had the hallmarks of truth. For the benefit of investigators, Cobb went through the routine of a security guard closing up the church. He would check the exterior doors first to see they were locked, then enter the church through the front door. After turning on the lights and locking the two interior side doors, he would walk up to the altar and finish by walking around the inside perimeter. It was a more conscientious routine than Crawford admitted to.

If the story of Jim Cobb had ended there, it might have remained a footnote to the murder. His statement did much to fix the time of death. But like so much else in the Arlis Perry case, his resume had coils that extended in a vexing pattern. In the mid-eighties, Cobb had the dubious honor of being labeled the "Tupperware Bandit" on campus. In his memoirs, *War Stories Down on Stanford's Farm*, retired Police Capt. Raoul Niemeyer told the story at length, using the pseudonym "Crabbe" for Cobb.

One of Cobb's jobs was to collect the quarters people paid into a lockbox when they parked in a Stanford lot. Once a motorist inserted quarters, a wooden gate rose to allow entrance. This system was plagued by technical problems. The gate sometimes failed, and parkers found ways around it. The biggest flaw in parking collections, however, was human. It came to light when a parking-enforcement officer filled in for Cobb one day and had to repair one of the gates. Instead of the regular lockbox, he found a six-by-four-inch Tupperware container with $7.50 in quarters inside and a black line drawn by a felt pen about two inches from the top. It didn't take the cops long to realize Cobb had inserted the Tupperware container into the mechanism, taking a cut before turning in the quarters for counting. By making himself an expert in fixing the machines, he made sure his scheme stayed secret.

A sting operation followed. Starting early in the morning, the cops followed Cobb through his routine in preparing the lockboxes. To guard against an accidental leak, Niemeyer obtained special radios from the county communications office. The Stanford cops even marked a few quarters with red fingernail polish and dropped them into the lockbox. Known as "bait coins," these were meant to trace where the money went. At the end of the day, Niemeyer and his team searched Cobb's scooter, which was carrying $100 in quarters, including bait coins, inside a thick paper bag. They theorized that Cobb was employing the "salami technique," taking a slice of the take—up to the felt marker line—but not so much as to trigger an alarm.

When the police brought Cobb in for questioning, they left him in an upstairs detective office where the investigators observed him for several minutes without his knowledge. "I just gonna tell 'em I'm bringin' em in," Cobb repeated, rehearsing a mantra about how he dealt with the quarters. The Stanford police employed a primitive but effective eavesdropping device—a Sony desk radio that actually played music. Hidden behind the "O" in the Sony logo was a camera. A separate hidden mic provided sound.

After Niemeyer told him he was under arrest, the veteran security guard invoked his Miranda rights, throwing the police into a difficult situation. For all his flaws, Cobb was a popular man. The

Stanford Police Officers' Association denounced the arrest. But an investigation by Santa Clara County Deputy DA Julius Finkelstein led authorities to estimate Cobb had taken at least $68,000 over four years, the equivalent of more than $325 per week. When the cops served a search warrant at Cobb's San Jose home, they found brand-new furnishings, a new Oldsmobile 88, and cookware, dining, and glassware. The security guard was living larger than his salary. With a black mark at the end of his career, Cobb died in 1988 at age sixty-seven.

Had Cobb lived longer, his venality might have created trouble for investigators in the Arlis Perry case. It was hard to put faith in the words of a man who had taken the university for $68,000 or more. Yet in the absence of something better, Cobb's account of his talk with Crawford in the quad at 12:05 am was probably as close to the truth as detectives could get. And that meant the murder probably happened in the space of twenty minutes.

CHAPTER 14

THE MAN WHO CHANGED HIS STORY

On the Sunday morning of the murder, the chat between Sgt. John Johnson and security guard Steve Crawford marked the intersection of the straitlaced and the scruffy, the careful and the careless. Johnson was ascending a career ladder. Crawford was scraping the bottom rung. At that moment, however, the two were no adversaries. Laying the template for a much-debated narrative, Crawford said he checked MemChu twice, once at 10:30 p.m. and then at 11:45. He walked to the middle of the aisle and announced that the church was closing. He told Johnson no one was in the sanctuary. The detective's report noted that Crawford had not seen Arlis before discovering her body beneath a pew in the east transept around 5:40 a.m. It seemed like a straightforward narrative. Johnson's report took less than two pages.

At 7:35 p.m. on Monday, thirty-six hours later, Sheriff's Sgt. Dave Pascual and Stanford Lt. Walt Konar talked to Crawford again at police headquarters to flesh out his story. By the time they sat down, Bruce Perry had passed a lie detector test, which eliminated him as a suspect in the eyes of investigators. The detectives began by telling Crawford they wanted to go through his activities step-by-step from his shift Saturday night through Sunday. Crawford then made a startling disclosure. He believed that he had seen "her"—meaning Arlis—late Saturday night. And he changed his story about inspecting the church. Between his first trip at 10:30 p.m. and closing up at 11:45, he had returned around 11:15. Now there were three trips, not two. As he walked down the main aisle on that middle visit, he said the visitor "did pull into a pew in the back of the church." When Pascual and Konar asked whether it was Arlis, he said, "I think it was the person I found." He described her as blond and wearing a three-quarter-length dark coat.

This wasn't the smart-aleck Crawford, the guy who described Arlis's body as "a stiff." It was a more penitent man confessing mistakes. In this second interview, Crawford was remorseful about his failure to search the church more carefully at closing time, saying he might have been able to prevent the murder. "He was sure that the person found was the person that walked in and that she may of (sic) been in there and that if he had checked the place, she wouldn't of got creamed," the sheriff's report said. ("Creamed" was another one of those 1930s-gangster words, not dissimilar to "a stiff.") Nonetheless, the revelation raised fresh questions. Why did he neglect to mention the 11:15 trip in the first interview? If Crawford had seen Arlis in the church during that middle visit, why didn't he tell Sgt. Johnson?

THE MAN WHO CHANGED HIS STORY

Most significantly, Crawford's statement contradicted what he had told dispatcher Charlie Papp at 3:00 a.m. on Sunday—that he had not seen anyone resembling Arlis. During the cursory search for the missing woman, Crawford repeatedly said that the church was locked, implying that it did not need to be searched. On the strength of Crawford's assurances, police were dissuaded from exploring the sanctuary. "Well, I'll keep an eye out for her," Crawford told Papp. Now he was saying he had seen her *before* he talked with the dispatcher.

If Crawford's new version was to be believed, it implied that Arlis was kidnapped or killed between 11:15 p.m., when Crawford saw her slip into the pew, and 11:45, when he concluded that the church was empty and locked the doors. This idea posed inherent problems. If the killer accosted Arlis while the church was still open, she might have screamed and alerted witnesses. It was always possible that the assailant had disabled her before she could cry out. In fact, Stanford Police Chief Marv Herrington theorized that Arlis was killed before the church was locked up. But several people remained in the church between 11:15 and 11:45 p.m., including Brent Davis and Mark Kral, who reported seeing a young, blond woman in prayer near the front of the sanctuary.

By the time of the second interview, the detectives still did not have a full transcript of the radio traffic early Sunday. On the surface, they had plenty of reasons to give Crawford a break as a witness. The twenty-eight-year-old was an air force veteran, a security guard who had been hired as a Stanford police officer. His brother, Bill, was a

Mountain View cop and an ex-Holy Cross brother. Crawford had been shaken by the crime, his memory ruffled by what he had been through. Neither detective interviewing him was a novice. Pascual, thirty-three, was a veteran who could play the stern cop, as he had done in the interrogation of Bruce Perry. Konar was a former Vietnam Green Beret, the son of an Auschwitz survivor. But they were operating at a disadvantage. Pascual and Konar had not interviewed Crawford initially. So the troublesome contradictions in the security guard's story did not resonate as loudly as they might have.

As the conversation unspooled, several new details emerged. Crawford explained that he had driven his car to his beat—the Old Quad—and started his rounds at 10:10 p.m. He first checked out the law school, which, in 1974, was in the northeast part of the outer quad, several hundred feet north of the church. Working his way through the Old Quad, the security guard entered the church around 10:30, walking down the west aisle. He said he tested the west interior door that later was found broken open. "The door was locked," he told the detectives. "I shook it." (The investigators did not record that Crawford shook other doors.) Crawford said he remembered seeing two couples in the church along with a man with a Prince Valiant haircut, whom deputies identified as Mark Kral. For the benefit of the detectives, he marked the latter's location in the east transept with an "X." Crawford remembered that only the altar lights were on. Most of the sanctuary was dark. Before he left, he turned up the transept lights "substantially enough so people could see."

After that first visit, Crawford said, he "went out to the trees" in front of the church and sat around looking at people. Then, at 11:15 p.m., midway between the first and third visit, he returned to the church. As he walked down the aisle, he saw a person with a dark coat—whom he later identified as a young woman—walk in behind him and "pull into" a rear pew. "I thought it was a male at the time," he said. He told the detectives she may have been the only person left in the church. After this second visit, he went outside again and saw several people outside the church, including a man on a bike. At 11:45, he returned to close up. This time, he spent five minutes walking through the church, going by the Round Room and leaving by the main aisle. He said he had "flash-lighted" the west door's dead bolt to ensure that it was locked.

At this point in the interview, the security guard turned rueful. Normally, Crawford said, he would have walked all around the church and checked the balcony. After all, sleepers had been found in the church. In the past, Crawford had found a man who played flute in one of the transepts. When Pascual and Konar asked him why he did not perform a full check on Saturday night, Crawford explained that he was in a hurry. The exchange went this way:

Q. What reason were you in a hurry?
A. Just to get out. I had some homework, and I had some homework, and I thought I would get my notes out and read through them, plus the fact I thought I was ahead of the game, by closing up a little early.

After closing up, Crawford "drifted around the quad," getting the keys from Jim Cobb, the security guard going off his shift. He returned to the Round Room between 1:00 and 1:30 a.m. He said he had gone downstairs, gotten a drink of water, and shined his flashlight around the basement. Later in his shift, he went for lunch at the Jordan Quad, a group of low-rise buildings about five blocks away.[1] Then, at 5:30 a.m., he returned to open the church. He noticed he had left the lights on—the same lights he had turned up earlier in the night—and that the interior west door was open. Stepping into the chamber behind the door, he sensed something was wrong. He knew the west door had been locked, he told the detectives. It couldn't be open unless someone had a key or "came in from the side."

Following around the west side of the church, Crawford then crossed in front of the altar and into the east transept, where he found Arlis's body behind a rear pew. At first, he told the detectives, he thought it was an overdose, because her clothes were in disarray. The logic of that comment was elusive. The candles used on Arlis's body were visible, as were bruises on her neck. An overdose victim was unlikely to have arranged the scene. Crawford remembered grabbing the body and pulling it out from under the pew—a distance he later estimated as six inches to a foot. Saying "hey," he bent down to tap her and got no reaction. Checking her chest and wrist, he found no heartbeat. He told investigators he remembered thinking that the body did not feel cold.

As Crawford recalled it, Arlis's chest was bare up to her breast line, and she was wearing underwear. But he noted that the newspaper had reported that she was nude from the waist down (which was correct). Crawford said he saw no blood, though there might have been blood under the pew. On her mouth, he saw something resembling burns. When he saw her face, Crawford said, "black became white, white became black, and I got the hell out of there." After trying to call communications from a spot near the east door, he left through the front doors and used his radio to inform dispatcher Charlie Papp that he had a "stiff." (Stanford police say their handheld radios, a brick-like Motorola HT 220 model, sometimes encountered problems in transmission from inside the church.)

When the detectives asked Crawford if he would take a lie detector test, the security guard refused. He told them that he was getting the "distinct impression that he was a suspect." He had gotten his job on the basis of trust, Crawford said, and he did not "murder people or rob safes." His refusal left the detectives skeptical and wary. But they had little to conclude Crawford was the killer. No physical evidence linked him to the crime. One detail, however, suggested that the detectives had not dismissed Crawford as a suspect. Konar and Pascual noted that the security guard appeared to be left-handed. By this time, the detectives knew about the ice pick and had reason to think the murderer was a lefty.

The biggest revelation was that Crawford was now certain he had seen Arlis in the church, at least during his 11:15 p.m. visit. The security guard invited sympathy by expressing remorse about not checking the church more carefully. Had she already been disabled or even killed by the time he returned at a quarter of twelve to close up? It seems unlikely. Brent Davis had seen her praying shortly before he left the church at 11:45. But if Arlis was still alive in the church at closing time, why did Crawford not see her? And why did he imply that Memorial Church wasn't worth searching when Bruce called the dispatcher?

In the days after the murder, the backup sexton, Bill Aaron, came across Crawford, who was still working as a security guard. Noticing that Crawford seemed dejected, Aaron talked to him. "They think I did it," he remembers Crawford saying. If the investigators weren't saying anything publicly—and a number of them came to doubt Crawford was their man—the security guard knew he was under watch.

PART TWO

CHAPTER 15

THE LADY WITH A PARASOL

No matter what Undersheriff Tom Rosa said, it was never possible to think about the murder without considering the setting. The facts were damning, the crime a violation of sacred space. Arlis visited the church to pray and emerged as the victim of a horrible murder. Seeking solace, she was defiled. At the least, the scene implied a killer who wanted to make a statement in surroundings of splendor. At the worst, it suggested a man who lifted a middle finger to God.

Those surroundings owed their origins to one woman: Jane Lathrop Stanford, the widow of Leland Stanford, the senator and governor who seized power and wealth as a railroad magnate—or a robber baron. Stubborn, dictatorial, impatient with delay, Jane did more than anyone else to create the setting in which Arlis Perry was killed. Memorial Church was designed as the focal point of spiritual life at Stanford. When the university opened in 1891, two years before Leland Sr.'s death, the Stanfords said they expected students to share a sense of "the highest teachings of morality and religion." Jane sought to translate that goal into a work of art that rivaled the cathedrals of Europe. With a matchless collection of mosaics, statues, and stain glass, marred by an instinct for the maudlin, she created an architectural jewel. So it was ironic that the last chapter of Jane Stanford's life echoed that of Arlis Perry's. Like Arlis, Jane was murdered.

Well before the church was dedicated on June 25, 1903, the family's story was carved in grief. Jane and her husband dedicated the university to the memory of their son, Leland Stanford Jr., who had died of typhoid at age fifteen during a European tour. One of the church's stained-glass windows, entitled "Lo, I Am with You Always," depicts a teenager believed to be Leland Jr. being lifted to heaven by angels. But the church was primarily Jane's tribute to her husband, Leland Sr., who died ten years before it was finished. Beneath the mosaic on the facade was a garish, theater-like billboard that said, "Memorial Church. Erected to the Glory of God in Loving Memory of My Husband, Leland Stanford." Jane was rich enough to afford bad taste. "While my whole heart is in the university," she told a faculty member, "my soul is in that church."

Already in her seventies when the church was built, Jane hefted a parasol when she inspected the work. It wasn't for the California sun, although she had a pale complexion she sought to shield. In Jane Stanford's hands, the parasol served as a yardstick of glory, an arbiter of angels, a cudgel of artists. Clutching the coat of the university's young, British-born architect, Charles E. Hodges, Jane climbed the scaffolding to the far reaches of the church. With a notch on the parasol, she then measured the depths of the carvings she had ordered. If they did not come up to her mark, she would demand that they be cut deeper.

A hybrid of Gothic cathedral and Mediterranean sanctuary, the Stanford church contained works of breathtaking splendor. The sanctuary was 152 feet long, with seats for 1,250 people on the main floor. Jane picked the stained-glass tableaus for the windows and hired the superb New York artist Frederick Stymetz Lamb to design them. For the front of the church, she chose the grand mosaic of Jesus blessing his followers, an artwork designed by the Venice firm A. Salviati & Co. Notably, Jane decreed that the mosaic have equal numbers of men and women.[1] Convinced that an undecorated wall squandered space meant for God, Jane filled the church with sayings that underscored her faith. A few feet from the spot where Arlis's body was found, an inscription read, "An eternal existence in prospect converts the whole of your present state into a mere vestibule of the grand court of life; a beginning, an introduction to what is to follow." If Jane's message did not sway everyone, her creation inspired visitors with its beauty. From the beginning, students and staff chose the chapel for wedding vows. The first couple to be married at Memorial Church, on February 22, 1903, was William Armfield Holt and Ethel Rhodes, from the class of 1902. Since then, there have been more than seven thousand unions.[2]

Nowhere did Jane Stanford's taste for the eccentric surface more than in the choice of God's Eye, or "All-Seeing Eye," a fresco painted at the top of the dome of the pre-1906 church. It showed a large eye staring down, complete with a teardrop. In the circle around the eye, cherubs frolicked next to a shooting star. One of them peered over the edge at worshippers below. Just where Jane got the inspiration for the design is unclear, but the all-seeing eye appeared often in religious and secular design. An eye confined by a triangle appears on the back of the one-dollar bill. It was frequently used by the Masons, whose members included Leland Stanford. "I am sure she (Jane) felt it was benevolent and protective," said Memorial Church historian Lesley Bone. "Could she have felt it was also representing her husband's watching over the university?"

The public reaction to the Eye ended well short of standing applause. A few critics thought it was creepy, a hint of heavenly surveillance. In 1906, George Hodges, the liberal dean of the Episcopal Theological Seminary in Cambridge, Massachusetts (and no relation to architect Charles Hodges), summed it up as "grotesque awfulness."

"I was told that by standing under the center of the lantern and looking straight up, I could see it if I would," Hodges wrote. "I saw people looking at it during the sermon, and probably guessing what would happen if the great tear should splash down upon the congregation. But I never looked."

The Rev. John Dinsmore, who gave the funeral homily for Jane, offered a stern but more charitable explanation, saying the faithful knew a steward must give an account to his master. "They understood they lived under the great Master's eye," Dinsmore said.

The fresco known as "God's Eye" adorned the tower of the
church until it collapsed in the earthquake of 1906.

A big piece of the church's design and mawkish features could be explained by Jane's Victorian background and the tragedy in her life. The third of seven children of merchant Dyer Lathrop and the former Jane Shields, Jane Elizabeth Lathrop was born on August 25, 1828, in Albany, New York. Reportedly her father's favorite, she was educated at home and briefly at the Albany Female Academy. She grew up to be a shy, self-conscious young woman who cared deeply about how others judged her. In 1850, she married an ambitious young lawyer four years her senior, Leland Stanford, who called her "Jennie." With him, she moved to Port Washington, Wisconsin, where he set up a law firm with a $3,000 bequest from his father (more than $95,000 in today's money). After a fire destroyed his office and library in 1852, Jane returned to Albany to nurse her sick and demanding father. Leland departed for California, where he joined his five brothers in the Gold Country, selling equipment to miners. The separation stung Jane, who worried, probably correctly, that Albany society considered her an abandoned wife.

When Dyer Lathrop died three years later, Jane joined Leland in Sacramento at the beginning of an extraordinary ascent that took them to the summit of California's social and political elite. In 1861, Leland was named president of the Central Pacific Railroad and was elected governor of California, a dual role that betrayed the vagaries of the young state's ideas about conflict of interest. At the couple's mansion at Eighth and N Streets, a Victorian confection that still stands, Jane established herself as a competent hostess, throwing parties that lasted into the early morning. For years, the Stanfords remained childless. Then, in May 1868, at the age of thirty-nine, Jane delivered a son, Leland DeWitt Stanford, whose name was later changed to Leland Stanford Jr. (A story, possibly apocryphal, has it that Leland presented his infant son at a dinner party atop a bed of blossoms on a silver platter.)

With an abundance of wealth and no other children, the Stanfords lavished attention on their son, who showed an early aptitude for collecting artifacts. On one floor of their Nob Hill home, Leland Jr. established a museum of his treasures—arms, armor, stuffed birds, and other curios. When the teenager died at the Hotel Bristol in Florence in 1884, the couple plunged into sorrow. Jane dabbled in spiritualism, trying to contact relatives through the netherworld. At one point, in an attempt to reach their son, the Stanfords consulted a famous medium, Maud Lord Drake. "The children of California shall be our children," Leland Stanford Sr. reportedly told his wife. By 1885, the two had donated land at their Palo Alto Stock Farm to a university to focus on science and engineering.

After her husband's death from heart failure in 1893—the sixty-nine-year-old founder had been in poor health for years—Jane faced the challenge of organizing and building the fledgling institution. Leland had run the university as part of his personal fief, a practice that saved time during his life but created massive headaches after his death. Because his estate was tied up by a claim from the federal government, Jane sought to pay the bills with her personal allowance of $10,000 per month, a little more than $300,000 today. It wasn't nearly enough. To bridge the gap, she tried unsuccessfully to sell her jewels at Queen Victoria's sixtieth-anniversary celebration in 1897. In the spring of 1898, Jane sought to advertise the gems by commissioning a painting of them by A.D.M. Cooper (1856–1924), a talented but dissolute San Jose artist. It was not a happy arrangement. After the teetotal Jane fired Cooper, he went home and finished the painting from his sketches, arranging to have it displayed in a San Jose saloon. (Cooper would typically trade his paintings for free drinks.) An embarrassed Jane felt obliged to retrieve Cooper's work, which hung in a prominent position for years in the university's Cantor Arts Center.

When the legal war over Leland's estate ended and the funds were released in late 1898, Jane embarked on a blitzkrieg of construction. She completed the Memorial Arch, the gymnasium, a museum dedicated to her son, and then, beginning with the new century, Memorial Church, the crown jewel. By spreading along Palm Drive, the main road between Palo Alto and the campus, her architectural choices defied the original plans crafted for Stanford by Charles A. Coolidge, a Boston architect who left after a rift with the Stanfords over design. It was the beginning of a helter-skelter approach to building that plagued the campus well into the 1980s.

Lacking her husband's experience with the treachery of California's ground, Jane pushed her builders and architects to move quickly, without the anchoring needed to withstand an earthquake. The church's most serious flaw was that the crossing structure supporting the eighty-foot tower was not adequately connected to the roof. That mistake left the church vulnerable to shearing in the earthquake of

1906, which devastated the young campus. The tremor felled the church tower, destroyed the facade, and blew out Frederick Lamb's rose window. It shattered the marble statues of the apostles around the altar. This last blow was tragic but not a complete disaster. In the rush of construction, the statues did not fit the niches designed for them in the walls. It gave the pre-1906 chancel the feel of a crowded waiting room in a train station.

And God's Eye? It was destroyed when the tower toppled. After the earthquake, there was no groundswell for it to be replaced. The tower above the church, always too heavy for the structure, was replaced with a modest dome and skylight. So, too, was the garish billboard at the front of the church, succeeded by a small plaque honoring Leland Stanford. Both changes were for the better. Historians say the refuse from the earthquake of 1906 was swept into the nearby San Francisquito Creek, where souvenir hunters trolled for keepsakes. After the Arlis Perry murder, the tear in God's Eye gained a starker meaning, seeming to fulfill Dean Hodges's prediction so many years before. Metaphorically, it had splashed down.

Jane did not live to see the havoc. In 1903, with the bulk of her building campaign behind her, she announced that she intended to travel and embrace a quieter life. A familiar photo in the Stanford collection shows her standing before the Egyptian Sphinx with several companions on New Year's Day, 1904. Two final dramas, however, awaited her. On January 14, 1905, as she was staying at the family's mansion on Nob Hill in San Francisco, she took a drink of Poland Spring water. Sensing a strange taste, she threw up. Traces of strychnine—rat poison—were found in the drink, and Jane decreed that she would no longer live at the Nob Hill home, which Leland had built in the 1870s. With her maid and her longtime personal secretary, Bertha Berner, she decamped to Hawaii, where she checked into Honolulu's Moana Hotel, a four-year-old luxury refuge with a library, a salon, and the first electric elevator in the then-territory.

There, on February 28, 1905, in a second-floor room that overlooked the trolley line, she suffered a lethal reprise. After a day of picnicking on sandwiches, eggs, and gingerbread, she returned to the Moana and asked Berner to mix up a bicarbonate of soda, then commonly taken to soothe an unsettled stomach. Jane had no sooner taken it than she felt a spasm. She told her entourage that she had no control of her body. She believed she had been poisoned. Her jaws were fixed. A doctor was summoned but could not help. At one point, the seventy-six-year-old Jane told him, "This is a terrible death to die." Within twenty minutes, she was gone.

A coroner's jury in Hawaii concluded that it was a homicide by strychnine, although it did not name the killer. Stanford's president, David Starr Jordan, selected by the Stanfords as the university's first leader, embarked on a mission to Hawaii to control the damage. Jordan found another doctor, who concluded that overeating and angina figured in Jane's death. A controversy ensued for years. In 2003, a respected Stanford doctor, Robert W.P. Cutler, published a carefully researched book that concluded it was murder—and that Jordan engaged in a cover-up to protect the university. Without accusing her of involvement in Jane's murder, Cutler questioned the credibility of Jane's personal secretary, Berner, the one person present at both poisonings. Berner, who died of natural causes at age eighty-three in 1945, has remained a suspect, although she was never arrested. Unexplained for so long, the demise of Jane Stanford offered a strange parallel to the murder of the young Bismarck woman who visited the church to pray seven decades later.

CHAPTER 16

SPECIAL DEPUTIES

In February 1971, nine months after he had received an honorable discharge from the air force, Steve Crawford was hired as a Stanford police officer. He had no law enforcement experience, and it's doubtful he would have survived the searching psychological background check most police departments employ now. Crawford had only a few scattered college credits. But his older sibling, Bill, was a Mountain View police officer who had been a brother in the Holy Cross order. In a first meeting, Steve Crawford could come across as intelligent and amiable. Stanford's police chief, Tom Bell, preferred to hire veterans on the theory that someone accustomed to military discipline could help control Vietnam War-era student protesters disrupting the campus. On the night of Arlis Perry's murder, Crawford's presence in Memorial Church owed much to Stanford's desperation to bring those protesters under control.

The force he was joining was branded by incompetence. The fledgling cops received no serious training. New officers were taken to the ROTC range for a few rounds of target practice. A ranking officer would provide an introduction to the department. Then they were given a badge, a baton, and the right to carry their own gun for work. The force was not legally recognized in the state of California—though for many years, the Stanford police had a cozy arrangement with the sheriff's department that allowed officers a "special deputy" status. (Then as now, that status was also conferred on big contributors to the sheriff's political campaign. It was a useful badge to have when the contributor was pulled over for speeding.) The Stanford officers *looked* like cops: they wore uniforms and drove patrol cars. The unusual arrangement, however, lacked the blessing of the state's commission on Peace Officer Standards & Training (POST). It became an increasing worry for Stanford officials and Santa Clara County Sheriff James Geary. Elected sheriff in 1970, Geary made policing at Stanford a central issue in his campaign, claiming the university was not cooperating with the sheriff in quelling disorder.

A hazing ritual imposed on new Stanford officers illustrated the quasi-outlaw culture of the force. In his book, *War Stories Down on Stanford's Farm*, retired Capt. Raoul Niemeyer, who joined the force in 1974 as part of the effort at reorganization, wrote about the trip to the medical school's anatomy lab that all new recruits endured. In the lab, a dozen cadavers might be laid out for dissection. The "trainer" for the new officer would whip the sheet off one of the bodies and say, "Meet your cadaver!" Then, according to the lore, the new re-cruit was taken in pitch-darkness to a cage that held a spider monkey who had learned to greet the officers. "The monkey would grab the recruit by the wrist and scare the crap out of him," Niemeyer said. It felt much like a secret rite at one of the fraternities the new officers were charged with policing—with the difference that the frats were higher-toned.

A hem of exaggeration might attach to the fabric of another story recounted in Niemeyer's book. But the tale is too revealing to dis-miss. Not long after Stanford hired a new police chief to reorganize the department in 1971, an event occurred that persuaded every-one that change was urgent. It began with a Stanford police officer who lived in an Escondido Village student apartment, an unusual arrangement itself. Late one night, he heard a suspicious vehicle in the parking lot. Wearing his bed clothes and gun belt, he went down to check on the car. Not understanding that he was a cop, the oc-cupants of the vehicle peeled out of the lot. As the story goes, the cop fired three times as he yelled, "Stop! Police!" It was the kind of incident that could easily have haunted the police, leaving a multi-million-dollar liability for the university. Worse, it was no fluke. It was the result of years of confusion and neglect.

The reasons for this poorly trained force were not hard to fathom. In the late sixties and early seventies, Stanford administrators urgent-ly sought to curb a series of antiwar demonstrations. The university's managers wanted to hire more cops quickly even if it meant they had to embrace lower standards. The protests centered on the university's classified research and lingering connections with the Stanford Research Institute (SRI), which held government contracts during the Vietnam War. A string of arson that began in the late sixties destroyed offices and rattled administrators. Among the most notable attacks was the April 1970 arson that hit the Center for Advanced Study in Behavioral Sciences, wrecking the work of several scholars. Usually, the culprits got away. The flames destroyed the evidence.

Under then-president Kenneth Pitzer, Stanford tried a tolerant approach toward the protests. Then, as the demonstrations turned ugly, the pressure increased to deal firmly with dissidents. The new attitude was embodied by Provost Richard W. Lyman, who succeeded the luckless Pitzer as president in 1970. Dick Lyman was an intelligent, impatient man who vowed to restore civility on campus. Acid-tongued, dismissive of those he considered his intellectual inferiors, Lyman understood how to summon a moral argument meant to cleave the appeal of the radicals. In his view, he was not stifling dissent but defending freedom. "We have to preserve order, because if we do not, someone else who does not understand the delicate fabric of the university will come in and do it," Lyman told *Time*. In a 248-page book entitled *Stanford in Turmoil, 1966-72*, Lyman cited chapter and verse of his strategy, leaving a record that reads more like a military memoir than a meditation on higher learning.

Behind the university's combative stance lurked a practical weakness. The tough policy relied on cops to enforce the law. As the demonstrations grew large and violent, it was clear that sheriff's deputies called to the campus lacked the numbers—and sometimes the strategic sense—to control events in the way Lyman wanted. So the demands on Stanford Police Chief Bell to hire more officers increased. Bell understood the weaknesses of his force and tried to obtain more training for his officers. But he was handicapped because Stanford paid less than other departments. With a shaky reputation for training and discipline, Stanford was not getting top recruits. The university was blessing the use of guns and batons by people who had no business wielding them. As a result, Bell was embroiled in a fierce political battle. Worried about the county's liability, Sheriff Geary began moving toward withdrawing the fig leaf granted to Stanford by the "special deputy" status. Then, in April 1971, two months after Steve Crawford was hired, Bell quit. Though he said the decision was mutual with his bosses, the chief acknowledged that the university had begun the discussions about his exit.

Three months later, the vacuum at the top of the Stanford University Department of Public Safety was filled by a trim, thirty-five-year-old named Marv Herrington, who had been the chief of campus police at the University of California, Davis, before stopovers at Northwestern University and the Cal State system. A man who looked like a grown-up Boy Scout from a Norman Rockwell painting, Herrington was recruited to Stanford through the ultimate insider connection. The brother-in-law of Stanford's influential vice president for business and finance, Robert Augsburger, was the dean of students at Northwestern, and he recommended Herrington warmly. With Stanford pursuing him, Herrington flexed his bargaining power. One of the first things he demanded was the right to report directly to Lyman. No longer would the uncompromising president automatically relay his wishes about protests through bureaucratic go-betweens. The chief would have the access he needed.

That turned out to be a wise decision for both men. In many ways, Herrington emerged as Lyman's chief diplomat, capable of dealing with students yearning to denounce authority. "The university really had not learned to take a deep breath and count to ten," *The Stanford Daily* quoted a dean of student affairs, Jim Lyons, as saying. "But Dick Lyman instituted principles that set the stage, and Herrington demonstrated that there was a new approach. Rather than bombard (protesters) and make arrests, Herrington was unafraid to talk to students."

The new approach was evident when students sought to block trustees from leaving a meeting at the Hoover Tower by lying in front of their cars. After learning the cars were mostly rentals, Herrington rounded up new vehicles for the trustees rather than carting demonstrators to jail.

"Aren't you going to arrest us?" a protester asked.

"We've decided not to," Herrington replied, a classic reply that burnished the chief's legend.

Herrington was under no illusions about the shabby quality of his force. "The department was in kind of a shambles," he said later in an oral history. "These people were untrained, and they were armed…It was not a very good situation."

Not the least of the problems was that the Stanford cops were allowed to equip themselves with their own guns, a risky policy on the best of days. One day, Herrington performed an inspection and asked to see an officer's weapon. The cop pulled out his gun and pointed it at the chief before Herrington took it away. The only fortunate part of the story was that the weapon was defective. The gun had corroded so much that the cylinder could not be opened. But that hardly said much for the competence of the force.

With the threat of liability hanging over the department, Herrington disarmed the great majority of the existing force, a deeply unpopular decision with the troops, particularly when police and fire unions were flexing their muscles. The chief gave the rank and file a chance to become full-fledged officers—but as he recalled it, only about 10 or 15 percent qualified.

The rest of the Stanford officers were given the option of becoming "community service officers," handling mundane duties like security and parking. After a couple of initial hiring mistakes, Herrington brought on a cadre of new officers and supervisors who emphasized basic law enforcement standards. The university forged a new agreement with the sheriff that allowed the trained officers to have reserve deputy sheriff status. The agreement provided, however, that the sheriff's office would handle serious cases, particularly murders. "They (the sheriff's department) would have an on-duty spot for homicide," Herrington recalled. "I didn't have a department big enough for that. We could call on them in those murder cases." No one thought that would happen very often. But it was an important provision on the morning of October 13, 1974.

The changes upset Steve Crawford, one of the officers demoted to CSO status. A gun was a symbol of authority, even virility. Losing it stung his pride. For the next few years, unhappiness festered in the ranks of the community service officers. And those who knew Crawford say it was magnified by his fear of strange characters who wandered around campus. "He was extremely bitter about this," retired Capt. Niemeyer recalled. "He hated Herrington."

The truth was that reforming the force—essentially building a new culture—could not be accomplished overnight. It demanded proper training, supervisors who could enforce discipline, and officers who did not emulate Rambo. Among the cops Herrington hired were the first two female officers on the Stanford force, Kristin J. Henderson and Debbie Whittemore. In his oral history, Herrington estimated that it took at least five or six years to remake the department. It wasn't until 1982, eleven years after the chief arrived, that *The Stanford Daily* proclaimed the campus police force had been refashioned under Herrington. In the meantime, Herrington faced problems that were exposed on the night Arlis Perry was killed.

Despite the pact with the sheriff's department and Herrington's pledge to subordinate himself to Sheriff Geary on law enforcement matters, not everything was spelled out in the relationship between the sheriff and Stanford. Both parties were learning whom they could trust. Confusion was inevitable. On the morning of the murder, a deputy sent to the scene had to be met by a Stanford cop to be guided to the church. The main work was done by sheriff's detectives, but Stanford Lt. Walt Konar conducted a parallel probe for the university. When news of the homicide became known Sunday morning, the competent Sheriff's Lt. Richard Saldivar dispatched teams of investigators to the church. The Stanford police lacked a watch commander on the scene, who could have taken local control.

Finally, Herrington was haunted by his decision to keep the untrained cops as community service officers—the "old guard," now deeply dissatisfied. In his oral history, the chief said they had been hired under a different system, and it would have been unfair to fire them outright. Stanford would have faced rebellion from its police and fire unions if he had tried to dismiss them. In creating the CSO positions, however, Herrington bestowed second-class status on people who had once wielded guns. And while the duties of checking buildings and supervising parking seemed harmless enough, the CSOs retained power in a place that operated on trust. The guards had keys to the kingdom—and Stanford was so wealthy that it did not always count its treasures.

CHAPTER 17

THE UNUSUAL SUSPECTS

Homicide experts say the first forty-eight to seventy-two hours after a murder are the most critical. It is the time when crucial leads surface, when significant admissions occur, when the physical evidence is assembled and weighed. In the first week after Arlis's body was found, no one could accuse the Santa Clara County sheriff's department of shirking on resources. At one point, the murder demanded the attention of at least eight detectives as well as several deputies summoned for special tasks. Under Capt. Frank Mosunic and Undersheriff Tom Rosa, the department formed a task force that pondered the case every morning between eight and nine in the sheriff's conference room in San Jose, a chamber with a long table and framed pictures of former sheriffs on the wall. Among the lawmen gazing down on the discussions was Sheriff John Hicks Adams, who delivered the notorious bandit Tiburcio Vásquez to the gallows in 1875. Rosa presided over the meetings, which filled the room to capacity and spilled into the hallway. Mosunic, a respected forty-one-year-old veteran who could deploy a sharp tongue, handed out assignments. A secretary noted the work on three-by-five-inch index cards. "We had a good captain, Mosunic, and he never pressured you," remembered Sgt. John Johnson, who led the first wave of detectives. "Of course, they wanted it done."

After the interviews with Bruce Perry and Steve Crawford, the detectives turned their attention to people with an incidental relationship to the murder—the witnesses in the sanctuary that night, the people who worked at Memorial Church, and the names emerging from the seemingly inexhaustible tips from the public. It was the triage of disappointment. But three men they interviewed illustrated the serendipity that coursed through the case. One was a would-be novelist who slept on a heating grate near the student union. Another was an ex-student who camped under an oak tree and kept a key to the church. And the third was an old running buddy of Bruce Perry.

Noel Joseph Rogers, known as "Jick" to family and friends, enjoyed his own version of tenure at Stanford, one rooted in his hostility to hygiene. His stench dissuaded police from trying to dislodge him from his sleeping perch on the heating grate outside Tresidder Memorial Union. It wasn't comfortable, but Rogers was not particular. When the weather turned cold or rainy, he found a place to sleep in the dorms. Telling people he was researching a novel about Stanford, he begged for money and food from students. Left alone by the cops, the thirty-six-year-old wanderer was free to observe events on campus.

Two nights after Arlis's murder, when he chatted with community service officer James J. Golden, Rogers offered an insight that assured he would be hauled in for questioning. The two men exchanged thoughts about the sensational killing in the church. When Golden mentioned that the media was describing it as a stabbing, Rogers asked, "Was it an ice pick?"

Golden's suspicions mounted when Rogers, noting that the picture in the Stanford news was unclear, asked whether Arlis was pretty. "To my knowledge, Stanford news has not published a picture of the victim," Golden noted. It was not clear what picture the two men were talking about. Rogers, however, was correct in one aspect. One of the first photos put out of Arlis was unclear—and did not do her credit.

By instinct or chance, Jick Rogers had guessed the murder weapon, a secret the deputies were striving to hide. From the undisclosed details that filled the detectives' meager purse, Rogers had plucked the most valuable coin. If Rogers was asking whether Arlis was killed with an ice pick, it made him a suspect, plain and simple. No one but the killer was expected to know the weapon. So at 3:00 a.m. on Friday, October 18, just hours before Arlis's funeral in Bismarck, Sheriff's Sgts. Johnson and Pascual brought Rogers in for questioning at the Stanford police station. Since they had been called out for the case five days before, the two detectives had worked overtime to explore leads, sometimes extending their toil past midnight. Jick was not at the top of their list, but Golden's report was intriguing, and the suspect wasn't very far away.

Tall, articulate, and handsome even in his shabby state, Jick did not fit the profile of a killer. Noel Rogers was born in San Francisco on Christmas Day, 1937, given a first name that reflected his day of birth. Family lore had it that his mother nicknamed him "Jick" because his older brother, John, went by "Jack." "Jack and Jick" had a ring to it. The two brothers and their older sister grew up in relative comfort in a San Mateo neighborhood behind the Hillsdale Shopping Center. Their father, Charles A. Rogers, was an insurance agent who had been a varsity tennis player at UC Berkeley before World War I. It was Charles's second family: Jick had a set of half siblings from the earlier marriage. Jick's great-great-grandfather, Nathan Olmsted Ferris Sr., was an Illinois businessman who reputedly introduced popcorn to Queen Victoria in England.

Jick inherited his father's athletic talent, one burnished at the country club his family joined. A photo from the San Mateo High School yearbook in 1953 shows a good-looking tennis player with an engaging smile sitting next to his coach on the bleachers. After graduating from high school in 1955, Jick joined the U.S. Air Force and later took up his father's pursuit of selling insurance. But he seemed to lack direction and focus. Before he came to Stanford to write the Great American Novel, he had at least three short marriages. Long after Jick's death in 1996, his relatives described him as a sweet guy who floated along in life—creative, a playboy, a drifter.

For all that, he *was* perceptive. At Stanford, even the homeless had intellectual heft.

At the station, Pascual and Johnson got down to business, asking Rogers if he remembered his early-morning conversation with Golden. Jick did but with different details. He said Golden had mentioned that the fatal blow was a *puncture* wound, which prompted Jick to ask whether it was an ice pick. Pascual then asked whether any of the Stanford officers had suggested weapons. A hatpin? Scissors? The ice pick? No, Jick said, he had come up with the ice pick idea himself. He also had a few other thoughts. When he first heard about the case, he thought it was a psychology-department joke.[1] A murder committed in a church with candles? It seemed too strange and time-consuming to be true. From his own experience, Jick knew the church was checked often by security guards. About a year before, he told the detectives, he had been thrown out of the chapel because of his dress and appearance.

Taking nothing for granted, Johnson and Pascual honed in on Jick's alibi. On the night of the murder, he explained, he lingered at the Tresidder Union coffee shop until its closing time, between midnight and 1:00 a.m. After that, he remembered staying in a dorm with a guy named Andy. Helpfully, he supplied Andy's room number. The detectives took Rogers's photo and a full set of fingerprints. After checking his alibi, the investigators concluded that he was telling the truth. He was strange, eccentric, but not lethal. For all his oddities, Jick contributed a significant insight about the killer. If the murder was committed by an outsider, a theory deputies were to pursue for years, it would have been strange for the murderer to have lingered in the church to lay out his victim. An opportunistic killer who followed Arlis into the church and hid at closing time would be more likely to flee quickly.

Jick was not the only long-haired man with an odd perch who was hauled in for questioning. That description fit the church's back-up sexton, twenty-two-year-old Bill Aaron, a lean Stanford dropout living under an oak tree in the foothills not far from the Stanford radio telescope, or "Dish." A voluble redhead who could expound on religion, politics, music, and rock formations, Aaron jokingly called himself "token white trash." A native of Birmingham, Alabama, he tested well as a middle-school student and won a scholarship to Phillips Exeter Academy in New Hampshire. Though prep school was a cultural shock for the young Alabamian, Aaron did well enough at Exeter to apply to Stanford. "Stanford thought it could build its reputation by admitting kids from prep schools," he told me in his self-deprecating way.

At Stanford, Aaron studied geology and embraced music. He was fascinated by Northern California's rock formations. Having received a scholarship, he also got a job as the sexton at Stanford Memorial Church, where his duties included making coffee for the choir, changing altar candles, and working with hostesses to prepare for weddings. The job gave him an intimate glimpse of the church's operations. It granted him access to a key piece of evidence. And it nearly got him booked for murder.

It was the early 1970s, when students at elite schools were rebelling against the demands of the larger society. Unsure what he wanted in life, Aaron grew his hair long and dropped out. "I wasn't the guy who wanted to write papers," he told me. After returning to Alabama briefly, he came back to Stanford to live under his chosen tree. Like Jick Rogers, Aaron understood that you can do almost anything at a university if you *look* like you have a purpose. Well-removed from the main campus, his spot in the foothills offered a commanding view of the Bay Area. For a young man pondering his future, it was not a bad post.

An encounter with an associate professor of geology, Dr. James Ingle, gave Aaron his alibi in the Arlis Perry case. In the fall of 1974, Ingle spotted the long-haired ex-student on campus and asked him if he wanted to join a geology field trip to Humboldt County on the second weekend in October. The trip had been canceled in a class Aaron had taken earlier, and this was a second effort. When Aaron said he wasn't enrolled anymore, Ingle asked him along anyway. One of the students who also went on that trip was Mark Dalrymple, the sound guru at Memorial Church, who contributed his own important clue to the Perry case.

Aaron returned to campus at about 5:00 p.m. on Sunday, October 13, less than twelve hours after Crawford reported finding Arlis Perry's body. Because he still had a key to the church, he opened up the door to the Round Room, the church office, to leave his belongings inside.

"You know what happened?" he remembered a security guard asking him.

"No, I don't know what happened," said Aaron, who had been gone for more than three days. It was then that he learned about the murder of Arlis Perry.

Leaving his gear at the church, Aaron headed for White Plaza, a five-minute walk away. When he arrived at the plaza, he was surrounded by five patrol cars with deputies flashing their lights and demanding identification. It took a while to explain to the detectives that he had been on a geology field trip and could not have been involved in the murder. After all, Aaron seemed to fulfill all the ingredients of suspicion. Here was a strange-looking guy with a key to the church, a tenuous Stanford connection, and no physical address except a tree. "If I hadn't been on that geology trip, no question I would have been a goner," said Aaron, who returned for a degree at Stanford in the eighties and went into a career in construction. "They realized I wasn't their murderer."

Shrugging off the status of suspect, Aaron emerged as a knowledgeable guide for detectives attempting to understand the routine of the church. A growing respect developed between the long-haired sexton and the straitlaced Johnson. Aaron told investigators that a locked church was hardly immune to intruders. Among other things, a flutist played his instrument late at night inside the sanctuary. It was common to find lost souls wandering around. "There were all these crazy people on (Palo Alto's) University Avenue," Aaron remembered years later. "The church was a magnet for these people."

One other note stood out in Aaron's account. He had replaced the altar candles on Friday, October 11, before a wedding. Though sheriff's deputies were unable to determine who left the palm print on the candle used on Arlis's body, the sexton's statement narrowed the window of timing. The candles had been on the altar for more than a day before the murder. It was always possible that the print, which came from the web of a hand, might have been left by a visitor to the church. It was not uncommon for the candles to be moved when there was a wedding or a ceremony.

The alliance between dropout and detective presaged an extraordinary moment. Several months after the murder, Dean Hamerton-Kelly offered Aaron a chance to stay in a second-floor room on the eastern side of the church. Although they were spartan quarters—a bed, a refrigerator, a hot plate, carpeting equipment—it marked a step up from his home under the tree. To reach his new abode, Aaron entered the church through what was called "the East Room," taking the stairway to his room, roughly on the opposite side of the church from the Round Room.

One night in October 1975, exactly a year after Arlis was killed, Aaron passed a large, dark sedan parked on the church's west side as he went to open the door to the East Room. Not long after he entered the church, he heard a banging on the door. Sgt. Johnson stood outside. On the anniversary of the murder, Johnson had waited to see whether Arlis's killer might return—a long shot, but something detectives check. Johnson relaxed when he saw Aaron. Under the pressure of a murder investigation, the two men had come to trust each other. Aaron even showed the detective his new sleeping quarters.

Immediately after the murder—that exhausting week in October 1974—Johnson still had a long list of potential suspects. One who did *not* fit the description of a homeless dropout was a Stanford junior and athlete, Rich Karlgaard, a member of the wedding party for Bruce and Arlis and the older brother of Liz Karlgaard, who had passed the news of the murder to her Bismarck acquaintances at Sertoma Park. A year older than Bruce and Arlis, Rich had gone to Bismarck Junior College before transferring to Stanford. He knew the Perrys well. Rich's and Bruce's fathers were friends in Bismarck. When Arlis went out to see Bruce at Stanford in May 1974, Karlgaard knew about her visit. He was able to tell deputies that she had stayed with another girl in a dorm while she visited Bruce. And he had recently accompanied Arlis once on her job-hunting.

What made Karlgaard an early suspect was an unlucky chance of newspaper circulation. In the dumpster to the west of the church, deputies found two copies of *The Bismarck Tribune* addressed to Karlgaard at his Stanford address. An avid reader who was proud of being from North Dakota, Karlgaard liked to keep current on the news from his hometown. Still, the coincidence seemed mind-boggling. A short distance from where a young woman from Bismarck had been murdered, copies of her hometown paper were found in the trash, addressed to a Stanford student who, only two months earlier, had been a groomsman at her wedding. True, a killer would have to be boneheaded to leave a newspaper with his name on it in a dumpster next to the murder site. But the detectives had seen dumb crooks before. And there was one more problem, reminiscent of the nosebleed that had stained Bruce Perry's shirt the morning of the murder. When the deputies saw him, Karlgaard had an eye injury. The detectives had to run it down.

On Monday, April 21, deputies Ken Kahn and Dave Pascual sat down with Karlgaard at the police annex to get his story in detail. His account had all the rough edges of truth. Karlgaard said he had picked up the newspapers at the post office while en route to see a girlfriend. After taking a tumble on his bike, he tossed the newspapers into the dumpster before he continued on his way. Karlgaard had an airtight alibi for the weekend of October 11–13. He had been on a chartered student bus that left Toyon Hall at about 5:00 p.m. Friday to attend the Saturday night UCLA game in Los Angeles. (After UCLA scored a late-game field goal, the contest ended with a 13-13 tie. The pundits proclaimed that it illustrated Stanford's ability to snatch mediocrity from the jaws of victory.) About midnight, the Stanford bus headed back to Santa Barbara, where the students spent the second night. The next day, they drove back north, arriving on campus around 6:30 p.m. on Sunday.

If that chronology was accurate—and it was—the young North Dakotan was three hundred miles away from Stanford Memorial Church when Arlis was murdered. To back up his story, Karlgaard provided the names of a couple of his companions on the bus, who vouched for his presence. And that eye injury? Karlgaard said he had gotten it when he tried surfing in Southern California.

Karlgaard was not the man deputies were seeking. Except for the prominence he achieved later in life—he became the publisher of *Forbes* magazine—he might have been just another footnote to the story. But in one of those odd links that haunted the case, his tumble on his bicycle figured in the debate over something else found in the dumpster: three rags that looked like they were stained with blood. The deputies carefully checked the alibi of the student whose address was on the newspapers. But they did not test the rags.

CHAPTER 18
CRIME AFICIONADO

Nearly a year and a half before the murder, while Bruce and Arlis were completing their senior year as sweethearts at Bismarck High School, a strange phone call came in to the Stanford police. It was four minutes after 11:00 p.m. on Thursday, May 17, 1973, the day that folksy North Carolina Senator Sam Ervin opened the U.S. Senate Watergate hearings. Perhaps trusting that the tape would speak for itself, a Stanford dispatcher noted the call in a two-paragraph report that offered little detail. Sadly, prosecutors believe that the recording did not survive. "Subject saying that there was a possibility that the chapel (Memorial Church) would be burned and that he had information that was limited to him," dispatcher Daniel Rodriguez wrote. The caller refused to give a name. "I could not get any further information from him," Rodriguez added.

It was hard to know how much credibility to ascribe to the call. But Stanford could not dismiss the threat. In the previous half a dozen years, the university had been wracked by a series of deliberately set fires. In May 1968, an arson destroyed the headquarters of the Naval ROTC building, causing $580,000 in damage. Two months later, arson hit the office of departing President Wallace Sterling, destroying mementos and rare books he had collected in his nineteen years in office. In 1971, a deliberate blaze struck a lounge in Wilbur Hall used for Black Student Union meetings. The following year, a suspicious fire ravaged Encina Hall, a nerve center for the administration. In the early seventies, arson wasn't an inconceivable act at Stanford. It was part of the political vocabulary.

Working from the tape, the police had little trouble putting the late-night threat into context. The dean of the chapel, Robert Hamerton-Kelly, had raised questions about allowing a Black Muslim minister, John Muhammad, to speak at the church. On Thursday morning, *The Stanford Daily* reported that Muhammad, the minister at the Black Muslim mosque in San Francisco, had "indefinitely postponed" a speech at Memorial Church scheduled for that evening. Muhammad's decision came after a week of controversy about whether the message of the Black Muslims was racist. As a white South African who battled apartheid, Hamerton-Kelly requested a meeting with Muhammad before allowing him to speak. To the Black Muslim's supporters, that demand imposed unacceptable political vetting, violating free speech. The police concluded the arson threat had come in retaliation.

In response, Stanford authorities assigned a couple of extra security officers to patrol the church. At least one guard, Steve Crawford, listened to the tape of the threat. In a 150-word report written in his characteristic block-letter style—he was a left-hander who wrote in a crabbed overhand fashion—Crawford said the voice "closely resembles" that of a young man he had talked with in the quad several times over the previous ten days. Without providing the name of his informant, Crawford described him in generic terms—white, five foot ten, slender build, short black hair, a clean-shaven face, and casual clothes. Strikingly, the security guard reported that he and the unnamed young man had talked about how eerie a site the church would be for murder.

As a lead about arson, Crawford's report amounted to a mumble, a rehashing of gossip in the quad. There was no way to connect the threat to Crawford's unnamed informant. With the church unburned, the case was filed away. As a prequel to murder, however, the Crawford account was an unheard shout. The report might have been forgotten except for Stanford police Lt. Walt Konar, who was poring through old reports late one night a couple of months after the murder. Konar flagged Crawford's report and the dispatcher's note for the Perry investigators. "The report(s) are of some significance due to the mention of Memorial Church as a likely murder scene," Konar wrote.[1]

After years of turbulence, most people assumed the Stanford campus in the spring of 1973 was returning to calm. No one was occupying buildings or firebombing the president's office, though the Encina Hall fire damage remained unrepaired for years. "When we got back to campus and 1973 began, we found that civility had broken out all over," wrote then-Stanford president Richard Lyman, who took a tough stance toward protesters before embarking for England on a sabbatical in the fall of 1972. "The mood was completely changed. Stanford had, somewhat belatedly, returned to the kind of normalcy enjoyed by most other campuses," he concluded in his memoir *Stanford in Turmoil.*

If Lyman's take was broadly true of political strife on campus, pockets of unease and violent crime lingered. In early 1973, nobody could ignore the broader topography of murder. Leslie Perlov had been killed in February in the Stanford foothills. And the campus was less than forty-five miles from Santa Cruz, which had been terrorized by two serial killers, Edmund Kemper and Herbert Mullin. A month before the arson call, the six-foot-nine Kemper, known as "Big Ed," had confessed to killing his mother and six hitchhikers he had picked up in Santa Cruz and the Bay Area. Mullin committed thirteen murders, including that of a Roman Catholic priest, Father Henri Tomei, whom he stabbed to death in November 1972 inside St. Mary of the Immaculate Conception Church in Los Gatos, less than twenty-five miles away.

All this unfolded as racial unrest mounted. Although angry protests against the Vietnam War were deflated by the draft lottery and the unwinding of American forces in Southeast Asia, the cultural wars that dominated college campuses for the next two generations were beginning to simmer. Once an overwhelmingly white refuge known as "the Farm," Stanford had made serious strides toward diversity by the early seventies, increasing the number of Black faculty and students. With that new diversity came a searing critique of the university's place in the world and inevitable tension between Blacks and whites.

A Black Muslim scholar named Cedric X (Clark), an assistant professor of psychology and communication, emerged as one of the foremost critics of the status quo. Behind wire-rim glasses and a polite manner, the professor prepared the sacred cows of academia for slaughter. Cedric X lambasted electrical-engineering professor William Shockley, an exponent of views widely seen as racist. Gifted with a sense of publicity, Cedric garnered national attention for an experiment in which he "discriminated" against white students in one of his classes, lashing them verbally as agents of racism. Most of the white students dropped out. The Black Muslim professor denounced whites as "devils" who had committed actions that were "some of the worst in the history of man."

With allies in the Black Student Union, Cedric X proposed having minister John Muhammad of the San Francisco Black Muslim Temple speak at Memorial Church on Thursday, May 17. It was a controversial choice. Born as John Peeples in Barnwell, South Carolina, the thirty-eight-year-old Muhammad was a stalwart follower of Black Muslim founder Elijah Muhammad, an unapologetic advocate of Black separatism and distrust of whites. That message distressed Dean Hamerton-Kelly, who had come to maturity in a South Africa dominated by white racism. The dean said he wanted to discuss "what I understood to be the racist element" of the Black Muslim message with Muhammad. In the end, Muhammad decided against appearing on campus—and black leaders criticized the dean for questioning Muhammad's appearance. The arson threat came on the same night the Black Muslim hoped to speak. Not long afterward, Crawford listened to the tape and wrote his report. Littered with misspellings, his language was uncanny.

The voice on the recorded call closely resembles that of a subject who was in contact with this officer on the nights of May 16, May 14, and several other dates since May 6," Crawford wrote. *Subject identified himself as West Valley College pt-time (part-time) student working in a plant near Bayshore Fwy. Subjects (sic) conversation dwelled on the murders at Santa Cruz, the "erieness" (sic) of Mem Chu as a likely murder scene. Subject showed a great deal of fascination with the archecture (sic) of the building, the fact that someone locked in inadvertently could not get out, & on each of the occassions (sic), he asked several questions about the nature of the security force, closing times and particularly how often the church is checked by the beat unit. My reply to this question was that we made constant checks throughout the night & early morning & that no particular schedual (sic) was followed. I did not indicate to him that the church could be vacated once it was secured.*

Did such a West Valley student exist? With Crawford's record of queasy credibility, it's possible he invented the character. His report gave detectives little to work with. The description was strikingly similar to one Crawford gave to Sgt. John Johnson seventeen months later, when asked if he had seen any strange characters around the church. About a week before Arlis's murder, Crawford said, he had seen a gay man looking for a pickup after a gay-liberation dance.

As the man left the church, he discarded a paper that Crawford described as a sermon on homosexuality. Neither the gay man nor the author of the homily was identified.

Because Crawford was one of the Stanford cops demoted after Chief Marv Herrington took over the department in 1971, it's conceivable that his report on the arson threat wasn't taken seriously. It's also possible that Crawford *did* have such a conversation and embellished the details. It's one of the curiosities of the case—perhaps irrelevant but worth noting—that his chats with his informant occurred around the time he married his first wife, Joyce. A municipal court judge presided over their ceremony on May 13, 1973, four days before the call. Crawford appeared to have taken little or no immediate honeymoon. Within days of his wedding, he was discussing murder.

In retrospect, several details in the memo stand out. The first is the "eeriness" of Memorial Church as a likely site for murder. (Crawford misspelled the word as "erieness.") The caller on the tape never mentioned murder, and just how the topic arose between Crawford and his companion was unclear. By his account, Crawford had extended conversations with the unnamed student about the church's architecture, the killings in Santa Cruz, and the likelihood that someone could be locked in the church. If nothing else, Crawford's memo seemed to validate the theories of those who believed the setting was a central piece of the Arlis Perry murder.

Outside the church, the fact that the interior doors could be locked wasn't widely known. That suggested the topic was raised not by the part-time West Valley student—unless he had some connection with the church—but by Crawford himself. From Crawford's report, it's unclear just why his student friend kept returning for conversations in the quad or how they happened to meet. The confidant's workplace near the Bayshore Freeway went unidentified. It's also possible that Crawford had heard of people locked inside the church. (Notably, this happened to Bruce Perry's freshman roommate in the 1973–74 school year.)

Crawford's relatives say he enjoyed dissecting crime and talking about the macabre. In later years, he enjoyed military history as well. The level of detail in his 1973 report, however, went beyond casual conversation. The security guard said that on "each of the occasions" he talked with the West Valley student—there appear to have been four or five encounters in less than two weeks—the young man asked about the security force, closing times, and how often the church was checked. Ordinarily, that intensity of probing would prompt a cop's inquisitiveness. Who needs to know how often the church was checked or repeatedly asks for details of the security? Crawford apparently did not obtain the young man's name. As a security guard, he was woefully incurious.

Finally, Crawford finished with the strange note, phrased in the negative, that he did not tell the student that the church *could* be vacated once it was secured. The language strikes a chord because of the interior church door, which was broken outward on the night of Arlis's murder. At the least, it suggested that Crawford had thought about the details of how an assailant might escape. Was Memorial Church an eerie place for a murder? Yes. Any ornate place meant for worship would be. It could also be argued that a person who thought of Jane Stanford's sanctum as a site for killing was eerier.

CHAPTER 19
THE OTHER VICTIMS

Even if they wanted to, the detectives called to Memorial Church could not shake the sense of being forced to see the same horror movie again. No one would let them forget it. The newspapers and television stations repeatedly blared that it was the fourth murder at Stanford or in its environs in the past twenty months. Four young people, all promising, had been killed in an unexpected fashion, leaving bewildered relatives and a stunned campus behind. It wasn't supposed to happen at a prestigious university. A story in *The Stanford Daily* described the mood: "To be sure, the latest tragedy didn't resemble the previous three in several key respects. But there were similarities: a person out alone, a sudden killer, police without suspects."

None of the three previous murders had been solved, though investigators had tantalizing leads—and, in one case, a persuasive suspicion. The victims, two women and one man, were all connected with the university. For reasons rooted in their reading of the crime scene, investigators came to believe that the Arlis Perry case stood alone. The murder was committed by a man with curiosity about ritual; the body was laid out in a way the others had not been. And the killer picked his setting for maximum impact. For a long time, however, the possibility that the other murders were tied to the killing in the church stoked suspicion in the media and frenzy in the public. To the fearful campus, the differences in method hardly mattered.

Though the university nurtured an image as a safe haven—and largely, it was—Stanford had a fraught history with homicide. In 1933, a Stanford University Press advertising manager, David Lamson, was convicted of fatally bludgeoning his wife, Allene, at their home on Salvatierra Street on Stanford's Faculty Row. Lamson, a 1925 Stanford graduate who had married Allene at Memorial Church, was sentenced to die at San Quentin prison, where his experiences on death row prompted him to write a book entitled *We Who Are About to Die*. An appeals court overturned the conviction, and after a fourth trial ended in a hung jury in 1936, the prosecution agreed to Lamson's release. Always a dabbler in literature and acting, Lamson turned to a career as a magazine writer. He died the year after Arlis was killed.

In 1969, less than five years before the Memorial Church murder, a promising resident physician at the Stanford Medical Center—Leslie Kulhanek, twenty-nine—was killed after an argument at a Christmas party at the hospital attended by two hundred people. A computer operator, Rudolph M. Gray, was charged in his killing. Witnesses told investigators that a clash had erupted after Gray danced with Kulhanek's wife. The physician, a native of Boulder, Colorado, died when Gray fired three bullets at his chest. The gunman surrendered to authorities not long after the shooting. In more lenient times, he served only twenty months behind bars. A few years later, when Gray was arrested in another slaying, in San Mateo, his criminal résumé became a prime exhibit for law enforcement advocates who sought to stiffen California's sentencing laws.

In the earlier Stanford cases, the victim and killer knew each other or had a fleeting acquaintance. The rationale for murder emerged from contempt, jealousy, or boredom. In the Lamson case, the prosecutors introduced love poems in an attempt to prove that Lamson was having an affair with a Sacramento divorcée. In the string of murders that began early in 1973, however, the killings were committed by strangers, a distinction that chilled the campus and vexed the deputies trying to dissect clues. The murder wave evoked the famous 1946 essay by George Orwell, "Decline of the English Murder," which bemoaned the casual brutality of a new breed of murderer. If homicide was not an unknown intruder at Stanford, it suddenly looked like a much more arbitrary and brutal visitor, a caller who did not bother with a doorbell.

The recent cases were distinguished by one other disturbing fact. None of the victims had done anything that invited violence. It is one thing to be killed doing something chancy—say, dealing drugs or participating in a gang. It's another to be killed at random. Because the murders were so unpredictable, so capricious, survivors felt more vulnerable. The lack of a link between killer and victim made the puzzle harder to unpack. In the mid-seventies, detectives lacked what we have come to see as critical investigatory tools—DNA, extensive closed-circuit TV, cell phone and computer records. The investigations stuttered because they involved at least three jurisdictions—Santa Clara County, San Mateo County, and San Francisco. Finally, the inability to access or even know about juvenile records from abroad hindered an understanding of patterns.

The first victim was Leslie Marie Perlov, a dark-haired 1972 Stanford graduate who was working as a clerk at the North County Law Library in Palo Alto. On the afternoon of Tuesday, February 13, 1973, Perlov left work early to go into the foothills above Stanford to take pictures, hoping to find the right scene for a painting she was commissioning for her mother, Florence Perlov. Leslie parked her orange 1972 Chevy Nova near the intersection of Page Mill Road and Old Page Mill Road, close to the entrance to an old quarry. Slipping out of her flats and pulling on her rain boots, she walked northwest into the hills. When she did not return home that evening—she had moved back to her mother's Los Altos Hills home after the death of her father from cancer—paralyzing fear struck her family. The twenty-one-year-old Perlov was not the kind of woman to disappear. Ordinarily, she told her mother where she was going and when she would be late. A kind, smart woman with a social conscience, she intended to enter the University of Pennsylvania law school in the fall. She and her boyfriend, a premed student finishing courses at the University of Utah, planned to study near each other on the East Coast.

By the next day, as sheriff's deputies began their hunt for the missing woman, they had the statement of one reliable witness. An off-duty Palo Alto police officer who was out driving with his family had seen a man with long, blond hair standing near Perlov's Nova at about 5:00 p.m. on February 13, the day the young Stanford graduate disappeared. Nearby was a beige or brown sedan. It wasn't much, but it suggested that a man had been involved in her disappearance and that he used a car to get to the scene.

In muddy conditions late Friday morning, February 16, a mounted horseback patrol found Perlov's body about three-quarters of a mile from the quarry, eight feet from an oak tree. She was lying face down, her left arm underneath her, her right arm splayed out. Her navy-blue miniskirt had been hiked up around her waist, and her panties and panty hose were stuffed in her mouth. She had been strangled with a floral-pattern scarf that she wore around her neck. Although deputies investigated whether she had been sexually assaulted—the scene suggested it—they concluded she had not been raped. In Perlov's car, they found her umbrella, her sunglasses, and the blue shoes she wore to work. Not far from her body were the rain boots she used on her walk. Her brown purse and the keys to her car were missing. The scene revealed that there had been a struggle. Near the body, the grass was matted down.

One other discovery complicated the search. As they spread out to look for Perlov, sheriff's deputies came across the body of a twenty-five-year-old suicide victim, Mark Rosvold, who last had been seen alive on Wednesday, February 14, the day after Perlov disappeared. Rosvold had suffered a gun wound to the chest. A shotgun was found next to the body. After samples of his clothing were sent to a crime lab in Sacramento and deputies searched his residence, they concluded that there was no connection between Perlov and Rosvold. Despite the assignment of fourteen sheriff's deputies to the probe, a huge number, the Perlov case went cold.

The second in the trio of unsolved murders ended the life of a brilliant physics student, David Levine, who was knifed to death outside Meyer Memorial Library on September 11, 1973, at the beginning of Bruce Perry's freshman year. A twenty-year-old junior from Ithaca, New York, where his father was a Cornell professor, Levine left the physics department at about 1:00 a.m. to return to his room. Apparently taken by surprise by his killer or killers, Levine was stabbed fifteen times in the back and side by a long knife. An early-morning jogger discovered the body. Although Levine's wallet was empty when it was recovered in his pants, deputies dismissed robbery as a motive for the crime.

A quiet, hardworking student who was expected to graduate in three years with a straight-A average, Levine had worked on a computer program for a project coordinated by physics professor William Fairbanks. It was a coveted assignment that went only to top students. While he preferred to work alone, Levine was not asocial. He had also taken part in student government. His room at Mirrielees House was less than half a mile from Quillen House, where Bruce and Arlis Perry lived the following year.

A significant parallel to the Levine murder unfolded at the University of California, Berkeley, on December 20, 1973, when Eric Abramson, a chemistry graduate student from Pennsylvania, was found murdered near the Cal Faculty Club. Like Levine, he was stabbed repeatedly with a knife estimated to be eight to ten inches long. A two-hundred-foot-long trail of bloodstains led to the body, suggesting that Abramson had tried to get help before collapsing. After Abramson was killed, Stanford officials distributed handbills warning that the cases were "very similar" and students should take precautions.

Initially, the motive in the Levine murder remained elusive. The possibility that the stabbing had a racial component arose in April 1974, when San Francisco investigators unraveled the crimes of a group of Black Muslim men known as the "Death Angels," who committed at least fifteen murders against white victims. Collectively, the cases were known as the "Zebra" killings, named after the special radio band that police used for their investigation. After one of the members of the group, Anthony Harris, came forward to save his own life, San Francisco Mayor Joseph Alioto announced that Levine's murder at Stanford might be linked to the Death Angels. Capt. Frank Mosunic of the Santa Clara County sheriff's department said, "What we have would coincide with what San Francisco has released to the media." Despite that statement, no arrest was ever made in the case. To honor Levine, Stanford established an award given to the outstanding junior physics student.

The final victim in the trio of cases that preceded Arlis's murder was Janet Ann Taylor, the twenty-one-year-old daughter of ex-Stanford athletic director Chuck Taylor. Janet was not a Stanford student—the 1970 Menlo-Atherton High School graduate had just taken a job with a Palo Alto maritime information firm—but in many ways, her murder resounded even more deeply than the other two. That had everything to do with her father, a legend at Stanford. An All-American football player who played on the undefeated Stanford team that beat Nebraska 21-13 in the 1941 Rose Bowl, Taylor went on to serve as both a head coach and an athletic director, a position he held between 1963 and 1971. At the time of his daughter's death, he was running a youth-sports camp not far from Pescadero, on the coastal side of San Mateo County's mountains.

On Sunday, March 24, 1974, nearly seven months before Arlis was killed, Janet visited a friend on the Stanford campus. When her car would not start for the return trip to her home in La Honda, she hitchhiked home. Wearing a rain jacket and bell-bottom pants, the five-foot-seven, 120-pound woman was last seen trying to catch a ride from Mayfield Avenue and Junipero Serra Boulevard at about 7:05 p.m. More than eighteen hours later, a passing milk-truck driver found her body off Sand Hill Road, near Manzanita Way. She, too, had been strangled—by her assailant's hand. A bruise from his thumb was spotted on her throat. Like Leslie Perlov, she had been killed after a struggle during Northern California's rainy season. San Mateo County authorities said there was no sexual assault.

The killer left a trail of evidence along the road. One shoe was found along Sand Hill Road about one hundred yards past the body. A second shoe was found another quarter mile on. A belt was found two hundred yards farther. The San Mateo County sheriff's deputies who handled the case concluded that the killer pushed Janet's body out of a car and then tossed out the other items as he drove onward. The deputies received a report that a nervous man was standing next to a white 1964 Pontiac Catalina at about 12:15 a.m. on Monday, not far from where the body was found later. According to news reports at the time, a witness stopped and asked the man if he'd had problems with his car. Told no, the witness drove on.

No one could miss the parallels between the Perlov and Taylor murders. Both women had their shoes off when their bodies were discovered. Their purses were missing. Both had Stanford connections. Both died of strangulation. And in both cases, deputies received reports of a man standing near the scene with a car. The investigators from San Jose and Redwood City met together to coordinate their probe.

No arrests were made. But the crimes left one notable piece of evidence the deputies had no way of fully understanding in the early seventies. Perlov had fought desperately with her attacker. Under her fingernails were scrapings of his skin. Those scrapings eventually yielded a full portrait of her killer's deoxyribonucleic acid, or DNA.

Forty-five years later, the investigators matched that DNA to a man who had been a security guard on the Peninsula.

CHAPTER 20

ODD FISH

If Jick Rogers and Bill Aaron helped detectives after surmounting suspicion, other characters lingered in the shadows, bolstering the idea that someone with a mental affliction had killed Arlis Perry. The murder scene was so revolting that more than a few people were convinced the killer had to be unhinged. From the psychiatric ward of the Veterans Affairs Hospital in Menlo Park and the street scene in downtown Palo Alto, a parade of strange characters passed under the reviewing stand of detectives, each straining believability with a more bizarre story than the last. With roughly 11,400 students, the campus also had its share, albeit a small one, of troubled people. To investigators examining these leads, the quest meant more than asking where suspects had been on the night of October 12 and the morning of October 13. It demanded revisiting reports of odd behavior in the past. With the help of Stanford Police Lt. Walt Konar, the detectives started culling files.

For all their work pursuing leads and excluding suspects—the punch list of any probe—a troubling pattern emerged for the investigators. They assembled a storehouse of fingerprints, interviewed scores of people, conducted dozens of lie detector tests, and collected bags of evidence. It was exhaustive and exhausting work. But a cohesive theory of the crime was lacking. The detectives could describe the metaphorical trees of the murder—the shapes of the branches, the girth of the trunks, the thickness of bark. A good picture of the forest eluded them. So the investigators were forced to pursue increasingly outlandish ideas, moving from one eccentric suspect to the next. The glut of tips revealed just how deeply the murder of a young woman in a church had struck public imagination. It also made the deputies' job harder.

One of the first people who came to their attention was a Stanford student named Larry B., a thin twenty-three-year-old with straight, brown hair, a well-worn green jacket, and an edge of menace. In May 1974, five months before the murder, Larry attended a 5:00 p.m. prayer meeting in the church's Round Room. Though not a big draw, these sessions still formed a valued part of the church's agenda, often attracting worshippers from outside campus. According to the participants, Larry was quiet at first. Then, as the group read from scripture, he interrupted with a fusillade of questions. What did the group think about the Bible? The role of the church? Jesus Christ? The four other attendees, three women and a man, urged him to hold back. Larry forged ahead. At one point, he turned to a twenty-four-year-old Portola Valley woman named Virginia and asked, "Are you a boy?" When the meeting ended, Virginia walked with Larry toward Tresidder Union. A devout and sincere woman, she believed in helping people search for God even if they were peculiar.

To the ranks of the peculiar, Larry brought deep credentials. He believed in Satan and was convinced of the depth of evil in the world. Confiding that he had terrible dreams, he told Virginia he was convinced that the devil's power far exceeded God's. He insisted that the four worshippers in the prayer meeting "cannot hold out against all the powers in the world." When Virginia asked for his name, Larry replied that she would not want to know it. Nothing about this was reassuring, and Virginia, feeling uneasy, was reluctant to let Larry know where she had parked. Minutes later, she broke off the conversation. She told Sgt. Johnson she had the feeling the man would kill her if he had the chance.

Two months after the Round Room incident, in July 1974, Larry threatened a forty-six-year-old woman who worked in the registrar's office. The woman told police that Larry wandered into her office just before a hold was placed on his registration. As he tried to shut the door, he told her, "I could make love to you right here on the floor anytime I wanted to."

The administrator coolly replied, "Don't be ridiculous. There are too many people coming in and out of the office." She told detectives that Larry talked about God and appeared to be on a mystical trip.

One or two days later, Larry returned and menaced her again. "God said it's all right to kill people, and I have a knife," she remembered Larry telling her. Although she saw no blade, she reported him to police. When he came back a third time, she told him she didn't want him around.

All of this elevated Larry as a suspect in the killing of Arlis. Waiting outside a math classroom, investigators cornered him to ask a series of questions. From the start, Larry seized their attention by saying that he had slept inside the church at least three times. His alibi for the night of October 12–13 seemed shaky. Initially, he told detectives that he had been in his room on Palo Alto's Hawthorne Avenue from 9:00 p.m. Saturday to noon on Sunday. He claimed his roommate could verify his presence. But the roommate had moved out, possibly as uneasy as everyone else about Larry's behavior. Larry also insisted that a student who lived next door could back his alibi. Not so: that neighbor was sure that Larry was *not* in his room Saturday night and early Sunday. To deputies, Larry was not simply an odd figure. He was a liar, obsessed with satanism, and given to threats of violence against women. And he had slept in Memorial Church. It wasn't until Larry came into police headquarters and passed a lie detector test that they could remove him from their radar.[1]

After Larry, the quality of the leads declined, but their eccentricity mounted. At the VA Hospital in Menlo Park, the detectives were alerted to look at a thirty-two-year-old patient named Joseph W., who was at the hospital voluntarily. Joseph had been reported absent without authorization on Saturday afternoon—and had been seen on the Stanford campus. In fact, he had tried to be admitted at the Palo Alto VA hospital late Saturday afternoon and evening, vowing to return to Stanford after he was refused entry. The Stanford police described Joseph as prone to hallucinations and religious delusions—which turned out to be an understatement.

Interviewed by a sheriff's sergeant, Joseph sketched a befuddling tale. He said he had arrived at Stanford at 2:15 p.m. Saturday, well before Arlis was killed, and walked past the church without going inside. After a cup of coffee at Tresidder Union, he wandered across the way to the Stanford bookstore, where he saw several pieces of clothing he wanted to buy for friends. Joseph claimed that he communicated without speaking with the person selling the clothing, delivering the message that he wanted the merchandise but could not pay for it. That was the first tip-off that his story had flaws. The second was that Joseph identified the sales clerk as Arlis Perry, who had never worked at the bookstore. Pressed for a description of Arlis, he had none. Not surprisingly, he lost credibility as a suspect.

On the Tuesday after the murder, Sheriff's Sgt. Neal Pate was dispatched on a lead that seemed to hold more promise. A thirty-five-year-old Palo Alto man, Robert W., had been taken to Valley Medical Center in San Jose after a report made by a Palo Alto woman who saw him sitting in his car, a light-blue 1962 Plymouth Valiant. Palo Alto police said he was trimming his beard and mustache by candlelight as he was parked outside a church. This rang alarm bells for two reasons. First, there were signs that Arlis's killer had engaged in a candlelight ceremony next to the body. And second, Robert was acting strangely near a church, behavior that echoed the murder in Memorial Church.

Robert's explanation was—no surprise—bizarre. Yet it had a rough believability. Claiming that he had suffered from headaches caused by a head injury when he was seven years old, Robert insisted that shaving by candlelight helped alleviate the pain. He told Pate that he lived in his car, avoiding vegetables and meat and surviving on fruit. Presented with this odd narrative, Pate checked it out, inspecting Robert's Valiant at a towing company in Los Gatos and confiscating a writing tablet that had psychiatric and religious ramblings. He also found three candles, two orange and one light-green. None of them matched the candles inside the church. It was clear to the detectives that Robert was not their man.

A more threatening suspect was a transsexual named Susan T., whom a Stanford counselor suggested that deputies investigate. She, too, had a strange past. On the Monday after the murder, Susan had called the police, offering to serve as a decoy in Memorial Church to help solve the homicide. She claimed to know how to handle herself in a fight. A Kentucky native who had served in Vietnam, she had once given a demonstration of her talent by breaking boards with her bare hands. Noting that Susan often carried a bowie knife in her boot and sometimes wielded a .22 caliber rifle, the counselor felt she was potentially dangerous. The hackles of investigators were raised further when they learned Susan had left town on October 16, three days after the murder. Sgt. Tom Beck (see chapter twenty-five) later traced her to Los Angeles. But there was no evidence linking Susan to the crime. She, too, was ruled out as a suspect.

Other leads teetered on the edge of credibility but demanded checking. On the Tuesday after the murder, Deputy Gary Meeker, who was emerging as the utility infielder of the task force, drove to the Oakland police department to pick up a recording of a woman who had called long-distance from a pay phone. Speaking in a heavy Spanish accent, she said, "We found the body in the back seat of a car on the road. We moved it to the chapel." The woman claimed to be with "an American woman" named Carol. Added to the growing murder file, the tape didn't lead anywhere. Nor did a tip about a VA patient named Jerry Y. who hung around Memorial Church with a tape recorder, verbally challenging the staff. Taken to jail to deal with an outstanding warrant, the twenty-five-year-old spoke rapidly as he was being transported, pretending to be a computer. "A very unbalanced individual," Sgt. Johnson noted dryly in his report.

A more credible lead came from a nineteen-year-old Stanford student named David R. who lived in the ZAP house, one of the university's row houses. The ZAP resident had taken a writing class in the previous winter quarter with Bruce Perry, a course that required students to write about something they would not normally do. David followed instructions by going to a strip club in San Mateo, which showed pornographic films. In one of those films, a man was shown "doing obscene things to a girl with a candle," as David described it. The class discussed his paper, which was read aloud. After David learned what had happened to Arlis, he filed a report with Stanford police, who collected a copy of the paper. "This coincidence seemed somewhat important," David wrote. But by this time, Bruce had passed a lie detector test. The investigators concluded that it was truly a coincidence—strange yet probably meaningless.

Among the other believable people detectives talked with was Sam Swartz, an assistant organist during the 1969–70 school year. After a year's hiatus in Germany, the Iowa native had returned to play occasionally at the church. Swartz said the only truly peculiar person he had come across at the church was a flutist who always chose a section of the church hidden from view. But the twenty-six-year-old organist had an intriguing tale about the last time he had played at the church, in October of 1972, two years before Arlis was murdered. Swartz said he had played a "Black Mass Halloween Recital," a parody or dark version of the traditional Catholic liturgy.[2]

At that Halloween performance, Swartz said, he was approached by two men who urged him to join the Society for Creative Anachronism, a Berkeley-based group that celebrated medieval European culture and insisted that its members wear pre-seventeenth century garb. Among other things, the society held tournaments in which the participants wore helmets and fencing masks to spar with one another. Swartz told Sgt. Dave Pascual that he was "spooked" by the two men, whom he did not know. Since that ceremony, he had not played at a Black Mass again. Memorably, the Black Mass was mentioned by Dean Robert Hamerton-Kelly after he viewed Arlis's body. But Hamerton-Kelly was not at Stanford in the fall of 1972.

The investigators had one final lead. One of the names on their list was that of Thomas Cordry III, a former Stanford student who had been convicted of a campus murder that occurred in 1958, sixteen years before the Memorial Church case. Cordry was a tennis player, the son of a successful insurance executive, and a man described by a Los Angeles newspaper as "deeply troubled by the dark and unexplainable urge to kill." The young Palo Alto native had a 1957 Chevrolet Bel Air convertible that he used to cruise around looking for a victim. He told police he thought of using an ice pick but decided a gun would be preferable. Unsuccessful at finding a victim at random, he persuaded his seventeen-year-old Palo Alto neighbor to drive him to the train station, saying he was taking a trip out of town. When they got to the Stanford campus, he grabbed a .22 caliber rifle from the back seat and shot her in the right temple. Jettisoning a plan to dump the body in the foothills, he pulled up at the Palo Alto Police Department and told the desk officer, "I want to report a killing. I shot a girl, and she's in the car."

What drew the attention of authorities in the Perry case many years after the murder was the threat of the ice pick. Even in 1958, an era only a generation removed from the gangland killings of the thirties, it was an unusual weapon. Could a former killer return with his preferred means of killing, a weird, twisted way of making up for past choices? At the time of Arlis's murder, Cordry had been released from prison, and police say there is evidence that he was living in Palo Alto. He would have been thirty-five years old, not out of the realm of possibility for a suspect. But despite his history, investigators concluded that Cordry was not the killer.

So went the parade: Larry, Joseph, Robert, Susan, Jerry, and the Spanish-accented caller could be dismissed, whatever strange echoes of the killing their stories had. Their behavior suggested they might have trouble putting together a sustained effort at murder. More than anything, they seemed to form strands of the odd tapestry of behavior in the Bay Area in the early seventies. But the emerging portrait of Memorial Church was more unsettling, particularly Swartz's story about the Black Mass. It suggested that Arlis's killer might have a connection to the occult, or at least that a piece of the church's milieu clashed with the evangelism so central to Arlis's life.

CHAPTER 21

A STRANGE FAMILY

Stephen Blake Crawford was born on February 11, 1946, at St. John's Hospital in Santa Monica, a six-story, white, art-deco building that had opened a little more than three years before, in the middle of World War II. His mother, thirty-two-year-old Maxine Crawford, a dance instructor, delivered the baby at 3:35 p.m. after twenty hours in the hospital. His father, thirty-eight-year-old William Edward Crawford, whom everyone called "Ed," was a musician who held a day job as a maintenance man at a dairy plant. Like many Californians, Steve came from a jumbled ethnic heritage. One of his mother's ancestors was a French Canadian who had drifted to Seattle, while his father's family included Scottish descendants who had settled in Ohio and Missouri in the mid-nineteenth century. Steve and his older brother, Bill, grew up in West Los Angeles and the San Fernando Valley in rental homes that the family exchanged with frequency. From first to third grade, he attended Our Lady of the

Valley Catholic School, the anchor of the biggest parish in the valley. (Lucille Ball and her husband, Desi Arnaz, attended services there around the same time.) Though he was a shaky student—he never learned to spell well—Steve went on to Notre Dame High School in Sherman Oaks, a tough and prestigious school that encouraged his brother's career in the Holy Cross order. After dawdling for a couple of years at Santa Monica City College, Steve enlisted in the air force, where he served four years at the height of the Vietnam War. He was assigned to bases in Korea and Texas, not Vietnam. With his military background and his brother's status as a Mountain View cop, he got a job with the Stanford police in mid-February 1971. He had just turned twenty-five years old.

Those were the bare details of Crawford's biography, the strands deputies traced after Arlis's murder. By the Friday evening after the homicide, Deputy Gary Meeker had filed a report on Crawford's past, noting that the security guard had a mediocre 2.88 grade point average at San Jose State University. At the three colleges he had attended before—Santa Monica City College, Midwestern University in Wichita Falls, Texas, and Foothill College—he had lingered on academic probation. This quick bio, however, did not begin to describe the strange embroidery of Steve Crawford's family, a weave of Hollywood, music, drinking, and deceit. As a young man, Crawford was surrounded by people who treated the truth as if it were a movie script that demanded a massive rewrite. His relatives changed basic details of their lives, adopted stage names, clashed with the law, and stayed one step ahead of the rent collectors.

The tale starts with Steve's grandfather, Barney Ambrose Rosselle, the father of Steve's mother, Maxine. Born in 1886 in Tennessee, Barney carved out a career as an adventurer, moving to Juneau as a young man. In his later years, he regaled his family with stories of the brawling Alaskan territory. By the mid-1920s, he was living in Los Angeles, where he called himself "an expert accountant," though his credentials seemed obscure. Barney and his wife, Josephine (née McGilvray), settled in Culver City with their daughters, Maddy and Maxine. A photo from the late twenties shows a ruddy man with hunched shoulders and Coke-bottle glasses holding a briefcase in front of his body. His only nod to fashion was a pair of pale slacks and elegant leather shoes. Barney *looked* like an accountant.

For a man who made his living counting other people's money, Barney took a casual view of numbers in his own life. Notably, he lopped a decade off his age. By the time the 1930s rolled around, he was reporting that he had been born in 1895, nine years after his real birth. When he died of an embolism in early 1943—a problem that his family linked to his diabetes—his age was listed as forty-seven. In truth, he was nearing fifty-seven. Fudging a birth date wasn't unusual in World War II, when Barney became a stateside navy lieutenant commander. Middle-aged men often subtracted a few years from their ages to join the military, which generally cut off enlistees at age forty-two. It was still strange for an accountant to lose nearly a decade.

The second discordant note on Barney's resume involved Gilbert Beesemyer, a good-looking entrepreneur whose family owned a ranch next to the booming movie town. Trading on his proximity and charm, Beesemyer built up a business called the Guaranty Building & Loan Association, which loaned money to Hollywood stars and businesses. Barney went to work for Beesemyer as an accountant. A 1929 *Los Angeles Times* piece described how Beesemyer dispatched Barney and a team of accountants to Bakersfield by airplane to perform an audit. In the pro-business *Times*, auditors taking flight was enough to merit several column inches.

People loved Gil Beesemyer, a seemingly honest and authentic man in a world built on artifice. But his ascent masked a gnawing problem. By the end of 1930, he had embezzled $8 million from the loan company, the equivalent of $120 million today. In the polite language of the day, authorities called it a "defalcation." Beesemyer was using the embezzled cash to invest in losing ventures, like oil wells on the coast. The financier got away with it until a state auditor began asking questions. After a grand jury was summoned, the tearful Hollywood entrepreneur pleaded guilty and was led away to San Quentin prison, insisting he alone was responsible for the fraud. Thousands of people lost money with Guaranty, a more severe blow for individual customers in the Great Depression than the savings-and-loan scandal half a century later.

Barney Rosselle was not implicated in his employer's embezzlement. But a fellow accountant and Guaranty vice president, Rupert Fleury, was enmeshed in the scandal. Fleury told a grand jury that he had falsified records for Beesemyer because he believed the chief's investments were in the interests of the firm. Fleury and Barney later went into business together in an accountancy firm in downtown Los Angeles. While the Beesemyer affair could not have helped their professional reputations, it did not destroy them. Barney bought a house on Horner Street near Robertson Boulevard, a West LA neighborhood for the upwardly mobile who could not afford Beverly Hills.

After Barney died and was buried at Holy Cross Cemetery in Culver City, his widow, Josephine, emerged as the real power in the family. She probably always was. Using the name "Joan Del Mar," Steve's grandmother had amassed a resume in dance and drama, performing supporting roles in community drama. One of them was in *The Peacock of the Underworld*, performed in 1924 at the Majestic Theater in downtown Los Angeles. She opened a dance studio herself, teaching in a converted home on Robertson Boulevard, two blocks from the Rosselle home.

In the Depression, when people flocked to movies for hope, relief, or distraction, Josephine competed with a better-known dance studio called Meglin Kiddies that was run by her rival, Ethel Meglin, a former Ziegfeld dancer. Though Meglin Kiddies taught Judy Garland and the young Shirley Temple, Josephine complained that Meglin's practices lamed the ankles of young performers. Holding recitals to show off her pupils, Josephine deployed her studio as her entrée into Hollywood. At one social event, she introduced her older daughter, Maddy, to movie director Robert McGowan, the nephew of the better-known director of the same name. (The elder McGowan directed most of the "Our Gang" shorts until 1933.) Maddy and the younger Robert had a turbulent marriage that produced two daughters, Nan and Mickie, Steve Crawford's first cousins.

Wearing a French tam and slacks, smoking a cigar, and driving a convertible, Steve's grandmother could be mistaken for a lesbian in postwar LA. She was not. Nicknamed "Big Bill" by her family, she simply nourished ambition for herself and her daughters. After Barney's death, Josephine showed no desire to remarry. She sold the dance studio and, in 1949, bought a lovely Cape Cod home at 32 Avenue 38 in Venice, now Galleon Street. Located a couple blocks from the Pacific Ocean, the house boasted a fascinating pedigree: in the 1920s, it had been the summertime retreat of the fighter Jack Dempsey, who liked to train on the beach. With a grand staircase that served as seating for orchestra players, the house was made for parties. In the Prohibition years, singer Rudy Vallée reportedly lived there as well.

Josephine was not sentimental about any of this. She divided the graceful old home into six units, moving into the front unit herself and renting the others out to students from the Jesuit-run Loyola University. Her real-estate dealings provided her with enough money to buy an imposing diamond ring, which she wore as she drove her convertible. According to family lore, a police officer stopped her one day and warned her that wearing the diamond as she made a manual turn signal invited the attention of robbers. Shaken by the warning, Josephine traded the diamond for a rental house in Canoga Park.

For all her steely ambition, Josephine also had a benevolent side, particularly toward the Catholic church. With regularity, Josephine had to help out Steve's parents, Ed and Maxine, who often fell behind on the rent. When Maddy's marriage failed, she assisted her older daughter too. For a while before her death in 1960, she considered leaving the Venice house to nearby Loyola University, but the by-then dilapidated old home eventually passed on to her two daughters. (It was torn down in 1988 and replaced by condos.) In real estate, Josephine had an exquisite instinct for place but a faulty sense of timing. When she died, Venice had deteriorated mightily. Only many years later was it revived as a refuge for the well-heeled. By the early 1960s, it was a seedy place, its once-graceful canals a breeding place for mosquitoes.

If Josephine was determined, her second daughter, Maxine, Steve's mother, shared Barney's flightiness. Like her mother, Maxine was a dancer. She was an attractive, dark-haired woman with a talent for playing instruments and telling stories. But a streak of deceit—and, when she was drinking, meanness—shadowed Maxine's life. A 1936 story in the *Los Angeles Times* reported that the young Maxine Rosselle was suing an unnamed Santa Monica hotel for $18,000 because she had fallen and injured her ankle on a dance floor that was waxed too assertively. "One, two, three, and then I slipped!" Maxine testified in court.

Mickie McGowan, Steve's cousin, was a rebellious teenager when her mother dispatched her to live with Maxine in Canoga Park in the mid-fifties. Many years later, Mickie recalled how Crawford's mother sent her with a note to the local liquor store to buy wine. In a more freewheeling era, the merchant sent the wine home with the teenager. "Maxine was generous, more fun than my mom," Mickie remembered. "She was popular with people. But boy, she could be nasty when she was drunk." One time, when Maxine was teaching Mickie to drive, the teenage girl ran over a postbox. Maxine got behind the wheel herself and drove away, leaving the property owners to deal with the damaged receptacle.

Maxine's guile echoed years later when Mickie, by this time grown, attempted to rent an apartment in Venice. The local power company rejected her request to turn on the electricity, informing her that she owed $1,000 in an overdue bill (more than $8,000 today). As Mickie recalled it, the bill was run up by her aunt Maxine, who had used Mickie's name and Social Security number to get power at her place. It was the kind of trickery that enraged relatives. It also hinted at the atmosphere in which Bill and Steve grew up. Mickie once thought of writing a portrait of her upbringing called "Mixed Nuts." (A 1994 movie starring Steve Martin used the title.)

One story about the young Steve Crawford in the fifties reflected his family's taste for a prank. It happened in the old Jack Dempsey house in Venice. As his cousin tells the story, the young Steve knew that his aunt Maddy was terrified of mice. One day, as the family gathered, he attached a string to a Brillo pad and pulled it past Maddy as she sat on the couch. "He knew she was afraid of mice, so he yelled, 'Mouse!' and almost died laughing when she shrieked and jumped off the couch," Mickie remembered. " In fact, he laughed all day about it." To a boy, it was funny—but there was a streak of meanness in the practical joke, a meanness that would never really disappear.

With both parents being heavy drinkers, Bill and Steve learned to fend for themselves early in life, making their own food and sometimes finding their own shelter. The people who might have offered protection to Steve weren't around consistently. When Steve was twelve, Bill graduated from Notre Dame High School and headed to the Midwest to join the Holy Cross order.

"Between the two (Ed and Maxine), life probably wasn't very good in that house," Mickie recalled. "Steve always smiled, which unnerved me. It was kind of, like, not real. He always had this joker look on his face." As she grew older, Maxine turned increasingly hostile, moving out of the old Avenue 38 house and into an apartment on Twenty-Ninth Avenue in Venice. When she died in 1966 at age fifty-three, she was alone. An autopsy attributed her death to acute bronchial pneumonia. But everyone thought the booze had contributed.

One final story about the maternal side of Steve Crawford's family, which might be entitled the "Saga of the Yellow-Tailed Black Cockatoo," actually occurred in the 1990s, well *after* the Arlis Perry murder. But it sheds light on the family's penchant for defying authority and defining its own code of ethics. It involved Steve's first cousin, Nan Crandall, the daughter of his aunt Maddy and the older sister of Mickie. (It's one of the curses of Crawford's family that so many first names are similar.)

In the poaching of generations that sometimes occurs in families, Nan Crandall was born in 1931, fifteen years before Steve. Nan grew up to be a bird-lover, and in later years, her home was filled with exotic birds. Her sympathy for wildlife also led to her undoing. As an employee of the U.S. Fish and Wildlife Service, she was convicted of accepting gratuities—five exotic birds—in exchange for releasing shipments of birds early from quarantine. This involved thousands of dollars. Exotic birds fetched absurdly high prices. Posing as a dealer, a U.S. Fish and Wildlife Service agent asked her to expedite the thirty-day quarantine for a yellow-tailed black cockatoo he was importing from New Zealand. Nan agreed, saying she was worried that the bird could contract the deadly beak-and-feather disease. During the investigation, the agents uncovered that she had accepted five birds from other dealers she had helped. Although Nan's case attracted the sympathy of Hollywood stars like Betty White and Doris Day, a video of her dealing with the undercover agent undermined their support. She was sentenced to eighteen months in prison by a judge who said he was bound by mandatory sentencing laws. Her lawyer described the sentence as being "like dogs piling on a rabbit."

By comparison with the Rosselles, the family of Steve Crawford's father, Ed, was more conventional and upstanding. As Scottish immigrants, the Crawfords traced their ancestry back to Baltimore before the American Revolution. In the Civil War, Steve's great-grandfather William E. Crawford (1842–1915) was wounded while serving with the Twelfth Ohio Cavalry Regiment, which saw action in Tennessee and North Carolina. After the war, the ex-soldier settled down on a 320-acre farm near Graham, Missouri. Ed was born in Graham in 1907, the offspring of the patriarch's son, John, and Myrtle (Charles) Crawford, a schoolteacher who had studied in the nearby town of Marysville. By 1925, when Ed turned eighteen, the family had moved to Los Angeles, part of a tsunami of migration to the sprawling young city. Myrtle taught for twenty years in the Los Angeles County school district, serving for a year as the principal of a school in El Monte. Ed's older sister, Marcelyn, was a superlative golfer until vision problems limited her playing ability. And she seemed to marry well. She and her husband, the union leader Jack S. Roberts, settled into a lovely house in Sherman Oaks.

The young Ed had musical talent, particularly as a trumpeter. Although he worked a variety of menial jobs through the thirties, his real passion lay in playing with bands. Many years later, Bill Crawford recalled that his father played with Ben Pollack, Jan Garber, and Benny Goodman. A search of the rosters of those bands doesn't reveal Ed Crawford as a regular, but he could well have been a stand-in. The bands he played for had a variety of styles—from the spiky jazz of Pollack to the dreamy, "sweet" sound of Garber—that spoke to Ed's versatility. In 1938, the young musician married Maxine Rosselle. Two years later, when their first son, Bill, was born, Ed and Maxine were paying $30 a month for a place on Westminster Avenue in West LA. Ed had a day job pumping gas at a filling station. Later, Ed got a job with North American Aviation in the Valley, a place where his brother-in-law, Jack Roberts, represented workers in labor negotiations. Ed built "jigs," platforms to hold tools. It paid well enough to support a family—or it should have.

Like Maxine, however, Ed had a problem with alcohol. Although Ed was likable, his relatives remembered him as slobbery when drunk. By Steve's account, he was also verbally cruel. After Maxine died in 1966, his son Bill persuaded Ed to move north to live in Sunnyvale, not far from St. Francis High School, where Bill, now a Holy Cross brother, was teaching. In 1969, in pursuit of a paycheck to support his father, Bill left the order to join the Mountain View police department. Less than two years later, a few months after his father's death, Steve took the job at Stanford. The focus of the Crawford family shifted to the Bay Area, where it remained for the next five decades. The baggage the brothers brought from Southern California never disappeared. If Steve's relatives bequeathed him a moral compass, it was the kind that spun out of control in a magnetic field.

CHAPTER 22

THE DOOR KNOCKERS

Two weeks after Arlis's murder, the Santa Clara County sheriff's task force had eliminated most of the obvious leads and dismissed the ludicrous ones. None of the physical evidence pointed to a particular suspect—not the palm print, not the broken door, not the kneeling pillow. The letters from the FBI fingerprint experts in Washington piled up without identifying the killer. What had been an all-hands-on-deck case fell back to the cargo hold of detectives John Johnson and Dave Pascual, weary sailors on an unpromising sea. After all, new felonies were occurring every day, summoning detectives to fresh crime scenes. As much as Sheriff James Geary's top people wanted to solve the murder, they faced urgent demands elsewhere.

At 10:00 a.m. on Tuesday, October 29, a cool and rainy day, Pascual and Johnson knocked on the door of the man who found the body, security guard Steve Crawford. With his wife, Joyce, Crawford lived in a Mountain View apartment a block from El Camino Real, a second-floor place with a vaulted ceiling and a view of an interior courtyard. It was nice but inexpensive—the one-bedroom apartments rented for $150 per month. The visit of the two detectives marked the third time that Crawford was interviewed, a sign that he was still a figure in their probe, one more "t" to be crossed. Two weeks before, at the Stanford police station, the security guard had declined a lie detector test. And he had altered his story about how often he visited the church on the night Arlis was murdered. First it was twice. Then three times—at 10:30, 11:15 and 11:45 p.m. In the second visit, he remembered seeing someone matching Arlis's description "pull into" a pew behind him. It was a muddy sheet of a story.

In hindsight, Crawford could have been put through a set of searching questions that morning. If he had seen Arlis, as he said in his second interview, why did he tell dispatcher Charlie Papp that he had not spotted anyone resembling her? Why did he not mention it in his first interview Sunday morning? Why did he tell Sgt. Johnson that her body felt warm after he had reported on the radio that it was a "cold stiff?" Crawford said he thought he had told "someone" on Sunday about visiting the church three times instead of two. Whom, precisely? And why did his story of seeing Arlis around 11:15 p.m. not match the account of witnesses who placed her entering the church around 11:35? Homicide detectives like to say a lie is as good as the truth in unraveling a story. Under intensive questioning, very few suspects can keep their fibs straight. Crawford's account contained enough conflicts to offer investigators a feast.

Their report did not reflect that the two detectives conducted that kind of interview. Instead, they rehashed Crawford's second version. Three trips to the church, with the middle trip featuring the woman matching Arlis's description. On the last trip, he had walked down the west side of the sanctuary and then returned up the central nave, locking the three front doors and checking them by hand. (This departed from his first version, which had him coming to the middle aisle and making an announcement that the church was closing.) He returned to the Round Room at about 1:00 a.m. and spent ten to fifteen minutes checking the office and the basement. "Crawford further stated that after receiving the missing persons report on Arlis Perry, at 0300 hours, he did not, at this time, check the church's interior or exterior," Pascual wrote in his report.

In fairness to Pascual and Johnson, the questions that could have been put to Crawford were the kind cops ask a suspect they see as the unquestioned killer, a man who can be coaxed or tricked into an admission. Even though he changed his account, Crawford had not reached that status. His landlady, Mildred Riveness, gave investigators a glowing review, saying Crawford was a nice person, "open and honest," with a "positive type of personality." After obtaining an associate degree from Foothill College, Crawford was majoring in psychology and minoring in corrections at San Jose State University, even getting an A in a course entitled "Psychology of Persons." Perhaps most important, he was a former gun-carrying Stanford cop.

At that point, the detectives had little idea that he was also a practiced liar. Crawford's acquaintances remember that he told a story that endured as a hardy untruth—that his parents died together in a car crash. In fact, his mother had died alone in her bed in Venice, California, in 1966. His father moved to Sunnyvale, where he lived for a sodden period before expiring at El Camino Hospital in 1970. No one questioned the car-crash story. Believing it was true, Stanford colleagues were sharing Crawford's version of his parents' death more than four decades after the murder. It seemed too tragic to have been invented. In retrospect, however, the lie revealed volumes. It showed a yearning to shed an unhappy childhood—and a willingness to manipulate truth to obtain sympathy.

To the homicide investigators, Crawford was still just the community service officer who found the body—a strange guy, yes, but a man who regretted that he had not checked the church more carefully. If anything, his behavior on the morning of the murder showed just why he had been demoted as a cop. Intent on matching physical evidence to the murderer, no one on the sheriff's task force was pounding the table for Crawford as the killer. Many years later, Johnson told me that he and Pascual had interviewed Crawford the last time without a full briefing on his contradictions, the dress rehearsal before a critical interrogation.

"We went on a cold interview," he said. "That's how we were directed."

Pascual and Johnson did try to establish what happened after Crawford got the missing persons report from Papp at 3:00 a.m. and why no one had checked the church. They assembled a rich portrait of incompetence with one more discordant note. Crawford said he thought Officer Art Nebgen might have checked the doors after following up a report of a couple of women strolling near the church. One of them reportedly matched Arlis's description, while the second wore what appeared to be red pajamas. The transcript recorded that Nebgen followed the two women and said, "I'm just now entering, uh, the rear of the church."

That prompted a wisecrack from Crawford on the air: "Tell her she can't take her friend home." It was hard to know exactly what Crawford meant, but the "her" seemed to mean the Arlis figure and the "friend" the woman in red pajamas. As a play on gender orientation—was he suggesting the two women were lesbians?—the jest was not very funny. If he was talking about Arlis, the remark suggested he did not take her disappearance seriously. For his part, Nebgen was reporting his general location, not describing an entry into Memorial Church. Nebgen told the investigators that he had *not* checked the church. He had not even stopped the women, whom he described as Hispanics not fitting Arlis's description. The story that went out publicly—that police checked the exterior doors at 3:00 a.m.—was wrong.

Crawford's story about how he found the body went unchallenged as well. He told investigators that he opened the front doors, entered the sanctuary, and noticed an interior door broken open on the west side, to the right of the church as a visitor faced the altar. That implied a burglary or at least an intruder. Where might Memorial Church keep money or valuables? The answer was the Round Room, the church office, which could be reached through a small vestibule to the right of the altar. At that moment, however, Crawford did not check the Round Room. Instead, he walked down the west side of the church, crossed in front of the altar, and went into the remote east transept, where he found Arlis's body under a pew. Crawford explained that he was looking for "sleepers," a common enough occurrence. Did Crawford have an idea that a body lay in the east transept? Like so much else in the case, it was a whisper, a suspicion, not a solid conclusion.

After the Mountain View interview, yet another question lingered outside the lines of the police report. Where had Crawford gone during the time he was missing from the crime scene? Shaken by the discovery of the body, the security guard stayed at Memorial Church until the first deputies arrived at 6:05 a.m. He gave Deputy Nick Consolo an initial statement, which might have taken ten minutes. Then he disappeared until past the time detectives arrived at 6:45.

While proof is scanty, my reporting convinced me that Crawford probably called two people from a Stanford telephone that morning, likely during the interval when he was missing from the crime scene. One was his wife, Joyce, although she told me she had no memory of talking to Steve before he returned home later Sunday. When dispatcher Papp asked her whether she had heard from Steve—Papp had gotten a busy signal when he first called their apartment—Joyce hesitated, saying, "Uh." There are signs that a second call went to a union steward and fellow security guard, Wayne Warwick, who, like Crawford, was often at odds with Stanford police administration. Years later, Crawford told a girlfriend he called Warwick that Sunday morning. In 2018, Warwick's widow told me her husband had mentioned such a call as well. The two women did not know the details of the conversation. Warwick and Crawford later became close friends, taking train trips together before Warwick's 2004 death.

Neither call would have been unusual by itself. Crawford was nearing the end of his shift, and he might have wanted to tell his wife he would be delayed—though Joyce did not relay that to dispatcher Papp. After the discovery of a murder victim in the church, a call to a union steward would not have shocked any police officer. Law enforcement unions teach their members to call the steward if they could be questioned pointedly by investigators at a crime scene. Unions exist not only to fight for better hours and wages. Above all, they seek to protect the rank and file from losing their jobs. It was a touchy point at Stanford, which had demoted a whole cadre of cops, including Crawford.

For a second time, Crawford declined in the Tuesday interview to take a lie detector test. Although his refusal bothered the detectives, it left them, at least as they saw it, with few other avenues to pursue the security guard. In many ways, the third Crawford interview marked a turning point in the case. Without physical evidence tying him to the crime, the investigators turned their attention to the idea that an outside killer followed Arlis into the church. The case was not closed—several developments unfolded over the next five years— but Crawford was not at the forefront. In an exchange of names in late October 1974 with a sheriff's office in Wisconsin that was investigating a case with parallels[1], the Santa Clara County detectives sent along the names of seventeen men who "have come to our attention as possible suspects" in the murder, including several whom they had cleared. Crawford's name was not on the list.

One other element, based more on instinct than evidence, dissuaded the investigators from concluding that Crawford was the killer. He did not seem capable of committing such a heinous murder. As one investigator put it, "He didn't seem to have the stones to do this." Crawford was a glib, talkative man with a surface charm. He seemed to lack the cold will of a murderer. His pretensions to intellectualism helped convince the cops that his patter masked weakness rather than a killer's callousness. Steve Mello, a Mountain View officer and friend of Crawford's older brother, Bill, remembered that Crawford liked to try to refute another person's observation. "Steve gave off the air of being smarter than you," Mello said. "He'd say, *Have you ever considered such-and such?"*

Pascual and Johnson eventually rotated to other assignments. Johnson was promoted to lieutenant, one sign that the conscientious detective's work was valued. Their successors, Sgts. Ken Kahn and Tom Beck, pursued the outsider theory, working with the FBI as they tried to flesh out evidence. If the outside-killer theory was correct, however, the investigators had hurdles to overcome. The first was how the killer had spotted and tracked his victim. No one knew in advance that Arlis was headed to the church. Had a murderer waited outside the church, spotted her entering alone, and then followed her to kill her? Had he been waiting inside? It seemed to demand a set of unlikely coincidences. True, the identity of the husky man who appeared at the law firm on Friday had not been explained. But if he was the killer, he had to have followed Arlis for thirty-six hours or agreed to meet her at the church near midnight. Both scenarios seemed unlikely.

The outsider theory also challenged the elaborateness of the crime scene. The positioning of the body, the use of the candles, and the possible ceremony all suggested that it took the killer thirty to forty-five minutes to lay out Arlis. That meant a murderer familiar with the rhythms of the church, a man who knew he would not be interrupted. A killer from outside would have been more likely to attack and flee, eager to escape capture. It was always possible an outsider might be familiar with how often the church was checked. In their initial investigation, the deputies had come across reports of sleepers in the church. But that universe seemed tightly confined. Lie detector tests had eliminated suspects like Larry B., the student who believed the devil would triumph.

Finally, there was the issue of the doors on the west side of the chapel, which became central to the case. On the Sunday morning after the crime, Sgts. Wes Bowling and Tom Sing—the H-4 undercover unit—had found an interior door on the west side of the church kicked outward with enough force to cause a couple of cracks in its heavy wooden boards. In the outsider theory of the crime, that was the route of escape for the killer. Locked inside with Arlis, he killed her and then escaped by breaking out. Throughout most of three decades, it formed a cornerstone of thought for detectives.

Yet doubts lingered. Crawford said he had locked the west interior door the night before, even "flashlighting" the deadbolts. But if the western door had been locked by a deadbolt, it would have been impossible to kick out. It was a sturdy lock. The next morning, when he dusted for fingerprints, Bowling noted that neither the inner or outer doors were locked. A floor latch was not secured. That left the question: If the door was unlocked, why was it broken out? Why didn't the killer simply let himself out? As Deputy Nick Consolo sensed from the start, there was something strange about the doors. If the murder scene was staged, then the breakout could be too.

CHAPTER 23

THE CROSS STEALER

At about nine-thirty on the morning of Friday, February 28, 1975, more than four months after Arlis Perry was murdered, a janitor making his rounds at Memorial Church noticed something missing from the chancel at the head of the sanctuary. The three-foot-tall gold cross that dominated the marble altar had disappeared. The cross had stood in its place since the church was dedicated in 1903, one of the few pieces to emerge unscathed from the huge California earthquake three years later. Designed by Italian artisans, it had been the personal property of Jane Stanford. It was such a hardy survivor, such an emblem of church life, that the theft befuddled the church staff. Aside from the value of the piece, nobody could forget that the cross stood next to the altar candles used by Arlis's killer. Jane Stanford's cross had been a witness to murder. Now it was the victim of kidnapping. Was there any link between the two crimes?

Stanford authorities put a value of $12,000 on the gold-and-mosaic piece, but it was almost certainly worth more. On a cross weighing twelve to fourteen pounds—my rough estimate—the gold alone would have been worth more than $25,000 in 1975, or $120,000 in today's money. More significantly, the cross was made with techniques that could not be replicated. The craftsmen at the Salviati studios in Venice had used bits of exquisitely ground glass known as "smalti" to fashion mosaics that displayed the four ancient basilicas of Rome: St. Peter's, St. John Lateran, St. Paul's Outside the Walls, and Saint Mary Major. In the middle of the work was the Lamb of God and a Chi Rho monogram, an early symbol of Christ. It was a long, imposing piece with bulbous arms that lent it the feeling of an Eastern Orthodox heirloom. Like the walls of the church itself, virtually every inch of the cross bore a decoration.

From the start, investigators had promising leads to the theft, which they pinpointed as having taken place on Thursday morning, February 27, five days after what would have been Arlis's twentieth birthday. Sheriff's Lt. Robert Bartoo said that three people had seen a man they believed to be the thief. He was described as being in his early twenties, five foot eleven, with a dark monk's robe and sandals. He had dark, straight, collar-length hair combed over his ears. Carrying a flannel bag and a sleeping roll tied with ropes, he had taken the cross to the woodshop at Sequoia High School in Redwood City, seven miles away, where he persuaded students to make a wooden staff on which to mount his trophy. Hefting the cross, he was seen hitchhiking south on Highway 101 at Whipple Avenue in Redwood

City at about 6:00 p.m. on Thursday. "He's acting rather strange," Bartoo said, a memorable understatement.

As they traced the sightings, investigators theorized that the thief was headed toward Monterey or Santa Cruz. An all-points bulletin was put out for his capture, though sheriff's deputies held out hope—fruitless, as it turned out—that he would return the cross on his own. The deputies also disclosed that they had found the door to the organ loft in the church unlocked and open. That detail offered a fractured rhyme with the Arlis Perry case. One of the students interviewed by the cops investigating the Perry case had heard shuffling sounds coming from the organ loft.

The man with the cross struck the police as no ordinary crook. The witnesses said he reminded them of a religious student or monk. If he intended to sell the cross, he was unlikely to have visited Sequoia High School, an errand that only made the piece more visible and the thief more vulnerable. One theory was that the thief believed himself to be a Franciscan friar and was following the path of Father Junípero Serra, the Spanish priest who had founded a string of missions in California. While this idea demanded imagination, it didn't strike people as absurd in the thicket of crime in the seventies.

At Memorial Church, one fact revealed the relaxed security more starkly than anything else. Nearly twenty-four hours elapsed before the theft was discovered, a delay that allowed the thief to escape and hitchhike south. In such an ornate sanctuary, the absence of the cross did not stand out immediately. Although it commanded a central place on the altar, the cross was one piece of art among many.

Church authorities seemed to have only a foggy idea of the cross's value.

In April 1975, two months after the theft, Dean Hamerton-Kelly sat down for an interview with *The Stanford Daily*—the *Daily* called it "Preacher Feature"—to talk about the missing cross and the murder. More than anyone else in the Arlis Perry case, the dean was cursed by an insensitivity to how his words would be received. He insisted that the church's reputation had not been damaged by the murder or the theft. "The reputation of a church like this is something that is formed over time and even dreadful things like the murder, I think, fit into a larger pattern," he told the reporter, a comment that made murder sound like a season in the church calendar. Stressing that observers should look at the whole of his two-year tenure to judge the church's stature, he added with a chuckle, "I hope it appears in relatively good repute."

Reflecting on the theft, Hamerton-Kelly sounded almost blasé. "It's a little embarrassing to realize that I had that much money standing around," the dean said. He insisted that there was no way the church staff could have anticipated the murder or the theft. "All of us had thought that the most threatening times had passed," the dean said. "We thought that everything had become quieter…There is nothing we could be blamed for except that we were not more careful." In retrospect, that was the point—and Stanford became more aware after the theft. In fairness to Hamerton-Kelly, the university suffered from an embarrassment of riches. No one believed a piece so central to the church would be so easy to steal. Even after the Arlis Perry murder, Memorial Church staffers had trouble regarding visitors as potential thieves.

With any luck, investigators should have had a chance of apprehending the thief. A hitchhiking monk with a gold cross on a wooden staff should have found it difficult to disappear. But the deputies never reported an arrest. And the cross is still missing, replaced now on the altar by a large brass cross that bears no decoration, a handsome but anodyne heir to the original. For the church staff, a moment of hope surfaced when they received a tip that the cross was spotted out of state. Bill Aaron, a sexton at Memorial Church, remembers that someone contacted the church office, passing on a picture of a cross—Aaron recalls it as being at Boys Town in Nebraska. "We got all excited, but on closer inspection, we determined it was a copy with a few changes to the design," Aaron said.

Was the theft of the cross linked to the murder? On the surface, the possibility seemed remote. The method behind the two crimes was very different. In the Perry case, the killer went to great lengths to disguise his tracks. In the theft of the cross, the would-be friar strove to advertise his. If one crime was motivated by a murky sexual craving, the second seemed rooted in an impulse toward evangelism. But there was a connection in the choice of implements on the altar—the candles in one case, the cross in another. Both killer and thief perverted or mocked the church's symbols. The theft of the cross was always one of the loose ends that made a conclusion to murder so elusive.

In August 1976, Sheriff's Sgt. Tom Beck, a gifted detective who had inherited the Arlis Perry case, got a call that proved that the story of the stolen cross and the hitchhiking monk had not been forgotten in law enforcement circles. A San Mateo county deputy reported that one of his family friends, a teller at a Palo Alto bank, had spotted a strange man trying to cash a check. Identifying himself as Michael Gilmore, he had a full beard, a burlap-style shirt, two black eyes, and a staff without a cross. The San Mateo County deputy remembered that a rustic man with a staff could be of interest to investigators in Arlis's murder. Not long afterward, Palo Alto police stopped a full-bearded man walking barefoot along El Camino Real. When the man told an officer that he was Christ and that his philosophy of life was no killing, no sex, and no materialism, he was taken to the Palo Alto police department for questioning. He was a twenty-two-year-old meatpacker from Wisconsin. As much as they might have wanted to arrest him in the theft of the cross, investigators had nothing to hold him.

The cross theft, however, magnified attention to crimes that occurred in or near a church. One murder that deputies looked at was the murder of Sarah Lou Gammons, the wife of a Presbyterian minister in Gustine, California, a town of three thousand in the Central Valley. The police chief in Gustine, Robert Belmont, called Santa Clara County investigators to report that the Gammons killing had similarities with the Perry case. On February 16, 1973, Gammons was working with an after-school program that helped kids with homework and art. That afternoon, the pastor's wife was heard practicing piano inside the church for the weekend's church services. Later in the day, her husband, Kenneth, found her body in a home that served as the church's youth center. She had suffered slash wounds to the neck and been stabbed in the face multiple times. The killer had left her head propped up by two Bibles. Santa Clara County authorities concluded there was no evidence connecting the two murders. More than four decades later, the Gustine murder remained unsolved.

CHAPTER 24

BILL

In those British TV shows that feature a quirky detective who solves the case with a flash of insight, the cops often assemble a board on which they pin the photos of victims and suspects, linking maps or documents by yarn or twine. I've never been able to find evidence that investigators in the Arlis Perry case used such a board. They *did* collect pictures of the key people in the case as well as documents and a map of the church. One set of photos that I found intriguing came from a trip to San Francisco in the mid-seventies by a group of friends from the South Bay. Along on the trip were Steve and Joyce Crawford and their friends, Sandy and Al Mize. Like Steve, Sandy also served as a Stanford community service officer.

The group seemed to be having a buoyant time as they visited the standard tourist shrines—Alcatraz, Chinatown, a boat on the bay. Steve acted as clown, holding up a couple of fingers behind his blond wife's head or embracing a ceramic lion in Chinatown. Joyce seemed to tolerate his antics with good humor. The collection also contained a shot of another person who went along, Steve's older brother, Bill, a handsome man in his early thirties who wore a brown, military-style jacket, aviator glasses, and close-cropped hair. When I assembled my own board on the case—a piece of butcher paper marked with a felt pen and a cluster of arrows—I displayed Bill's photo prominently. He knew Steve better than anyone. Certainly the Memorial Church investigators knew who he was. Bill was the Mountain View cop who had been a Holy Cross brother. The brother who had been a brother.

To understand Bill, it's necessary to go back to Sunday, August 16, 1964, when seven young men of the Congregation of the Holy Cross took their final vows at St. Francis de Sales Church in Sherman Oaks, a well-lit church with engravings of saints on the white-washed walls. It was a solemn occasion. As they vowed to lead lives of poverty, chastity, and service, the seven brothers lay face down before the altar. They formed the backbone of an extraordinary generation of Notre Dame High School graduates who entered the priesthood or a Catholic brotherhood. From the classes of 1957 and 1958 alone, at least seventeen young men embraced Holy Cross vows. Although the great majority of them eventually left the priesthood or their order, sometimes to be married, the moment affirmed the times. In the late fifties and early sixties, before Vatican II opened the church to a fresh stratum of laypeople, taking vows was a coveted goal, granting admission to an elite brotherhood devoted to teaching, music, and fellowship.

One of those men, twenty-four years old on that August day, was William Edward Crawford, a trumpeter who had graduated from Notre Dame six years before. Bill, as everyone knew him, clung to a different set of beliefs than did Steve. Bill was a man of faith, while Steve was an unapologetic atheist. Bill lauded the cops. Steve saluted the American Civil Liberties Union despite his own stint as a police officer. In later years, the two quarreled about the Catholic faith in which they were raised. "Steve was *a*-church," Bill explained to me. "It was not a question of hating the church. It wasn't hatred. It was a general discounting. No matter what the religion, (he felt) they're all a bunch of nuts."

Nonetheless, the careers of the two men converged at key points. For half a decade after taking his final vows, Bill taught band, religion, and English at Holy Cross high schools, first in Long Beach and later in Mountain View. Then, in 1969, he became a Mountain View police officer who went by the nickname "Brother Fuzz." Steve, meanwhile, followed his brother to Notre Dame High School, graduating the same year Bill took his vows. Like Bill, he joined the band and enjoyed the protection of Brother Eugenio, the effervescent Notre Dame band leader. Like Bill, he enlisted in an organization that demanded discipline—in his case, the U.S. Air Force. And like Bill, he migrated north to join the law enforcement fraternity in the Bay Area. The similarities extended to the mundane: Bill remembered that Steve commuted to Notre Dame from Venice in Bill's 1949 Buick Roadmaster, a car whose chief asset was a working radio.

In the eyes of his parents, Bill enjoyed one advantage that Steve did not. He was a talented musician. A picture from the early fifties shows Bill as a goofy boy holding a trumpet and standing outside with his parents. His father, Ed, a slim man with an open-collar shirt, held his trumpet with the assurance of a professional, while his mother, Maxine, played an accordion, an exuberant look on her face. Steve, who would have been four or five, was absent. "Bill, by family standards, was supposed to be a star," said their cousin Mickie McGowan. "He was very musically inclined. I heard he had perfect pitch, and he taught himself to play trumpet, the piano, the accordion…it was thought he inherited [Ed's] talent…Perhaps being the younger brother, Steve got thrown to one side for Bill all the time."

In joining the Holy Cross brotherhood, Bill selected an order that traced its beginnings back to the effort to rekindle the fortunes of the church in France after the French Revolution. Its most famous institution in the new world was Notre Dame University in South Bend, Indiana, a haven for academic rigor and Touchdown Jesus. But the order had a more profound impact through its network of high schools. Showing remarkable foresight in buying real estate in the fifties, the Holy Cross Congregation expanded in California, building Notre Dame High School in Sherman Oaks and St. Francis High School in Mountain View. After his stint in Southern California, Bill spent several years in the sixties at St. Francis, which then relied on the Holy Cross brotherhood for faculty. He even did a stint as the school barber. A popular teacher, Bill forged tight relationships with the families of his students, particularly those with musical backgrounds.

One of them was Steve Mello, a St. Francis sophomore who took Brother Bill's band class. One day in the mid-sixties, eager to show off for his friends, the youthful Mello called the close-shaved Brother Bill a "skinhead," a term that did not have the white nationalist overtones of today. Bill responded by giving Mello ten hours of detention to be served on a weekend by cleaning the school bus and picking pebbles off the track. When Mello's father dropped his son off to serve the detention, he told Bill to feel free to exact the required penance. In part because of their mutual love of Frank Sinatra, Brother Bill and the young Mello became good friends, with Bill frequently visiting the Mello home. Within a few years, both became Mountain View cops.

After Bill and Steve's mother, Maxine, died in 1966, the twenty-six-year-old Bill inherited responsibility for his father, Ed, whose drinking had become worse. (Ed's full name, like that of his son, was William Edward Crawford, but nobody used his first name.) While he taught at St. Francis, Bill coaxed his father to move north from Los Angeles to take an apartment in Sunnyvale. For a while, the senior Crawford stopped drinking. Then Ed relapsed, and in 1970, he died at age sixty-three, a victim of cancer and malnutrition. By then, Bill had left the Holy Cross brotherhood, in part because supporting his father demanded more money than his oath of poverty would allow. When he joined the Mountain View police force, it became national news, particularly because the department also hired an ex-nun. In 1972, the *National Enquirer* ran a story entitled "Ex-Monk and Former Nun Work on Same Police Force." Asked whether his years as a brother were an asset in becoming a cop, Bill answered, "One thing that happens to a lot of policemen is that they become unfeeling, cynical. A man of God is taught to be tolerant, and I have never lost that feeling. I'm glad I haven't."

Bill's long career as a cop was marked by stories that made for legend. One night, while waiting for a traffic light to change at 3:00 a.m. at San Antonio Road and El Camino Real, he fell asleep in his patrol car. His sergeant, who came across him a short while later, left a note asking him to call when he awoke. The sergeant parked nearby to keep a watch on his slumbering colleague. How long Bill slept was not disclosed—though it's doubtful it was very long. Another time, Bill accidentally shot himself in the leg with a stun gun, an early version of a Taser. He packed it back in the box and told friends he was going to return it to the department's acquisitions manager as faulty equipment. In yet another blunder, Bill dropped a trail of bullets from his bullet pouch at an accident scene—bullets that were picked up by firefighters attending the accident. Bill took it all with good humor. He even embraced the role of the bad guy by showing off the department's canine unit, wearing a phony black beard and a protective sleeve on his arm. Always genial but often klutzy, Bill offered a rich target for practical jokes. On his first night of patrol, his colleagues rigged his squad car so the lights and siren turned on with the ignition. "I got yelled at," Bill recalled later. "They denied everything."

As a school resource officer for much of his thirty-six-year police career, Brother Fuzz, who also went by the names Father Flanagan and Pops, devoted himself to the juvenile offenders he arrested. He created programs called "Fishing with the Fuzz" and "Camping with the Cops." "Bill never gave up on any child," recalled Steve Mello. "Even when they were sent to do their time, he would go on his own to visit them." It wasn't unusual for Bill to take kids to baseball or football games or to San Francisco's Steinhart Aquarium. To bolster his work with the Police Athletic League (PAL), he used his cousin Mickie's connections in Hollywood to create a talking dummy to chat with his young charges. It was known as "Officer Pal," a name extended to Bill himself. Asked about his approach to the problems of high school kids, he said, "I don't approach them from a religious as much as an ethical perspective. We spend a lot of time talking about gossip because it really hurts kids."

Even with that commitment, Bill's friends and colleagues remember a man with enough flaws to fall short of sainthood. Despite his service as a Holy Cross brother, he had not always shown respect to the church. As a teenager, he had joined Steve in disrupting the funeral of his aunt's husband at St. Vibiana's Cathedral with cackling laughter. Perhaps because of the enforced poverty of his young adulthood, Bill avoided picking up the check at a restaurant. His cousin Mickie McGowan remembers that he would head for the bathroom when the bill arrived. In later years, he liked to nurse a vodka drink in his garage, though no one accused him of having the same dimension of drinking problem as his parents. Because he

Bill Crawford, a Mountain View policeman
and Steve Crawford's brother.

was sometimes an unreliable witness, his version of facts had to be checked. (Then again, memory is a fickle servant, prone to betrayal and absenteeism.)

After his marriage in 1982, Bill, then in his early forties, settled into family life, helping shape the direction of his wife's son from a previous marriage. A photo from the early eighties shows Bill in his police uniform, with his arm around the boy, genuine affection between them. A fan of Sinatra and Count Basie, Bill found solace in music, continuing to practice trumpet. In retirement, he drove a bus for St. Francis High School, labeling himself "busjock" in his email address. His protectiveness extended to Steve, who traded on Bill's status. In later years, when Steve was stopped for speeding, he produced a leather folder that had his license on the right-hand side and Bill's business card as a Mountain View cop on the left. It usually produced a genial conversation—and often a reprieve from a ticket.

On the Sunday morning when Steve found Arlis's body inside Memorial Church, Bill was on duty in Mountain View, where word of the murder spread on the police radio. Mello, one of Bill's closest friends on the force, says Bill talked with Steve on the telephone that morning after the younger Crawford was quizzed by sheriff's investigators. "Steve was complaining that they seemed ready to blame this on him," Mello said. "Bill told him, *Don't worry, this is standard procedure, they have to clear people.*"

Decades later, when he was in his late seventies, an ailing Bill invited me into his San Jose house to talk about Steve. I think he mistook me for another *Mercury News* reporter, Ed Hering, who had done a story in 1977 about Bill leaving the Holy Cross order and becoming a cop. If it was a mistake, I did not correct him. Bill was a cordial man who was interrupted by bouts of a racking cough. Recalling how the sheriff's department renewed its interest in the murder in the early years of the new century, Bill talked about Steve's isolation and his initial unwillingness to give a DNA sample to investigators.

"He was disconnecting his phone because he didn't like telemarketers," Bill recalled. "I told him, *Call this deputy.* He didn't want to do it." (Steve eventually did give up a buccal swab to deputies in

2006.) Bill insisted that Steve had never told him anything implicating himself in the crime. "I've turned this over in my head," Bill told me. "The only thing I can think of, he had this demon in his head for all these years and never said anything, did anything, indicated that anything was wrong." Of course, it's legitimate to ask how much Bill wanted to know of Steve's darker side. No brother—holy or otherwise—wants to turn in his only sibling for murder.

CHAPTER 25

THE BULLDOG

For years before and after Arlis's murder, the word friends used most often to describe Sheriff's Sgt. Tom Beck was *tenacious*. "If he had an idea, he was like a bulldog," said his longtime partner, Sgt. Ken Kahn. "He wouldn't let go." In a search of a home, Beck would instruct officers to check behind wall pictures. After all, a criminal might hide a safe behind a portrait of Grandma Mildred. The sergeant could spend a day listening to a tape to parse what a suspect had said outside the presence of detectives. Beck was known for having lifted a fingerprint from an onion. Smart, caustic, and slow to forget a slight, the sergeant did not always win friends. He was prickly around the media, resentful among politicians. But no one ever questioned his talent as an investigator. Honing in on an overlooked facet of a case, he wrote with clarity and force. If other detectives weighed the evidence they had, Beck searched for the missing piece. He had an uncanny instinct for the unrung bell.

After the initial investigation sputtered, the case fell to Kahn and Beck, two veteran investigators who were promoted to sergeant in April 1975. The duo melded talents, in many ways as classic good cop-bad cop. Kahn was the judicious, diplomatic partner, a man who later became the public-information officer for the sheriff. In the Arlis Perry investigation, he was often assigned to work with other departments or the media. Beck, meanwhile, focused on the evidence at hand, trying to squeeze a drop of insight from an exhausted rind of facts. In September of 1976, nearly two years after the murder, Beck wrote a two-page memo that unearthed a key clue—or rather the absence of a critical item. The Beck memo informed how investigators behaved and shaped how the public thought of the case. It made Arlis more human. It played a role in two searches that deputies performed long after the crime. And it may have revealed something telling about her killer.

In retrospect, Beck's contribution surprised no one. Even as a young cop in Menlo Park, he had shown an ability to think quickly. At 2:00 a.m. one night, a dozen years before Arlis was killed, he was patrolling El Camino Real near Ravenswood Avenue when he saw a car swerve. A nearly three-year-old boy in a yellow jumper was pedaling his blue tricycle down the busiest street in Menlo Park. Spotting another car bearing down on the young traveler, Beck sounded his horn, turned on his red lights, and pulled to a stop, halting the threatening car fifteen feet from the toddler. When an attempt to find the boy's home proved futile, Beck brought the child back to the police department, where a sergeant took charge and bedded the boy down at his own home. It wasn't until six-thirty in the morning that the child's parents discovered him missing. The boy had decided that 2:00 a.m. was a good time to go for a joyride.

A tall, dark-haired man with a high forehead, a prominent nose, and a luxuriant mustache, Beck brought the same alertness to murder cases. Like all the detectives who labored on the Arlis Perry case, Beck was bothered by the way the killing was done. Calling it "a particularly heinous" crime, he was driven forward by its ugly details. Beck began by immersing himself in the transcript of the Stanford communications tape from the morning of Sunday, October 13, 1974. When Bruce Perry called Stanford police at 3:00 a.m. to report Arlis missing, dispatcher Charlie Papp asked for a description of his wife. Bruce described her as having shoulder-length hair and then added, "She's got, she's got glasses." Arlis was nearsighted. In pictures from the time, she wore big, dark, stylish glasses under her sweep of blond hair. Though she had contact lenses, she relied on the glasses. Her friends said she rarely went anywhere without them.

In the heap of evidence from the scene, investigators had not found those glasses. The missing eyewear did not form a critical part of the early investigation. The detectives were chasing down other leads: the source of the ice pick, the alibis of suspects, the chronology of the night, the appearance of a stranger at the law firm where Arlis worked. Beck was unwilling to leave matters at that. His memo noted Bruce's mention of the glasses and added, "No further mention was made about the eyeglasses in the reports." Though Beck did not

Mon., April 21, 1975 San Jose Mercury

Nine New Sergeants — Santa Clara County Sheriff James M. Geary has announced the promotion of nine deputies to sergeant, effective today. They are (from left) Robert Wilson, 29; Ralph Rivas, 36; Steve Marino, 28; Thomas Sing, 34; Sheriff Geary; Robert Jones, 26; Kenneth Kahn, 35; Gary L. James, 33; Thomas Beck, 36, and James Arata, 29. All live in San Jose except Sing, who resides in Milpitas, and James, who lives in Campbell.

A group of Santa Clara County sheriff's sergeants, including Tom Beck and Ken Kahn, who were promoted in 1975.

criticize his fellow investigators, you could almost hear him asking, "So what happened to the glasses?"

Displaying his instinct for detail, Beck then tried to determine the fate of Arlis's glasses. Though it was unlikely, it was possible that Arlis was *not* wearing them on the night she was killed and had worn contact lenses instead. It was possible, too, that the glasses had been returned to the family after the crime. So Beck reached her survivors to find out. The sergeant began by calling Bruce Perry's parents in Bismarck. Donna Perry, Bruce's mother, told Beck that Bruce was now attending Amherst College in Massachusetts. Three days later, Bruce called back. He told Beck that he had Arlis's contact lenses at one time, but not her eyeglasses, a fact that seemed to rule out the idea that she had been wearing contacts to the church. (Throughout the years, despite his bruising first experience with the cops, Bruce cooperated with investigators.) In the days that followed, neither the Perrys nor the Dykemas found the glasses in their searches.

Donna Perry and Arlis's sister, Karen, then embarked on a mission of sleuthing for Beck. The two checked with Dr. Paul Springan, Arlis's optometrist, who had last seen her in July 1972, when she was seventeen and about to enter her senior year at Bismarck High. As an officer in the Bismarck Lions Club, a longtime member of Good Shepherd Lutheran Church, and a former high school basketball star, Springan was a well-regarded figure in Bismarck. Like everyone else, he was shocked by Arlis's murder. Afterward, he disposed of most of her records, thinking it unlikely anyone would need them. A clerk in the office, however, found the paperwork about her prescription. Arlis wore Victory Barone glasses, style 502, a pewter color. Her prescription was -4.00 in the right eye and -4.62 in the left, which made her very nearsighted. Beck went to an optometrist in San Jose and obtained a picture of the glasses.

The bulldog now sniffed his bone. If the glasses were not at the scene and had not been returned to the families, the killer almost certainly had taken them. Aside from the ice pick handle, the Victory Barone glasses were one of the most significant clues for the police. Investigators eventually let the media know that they were searching for the glasses, though they offered no details about the prescription.

Still unresolved was what the disappearance of the glasses meant, the kind of puzzle that has animated the literature of homicide for a century or more. The most famous film featuring eyeglasses and murder is probably Alfred Hitchcock's *Strangers on a Train* (1951), which starts with an arresting premise: What if two strangers agreed to commit each other's murders, eliminating the symmetrical thorns in their lives? In the movie, the psychopathic killer (played superbly by Robert Walker in his last major role) strangles a woman who wears roundish glasses. As her glasses fall to the ground and break, a close-up of the lens reflects Walker strangling his victim, played by Kasey Rogers. The killer then picks up the shattered glasses and takes them with him.

It was always possible that Arlis's glasses were damaged in the struggle and disposed of quickly. In that case, their disappearance would count for less, an attempt to clean up. Investigators found no frames or glass in their search of the scene. If the eyeglasses were kept as a trophy, their disappearance could reveal much more. Why did the killer pick glasses? Did it comfort him to envision his victim as blind? Did he wear glasses himself? Former FBI agent John Douglas, who wrote the book *Mindhunter: Inside the FBI's Elite Serial Crime Unit*, says a keepsake helps a killer nourish his fantasy of the crime. A 1979 FBI profile done of Arlis's killer said the killer could take a souvenir—including "earrings, keys, wearing apparel, cosmetics."

Five years after the murder, Beck and his partner Kahn flew to Bismarck to talk once more to the Perry and Dykema families. The visit produced no breakthroughs, though the investigators got a better picture of Arlis's life. It was on this trip that they learned that Arlis had a premonition that she would die a violent death before she was thirty. Kahn later told me that one of the reasons they went was to ask again whether the glasses had been recovered. If the unrung bell mattered, it needed to remain unrung. The two detectives got no further in finding the eyewear. But the glasses played a role nearly four decades later, in the last search deputies performed in the Perry case.

For Beck, the Arlis Perry case never went away. In a 1980 interview with San Jose *Mercury News* writer Maline Hazle, the sergeant talked about the victim with feeling. "Arlis Perry was young, beautiful, popular, recently married and had no known enemies," he said. "That makes it all the more difficult to accept that somebody would kill her." Hazle recorded that Beck shook his head as he continued: "There's a brutalness about a molestation murder that you don't have in the others. I often think of the unsolved cases, especially when a case is as heinous as that one. I don't think I'll ever forget." Gesturing toward a bulletin board covered with wanted posters, Beck said, "I keep it in mind each time I go to the clipboard to look at descriptions of other murders throughout the country. And if my partner and I aren't here, somebody is bound to remember the case if something comes up. They'll check and the evidence will still be there." Then he paused and added one word: "Waiting."

CHAPTER 26

THE DRUM MAJOR

One day in the 1962–63 school year—it could have been a few weeks before Christmas—His Eminence Cardinal James Francis McIntyre of Los Angeles arrived at Notre Dame High School in the San Fernando Valley to confer with administrators and inspect the school band. In those days, The Irish Knight Band was a powerhouse, playing at every home and away football game except the first of the season. Under Brother Eugenio Cassano, a rotund man in his mid-forties whose weakness for chocolate and spareribs ravaged his diet, the band won a string of awards in Southern California band contests. The elite all-boys school, built on a prime location at Woodman Avenue and Riverside Drive in Sherman Oaks, served as proof of Cardinal McIntyre's vision for the Catholic Church and its educational mission.

A picture of that moment showed Brother Eugenio directing on the left, Cardinal McIntyre holding a baton in the center, and seven

Notre Dame band members running through a pep number. All of them wore white shirts, dark slacks, and bow ties. To the cardinal's left stood a tuba player, Steve Crawford, a tallish, bespectacled junior who showed no zeal to join the music. With his mouthpiece turned away from his lips, he stared at Brother Eugenio. It could have been the dictates of the score. But for anyone who knew Steve Crawford, the image of the turned-away mouthpiece was fitting. He loathed the church and its hierarchy. Like many of his Catholic-school contemporaries in the fifties, he had experienced the discipline of rapped knuckles. He once argued with a priest about why Catholics should not eat meat on Fridays. Crawford was not ready to give His Eminence anything more than obligatory recognition.

When the Arlis Perry case cooled, the detectives had not deeply explored Crawford's background. He lingered on the periphery of the investigation, not dismissed, but not the focus of attention. The motive in the Memorial Church murder was less pressing to investigators than the physical evidence. The detectives believed an answer to the crime would come from fingerprints in the sanctuary, the palm print left on the candle, or the semen deposited on the kneeling cushion. None of those clues led to Crawford. The detectives knew he had graduated from Notre Dame High School and taken a potpourri of courses at several junior colleges. If they had explored his critical high school years, they might have gleaned a better idea of his strange personality—a young man distant from his peers and suspicious of authority. They might have understood more of the Hollywood-influenced milieu in which Crawford came to manhood. At Notre Dame, he was the drum major during his senior year, 1963–64, the year after the cardinal's appearance. But he led a one-man band in his own direction.

With close to eleven hundred students in the early sixties, Notre Dame was a stern but academically superb institution, a school that turned out great sports teams and graduates with impressive connections. One of Crawford's classmates in the class of 1964 was a basketball player and student council member, Mike Mullen, whose father was a Hollywood press agent for Ann-Margret, Anthony Quinn, and Julie Andrews. More than four decades later, Mullen served as Chairman of the Joint Chiefs of Staff from 2007–2011.[1] The school was led by Brother Robert Hampton, an exacting administrator unafraid to enforce discipline. Notre Dame was salted with the sons of the Hollywood elite, and the brothers themselves had Hollywood connections. The school emphasized community service, insisting that every freshman or sophomore perform twenty hours a year. With students expelled for disciplinary infractions or poor grades, it wasn't uncommon for a class to start with more than three hundred boys and lose a quarter of the students by graduation.

In this heady and rigorous atmosphere, Crawford was not a ready fit. Like almost everyone else in Notre Dame, he had attended a Catholic elementary school—in his case, for three years at Our Lady of the Valley Catholic parish, the domain of Father John Hurley, a big, deep-voiced man who would come in to deliver report cards to the kids. Although classes had as many as sixty children, there were few discipline problems. Wielding rulers, the nuns and a few lay teachers at Our Lady wouldn't allow it. But there was always something different about Crawford, both at Our Lady and Notre Dame. "He did not fit in with other kids," said his first cousin, Mickie Mc-Gowan. "Part of it was his screwed-up home life. He dressed funky. His hair was stupid. Other kids looked at him, and said, *ew*." In the Notre Dame yearbooks of the time, Crawford appears in his class pictures and band photos—but in nothing else.

Young Crawford, however, did have one ally at Notre Dame—Brother Eugenio. Unlike most of the brothers at Notre Dame, the band director went out of his way to show kindness toward students. Brother Eugenio was a Los Angeles native who had worshiped at St. Vibiana's Cathedral downtown before joining the order and becoming a mainstay at Notre Dame. Famously Italian, a lover of food and opera, Brother Eugenio was a diabetic who deserted his diet, devouring the chocolate bars in Notre Dame's fundraising drive. A nonconformist in the brotherhood, he chafed at discipline, sneaking out at night with a friend to the movies or a restaurant. Eugenio also had a couple of strange tics. No matter how hot it was outside, he insisted on having a fire in the fireplace when he visited the homes of students. And he sometimes fell asleep in class. Several years before Crawford joined the band, his older brother, Bill, spotted Eugenio asleep in his office and woke him with a trumpet blast. Eugenio gave him detention on a charge of "waking the brothers."

On a jockish campus, the band attracted a geeky kind of student. "It was actually a pretty good band," said Louis Dow, a drum major a couple of years ahead of Steve. "It wasn't a place where the big guys on campus would be." On trombone and tuba, Crawford was not the player his brother Bill had been on trumpet. But at six feet tall, he was a good-sized young man who filled out a uniform. Remembering Bill, Brother Eugenio selected Crawford as the drum major. In his senior yearbook, a picture of Crawford shows him marching with his baton raised, body tilted backward, white shako hat on his head. It was not the same as being a basketball star, but being the drum major was *something*.

In truth, Crawford was a below-average leader. Only a mediocre musician, he lacked the ability to inspire the band. Dow remembered that Crawford once led the Irish Knights onto the football field when an opposing band cut them off. "It was a rude thing to do," Dow recalled. "Steve stopped the band, which I recall was the polite thing. I would have plowed right through them." As a drum major, Crawford had a couple of other counts against him. Because he lived at a distance—Venice, even in an era of lighter traffic, was half an hour away—he rarely returned to campus for extracurricular events. When the Notre Dame musicians were invited to perform in the All-Catholic Band at the Shrine Auditorium, Crawford was absent. He may have owed fealty to Brother Eugenio but little more to the school. And he did not always get along well with his fellow band members. "I thought he had an attitude," said Joe Vera, who also played tuba. "He seemed to have a need for dominance." Even then, odd conflicts surfaced in Crawford's personality—meek at times, imperious at others.

Halfway through his senior year of 1963–64, Crawford lost his protector. There are various stories about this, but one widely repeated theory was that Brother Eugenio had a blowup with Brother Robert Hampton, the stern Notre Dame principal. Eugenio was shipped out of the Sherman Oaks campus and designated as a Holy Cross representative to the Vatican. The stated explanation was that Eugenio's ability to speak Italian made him a logical candidate to send to Rome. But it was unusual for a replacement to occur halfway through the academic year, particularly for a man who had been such a backbone of the school. Eugenio's Italian, while fluent, was a guttural kind not heard at the Vatican. The yearbook showed a picture of Eugenio conducting the Christmas concert—but in a band photo taken in the spring, he was missing. Eugenio was replaced by Brother Roberto Muller, a transplant from another Holy Cross school. A thin man with a fine singing voice and a sense of command, Brother Roberto was a far more demanding instructor than Brother Eugenio had been.

Bill Hrnjak, a Notre Dame student who became drum major the year after Steve, remembers the first day that Brother Roberto took over. As the band members gathered for practice, Brother Roberto remained in his office reviewing the roll of the students. Someone suggested Crawford lead the band in the Notre Dame victory march, proving to the new band director that they knew their business. A ho-hum rendition drew no reaction from Brother Roberto. Crawford told the band to play it again, louder. At the end of the march, Brother Roberto stood behind the drum major. "What in the hell is that?" he demanded. "Pull out the music." It turned out the band had been playing the victory march with melody only—no harmony. The correct music was found in a cabinet, and harmony returned to the song. More than fifty years later, when I asked Brother Roberto about that story, he confirmed it, saying, "That sounds like me." It could not have cemented Crawford's pride in his role.

Never an outstanding student, Crawford graduated from Notre Dame in 1964 and then spent a couple of years taking classes at Santa Monica Junior College. Steve was a B and C student overall, flirting with academic probation. He may have wanted to stay near his mother, Maxine, whose health was fragile. Maxine died in Venice in December 1966, about the same time that Steve enlisted in the air force. (Bill Hrnjak told me that Crawford lived in a trailer with his mother during the time he was attending Notre Dame. That could imply that his parents, Ed and Maxine, were separated. Family members, however, insist that Ed and Maxine stayed together until her death.)

At the time of Crawford's enlistment, the Vietnam War was expanding rapidly, but the air force retained enough popularity not to rely on a draft. Avoiding duty in Vietnam, Crawford served as a material-facilities specialist, an airman handling equipment and supplies. His four-year stint showed no record of discipline or special-forces training. His brother remembered that he was assigned at Sheppard Air Force Base in Texas, where he reported that he was surrounded by a clutch of "good ole boys." He also served at Osan Air Base in South Korea, where Hrnjak saw him in 1969, marching along a road while Hrnjak rode in a bus. It was that way for many who crossed his path. People caught glimpses of Crawford, but very few saw the full scope of his life.

Mickie McGowan, Crawford's first cousin, remembered seeing him once during this era. It was during a break in his air force service, when Steve showed up at her place in Playa del Rey looking for a place to stay for a couple of weeks. He was driving a Cadillac convertible, perhaps in unconscious mimicry of his flamboyant grandmother, Josephine Rosselle. "It was the wrong car for a young guy to drive," Mickie told me. "It looked like Elvis, like he was a redneck. It just didn't work. Most kids in that era wanted to drive a Jeep." Steve was unfazed, she remembered. The idea that he would not fit in didn't seem to bother him.

CHAPTER 27
THE PROFILER

In one of the odd footnotes of criminal history, a jagged line ran between the personality of Nazi chieftain Hermann Göring and the attempt to find Arlis Perry's murderer. It crossed the case in the person of a tall, serious FBI man named Howard Teten, the first law enforcement figure to write a profile of what Arlis's killer might be like. Teten came to the task and his profession through his exposure to a UC Berkeley forensic psychiatrist, Douglas Kelley, who did a series of psychological profiles of Nazi leaders for U.S. government authorities at the Nuremberg trials. Against the weight of popular opinion, Kelley concluded that Göring was no monster. Though the Luftwaffe chief was cold, brutal, and deceitful, Kelley believed his personality fell within the boundaries of the sane.

Denounced by critics at the time, Kelley's analysis of Göring intrigued Teten, a student in the mid-fifties at Berkeley's School of Criminology. Guided by Kelley, who suggested he try psychological profiling rather than the crime lab, Teten embarked on a career that made him the FBI's behavioral profiler, the man who tried to unlock the secrets of a killer from a discarded food wrapper, the choice of weapon, or the setting of the crime. Often called "the godfather of profiling," Teten looked hard at the Memorial Church murder in early 1979, when investigators were grasping at straws. Although several of his conclusions turned out to be faulty—he acknowledged they were a "calculated guess"—his insights tallied closely enough with the truth to produce a shiver of recognition years later.

Working from crime-scene photos and sheriff's reports, Teten sketched a portrait of the killer as a loner, likely a white man, seventeen to twenty-two years old, maybe a part-time student. In a letter to the sheriff's office early in January 1979, Teten said the murderer was probably unmarried and living or working nearby, with little or no social contact with women. While he might patronize local bars, he did not mix with the crowd, and he was often better at describing his activities in writing rather than orally. The FBI expert also wrote that the killer might well take a souvenir from the scene of the crime—an earring, keys, wearing apparel, a pubic hair, or cosmetics. And he suggested the murderer was likely to keep a diary. Using a bullet-point style for his findings, Teten added: "Often enjoys 'girly books' such as Playboy, Penthouse etc. but would probably not enter an Adult Book Store."

The profiler concluded the killer would seldom flee the city because of the crime—though he might well do so for other reasons. "By and large the type of person I'm trying to portray is a loner, introverted and shy, who feels that he will be consumed by the attraction that he feels toward the opposite sex," Teten wrote. "This is particularly true if he is greeted in a friendly manner or in some way which he in his ultra-sensitive state, interprets as being 'too' friendly. He is then torn between his desire and his fear of being overwhelmed and he reacts by destroying the source of his desire." Teten's conclusion that the killer was likely to be living or working locally seemed to contradict the direction of the probe in the late seventies. At the time of Teten's letter from Quantico, sheriff's investigators were pursuing the outside-intruder theory, looking at name-brand killers. They had even checked out mass killer Ted Bundy, who pretended to be a law enforcement figure to gain the trust of his victims.

It was a bold letter, and it was fair to question how Teten could reach his conclusions. By early 1979, the six-foot-six FBI man was no neophyte to ugly crime scenes. A mix of curiosity about the abnormal and dedication to forensic analysis propelled him toward his hunches in the Perry case. Born in 1932 in Nebraska, the son of a construction foreman, Teten enlisted in the U.S. Marine Corps out of high school and was released four years later in Southern California, where he enrolled at Santa Ana College. While shooting at a local pistol range —he was a crack shot—Teten caught the eye of the Orange County Sheriff's Department, which gave him a job as a paid reserve. Eager to obtain a higher credential, he switched to the School of Criminology at UC Berkeley, which had been designed as a West Point for domestic law enforcement. (Having offended its law enforcement base with a radical turn in the late sixties, the school was shuttered in 1976.) To support his family, Teten worked at the San Leandro Police Department as an identification officer, the forerunner of a crime-scene investigator.

It was at Berkeley that Teten met Douglas Kelley, who introduced the young officer to the strange persona of Hermann Göring and the concept of profiling criminals. Kelley told Teten he didn't have the personality for the lonely toil of the crime lab. He was better suited for probing the psychological underpinnings of crime. (In one of the sadder chapters of this story, Kelley committed suicide on New Year's Day in 1958 in the same way that Göring had in 1946—by taking a cyanide pill.) At times, serendipity guided Teten's path. Looking for a better-paying job, he trekked to the federal building in San Francisco to apply for the Secret Service. When their regulations blocked his entry—Teten remembered the service wanted no one taller than six foot four—the aspiring profiler stopped by the FBI office in the same building. Within hours, Teten received an order to report to bureau headquarters in Washington, D.C.

After stints in Oklahoma, Cincinnati, and Memphis, where he was the first FBI criminal agent on the scene at Martin Luther King's assassination in 1968, Teten was switched to the FBI's fledgling new academy in Quantico, Virginia. There he combined forces with another FBI man, Patrick Mullany, to deliver a series of lectures on the psychology of killers. They were known as "Frick and Frack," the name originally given to a pair of Swiss skaters who formed a comedy duo in the Ice Follies. Teten and Mullany preached that the crime scene offered clues to the workings of the killer's mind. Even before he joined the FBI, Teten had begun assembling a database of the cases he examined. Based on his experience, he would make predictions about the murderer from the crime scene. If there was an arrest or conviction, he would compare his forecast with the characteristics of the killer.

The idea of psychological profiling wasn't new.[1] In the Jack the Ripper case nine decades before, a London surgeon, Dr. Thomas Bond, had looked at the evidence and concluded that the Ripper, while prone to attacks of homicidal or erotic mania, was likely to be a quiet, inoffensive man who led a solitary life. Frick and Frack refined the concept. At lectures for local police officers, Teten would describe the evidence, including such things as the pattern of slashes, the direction of a bullet, or a cigarette discarded at the crime scene. Then Mullany, a former Christian Brother, would delve into the pathology of the killer, trying to explore the forces that led to the crime. The two lecturers encouraged the police officers who attended the academy to bring them their cold cases—"old dogs," as they were known—and Frick and Frack became a hit. Teten emerged as an anchor of the FBI's Behavioral Health Science Unit, formed in response to the increasing number of sexual assaults and homicide cases in the 1970s. Broad-shouldered, personable, willing to help local police, he became one of the nation's best-known specialists in sexually motivated homicides. To the surprise of no one who knew him, he approached his job with a dose of humility.

One of the first big cases addressed by the FBI profilers was the murder of seven-year-old Susan Jaeger, who was snatched from her family tent during a camping trip to Montana in June 1974, four months before Arlis Perry was killed. Teten theorized that the killer was a young, local man who might brag about the crime and was likely to have taken trophies. When an anonymous tip focused attention on a polite twenty-three-year-old named David Meierhofer, Teten's predictions offered a guardrail for investigators, giving them an idea of what to search for. After Meierhofer teared up in a phone call with Susan's mother—FBI officials had urged her to keep a tape recorder by her phone—investigators had enough to get a search warrant and discovered parts of Susan's body. Meierhofer committed suicide in custody. But it was a signal victory for law enforcement. As murders by strangers rose sharply in America, profiling offered fresh hope for cold cases, even though Teten always cautioned that it was to be used only when more promising avenues were exhausted. In later years, as the field became crowded with less-trained soothsayers, he mourned that his specialty had become a "runaway train."

The FBI man's popularity as a speaker came at a steep cost. From repeated lecturing, Teten lost his voice in 1977. After rupturing a disc, he needed an immediate operation. While he was recuperating, he spent time developing and refining profiles. As he juggled other pursuits—among other things, he was striving for a PhD—Teten took a look at the Arlis Perry case at the request of the Santa Clara County sheriff's office. Teten addressed two central issues: Did the killer know Arlis? And what did the location of the crime say about the man who wielded the ice pick? Teten argued first that it was likely that the killer lived or worked in the general area of the church—

within eight to twelve blocks, tops. "In many cases this individual is a complete stranger to the victim who by chance encountered him just prior to the crime," Teten said in a more speculative finding. "In other instances, the perpetrator has seen the victim on several occasions 'from afar.'"

The choice of venue took the FBI expert deeper into the thicket of conjecture. "Due to the location of this offense, this particular individual is either; 'a total atheist (unlikely); or b) a highly religious individual who considers lone women entering the church at night in the type of dress noted, to be sacrilegious," he wrote. That hedged analysis offered the detectives little grist. It did, however, underscore that setting mattered to the killer. In retrospect, Teten may have come closer to the truth in his first point than in his second. It appeared unlikely that the killer acted because he had found something sacrilegious in Arlis's appearance—unless a young woman entering a church alone at night inspired a sense of sacrilege. She was, after all, wearing an inoffensive ensemble of blue jeans, a beige top, and a brown jacket.

At several key points, Teten couched his report so carefully that it was difficult to select a thread leading to a killer. But the FBI man highlighted a central question: Was the murder committed by an insider—that is, someone who had access to the sanctuary—or by an outside intruder who followed Arlis into Memorial Church? Though it was hardly conclusive, Teten's theory that the killer lived or worked nearby pointed to an insider. It suggested the killer had a link with Stanford.

Among Teten's most intriguing conclusions was that the killer could have toyed with the cops: "Depending upon other aspects of their personality, they are not above 'playing games' with the police—observing the crime scene investigation, listening to police discuss the case while at coffee, writing letters, etc. In this sense, he usually feels he is smarter than the police and receives some satisfaction in the fact that he is the only one who knows who committed the crime."

The possibility that the murderer was teasing the detectives suggested new ways of understanding how Arlis's body was laid out. Over the years, crime theorists expounded various ideas about what the layout of the body meant. One theory was that it was akin to a Freemason's symbol. Others professed to see a cult meaning in the symbol, something like the carvings done on Charles Manson's victims. All of these ideas depended on the killer being sincere in professing his hatred for an organization. But there was another, potentially more persuasive idea—that the body was staged to misdirect investigators, leading them to believe the murder was motivated by antireligious or satanic stirrings. Teten concluded his report by saying, "Individuals of this type do not necessarily follow a specific pattern and they may or not kill again." In an age dominated by serial killers, it was a useful admonition.

In the end, Teten's hunch that the killer was local did not dissuade investigators from pursuing the theory that Arlis was killed by an outsider, a homicidal crazy. Until Bundy was executed ten years later, Santa Clara County investigators hoped to interview him at a prison in Florida. And later in the same year that Teten delivered his report, detectives Ken Kahn and Tom Beck got on an airplane to pursue one the strangest leads of all—this time at Attica Prison in New York.

CHAPTER 28

THE CONSPIRACY BUFF

In the spring of 1977, a continent away from Stanford, a thirty-year-old house journalist for IBM was transfixed by a sensational set of killings—the New York murders attributed to the "Son of Sam." As each killing occurred, the writer, Maury Terry, culled the newspapers for clues, debating with friends where Sam would strike next. Perceiving hidden meanings in a letter the killer sent to *New York Daily News* columnist Jimmy Breslin, Terry came to believe that the accused killer, David Berkowitz, did not act alone—that he was tied to a filigree of satanic cults that had claimed victims across America, including Arlis Perry. Discontent with a role as kibitzer, Terry devoted his energy to pursuing what he saw as a sprawling conspiracy.

A decade after the last Son of Sam murders, Terry published a book called *The Ultimate Evil*, a jeremiad for readers who saw America slipping into the grip of satanism. His book began with the murder of Arlis, setting up the story of a placid Stanford campus shocked by the crime. The theory that she was linked to Berkowitz through a web of shadowy characters inspired cult theorists for decades. And the dust cover of Terry's book—which showed an angry wolf howling, fangs bared—made an appearance in the last search done by Santa Clara County sheriff's deputies.

The New York writer entered the story at a time when Sgts. Ken Kahn and Tom Beck clung to few promising leads. Beck had established that Arlis's glasses were missing, an important but not decisive clue unless the eyewear was found. Kahn pursued the history of Ted Bundy, the mass killer arrested in Florida in February 1978. The assumption that the killer was a crazed outsider had shortcomings, primarily the issue of how the murderer knew when Arlis would go to the church. But the two detectives could not ignore a lead about the Son of Sam, one of the most famous killers of the seventies.

Terry grew up in Yonkers, New York, the son of Regina and Maurice Terry. Young Maury went to a Catholic grammar school and then on to Iona College, a private Catholic college in New Rochelle. As a young man, Terry competed in sports, particularly baseball. He rooted for the Giants—New York and San Francisco—and commanded an encyclopedic recall of rock 'n' roll. With a stint as a suburban newspaper reporter behind him, he held down a good job at IBM headquarters in White Plains. A man with thick, Beatles-like hair, pursed lips, and inexhaustible energy, Terry was born for argument—and he turned his considerable reportorial skill to unraveling a chain of murder. As he later wrote, the day of Berkowitz's arrest in

August 1977 was the "beginning of a journey of a lifetime"—painful, rewarding, harrowing.

Claiming he was influenced by the dog of a neighbor, Berkowitz pleaded guilty in May 1978 to six murders committed in 1976 and 1977. The killings were attributed to a young man wielding a .44 caliber handgun and preying on young couples in lovers' lanes. As Terry traced the murders, he became convinced there were too many discrepancies in the descriptions of witnesses and police accounts for Berkowitz to have been the lone killer. Terry saw Berkowitz as a gullible partner in the crime spree rather than as its mastermind. In particular, the writer was fascinated by two brothers, John and Michael Carr, who lived in a house behind Berkowitz's apartment building in Yonkers.

Assembling a bewildering jumble of clues, Terry alleged that the Carr brothers—whose father was named Sam—had links to cultists in North Dakota and California. When both brothers died under suspicious circumstances within the couple of years after Berkowitz's arrest, Terry came to see the New York murder spree as the work of a cult with tentacles across the country. And he managed to persuade at least some law enforcement authorities that his theory had merit. Queens DA John Santucci said he was convinced Berkowitz did not act alone.

To forge the link with Arlis, Terry focused on a remark the imprisoned Berkowitz had scribbled in the margins of an obscure book about satanism: "Arlis Perry, hunted, stalked and slain, Followed to California." At the top of the page, the killer wrote, "Stanford University." After corresponding with Berkowitz, Terry came to believe the Son of Sam knew things about the Perry murder only an insider would know. To Terry, the mastermind behind Arlis's murder was a shadowy figure he called "Manson II," who arranged the killing as a favor to cult members in North Dakota. Terry attributed this information to a source he identified as "Vinny," whose real name he withheld. Convinced of his own probity, the New York writer lambasted the Santa Clara County sheriff's deputies' handling of the case. (He and sheriff's investigator Tom Beck famously clashed.) In Terry's view, the detectives should have paid much more attention to the husky young man who visited Arlis at her law firm.

The Son of Sam came to the attention of Santa Clara County investigators through a Staten Island attorney, Felix Gilroy, who in late 1979 forwarded a copy of a letter he had received from the imprisoned Berkowitz. Gilroy was a believable figure, a prominent trial lawyer who dabbled in Staten Island politics. In the letter, Berkowitz made a striking assertion: at a meeting in Queens, he said, he met a man who was involved in Arlis's murder. The Son of Sam focused a diatribe on "Satanists," saying that "they will even kill in a church." He urged Gilroy to call the sheriff's office and ask for details of what happened to Arlis, including the autopsy report. He also instructed the attorney to ask whether a religious item was stolen from the church a short time after her death. That seemed to refer to the theft of the gold cross from the altar late in February 1975. Finally, the New York killer instructed Gilroy to ask where Arlis came from. "Doing this will solve the whole case," Berkowitz wrote. "Back in

Little Tiny B___. This is where the answer lies." If it was vague advice, it was still intriguing.

In early December 1979, sheriff's investigators Beck and Kahn flew to New York to interview Berkowitz at Attica State Prison. That meeting occurred despite protests from Terry, who thought it would dissuade Berkowitz from talking further about the occult connection. The detectives' interest was heightened through a circuitous channel that Terry already had explored. The Santa Clara County investigators learned that an investigator for the Ward County sheriff's office in Minot, North Dakota, Lt. Terry Gardner, was looking into the February 1978 gunshot death of John Carr at Minot Air Force Base, initially classified as a suicide. Gardner had received a book in the mail, *The Anatomy of Witchcraft*, which apparently was sent to him by a Berkowitz friend. In the margin on page 114, Berkowitz had written the words about Arlis being "hunted, stalked, and slain." Could her death be part of a bigger plot? Was she linked to John Carr? To background himself in the Son of Sam thesis, Kahn talked with Maury Terry, who believed Berkowitz knew who killed Arlis.

All this was heady stuff, potentially a sensational break. At Attica, Beck and Kahn sat down to talk with a fidgety and defensive Berkowitz. The interview was not very enlightening. The twenty-six-year-old inmate told the detectives that all he knew about the case came from newspaper clippings sent to him by a woman named Dee Channel—though he seemed to hint at other sources as well. When the detectives asked whether he had talked with Arlis's killer, Berkowitz evaded the question—and by their account, he became "very nervous." Then he embarked on a rant about his fears that he could be identified as a police informant. "We thought we were close to having him name somebody, but he abruptly said, *If I'm talking to you guys any longer, they're gonna think I'm a snitch,*" Kahn later told documentary filmmaker Josh Zeman. "Then he says, *Well, if I tell you the name, they'll kill my father.*" (In fact, Berkowitz did have a scar on his neck from a prison attack.) Kahn noted later that the Son of Sam seemed to have "considerable knowledge of the occult."

"We thought he was playing with us," Kahn told me.

Before they returned to California, the two detectives stopped in Bismarck, where they talked with Arlis's parents, Marv and Jean Dykema, who dismissed the theories of the occult. If Arlis had contact with cultists in Bismarck, they said, it was likely accidental. The investigators noted, however, that Arlis's sister, Karen, said she did not think it was "far-fetched" to think there might be a link between satanic ritual and her sister's murder.

Whatever the merits of his Bismarck theory, Maury Terry's obsession revealed bits about Arlis's background not commonly known. In his book, Terry focused on a cult he claimed operated behind Mary College, a Catholic school on a bluff just south of Bismarck. The author learned that Bruce's parents had passed on a rumor about Arlis's evangelism to investigators Beck and Kahn. While the Perrys cautioned that they did not know whether it was true—and thought it was probably just a rumor—the story was that Arlis had tried to convert cult members to Christianity, crossing the Missouri River with a friend to proselytize in the town of Mandan, where the Dyke-ma family had once lived.

Terry reported that a young man in Bismarck had followed Arlis around taking pictures of her—some of which she liked well enough to display in her room at home. He quoted Rev. Don DeKok, the minister who married and then buried Arlis, as saying that a man with a black cape was seen trying to break into the Bismarck Re-formed Church before dawn on Friday, October 18, 1974, the day of Arlis's funeral. And two weeks after a makeshift marker was put over her grave in Bismarck, it disappeared without explanation. To Terry, all these events were part of a pattern. "If there was in fact a motive for the killing, it would be hidden in Bismarck, not Palo Alto," Terry wrote.

On the West Coast, Terry uncovered other facts that seemed to deepen the mystery. He talked to Guy Blase, the personable Palo Alto attorney who had seen the husky young man who came into the law firm the day before Arlis was murdered. Giving Blase the pseudonym "Mark Connors," Terry revealed details that were not in the police report. The husky young man was wearing a plaid shirt, and his hair was neatly trimmed. He was, according to Blase, not a "hippie type." Making use of Arlis's letters, the writer revealed the existence of the second Bruce Duncan Perry on campus, a man whom Arlis's rela-tives and friends called by mistake. Terry contended that the second Bruce Duncan Perry might have signed up for a telephone so that he could encourage Arlis to contact him. It would have been an unusual ploy, and there is no evidence for his theory.

At points in his book, Terry told the story from the viewpoint of Bruce Perry, describing the contours of a marriage the young couple was still sorting out. "Life would be good, Bruce believed, with children and a comfortable home. But first they had to survive Stanford and cope with the added demands that came with preparation for a career in medicine or dentistry." *The Ultimate Evil* contained a moving description of Bruce sobbing at Arlis's memorial service at Memorial Church. If Terry had not talked with Bruce, he had interviewed someone very close to him.

Terry nonetheless made several mistakes that undermined the strength of his argument in *The Ultimate Evil*. In this, he was not alone. Terry's most obvious error was to report that the handle of the ice pick protruded from Arlis's skull. It did not. In fact, the killer had broken off the handle. In a more forgivable bit of sloppiness, Terry wrote that Bruce Perry had graduated from Stanford. After an attempt to return to Stanford, Bruce transferred to Amherst College.

In attempting to show that Berkowitz knew things about Arlis that had not been made public, Terry also erred in his physical description of the murdered woman. He quoted from a letter Berkowitz sent to a female friend. "She sure was a skinny little thing," Berkowitz wrote. "She was so tiny." Terry then added his own judgment: "Both these assertions were true." To Terry, Berkowitz had revealed an important fact missing in the newspaper stories. In fact, it wasn't accurate. Arlis was 5 feet, 5.5 inches tall and weighed 125 pounds, a well-proportioned young woman. She was hardly skinny and certainly not tiny. Terry had decided on his theory first—that

Berkowitz had inside knowledge of the Memorial Church murder—
and squeezed the facts to match his premise.

Berkowitz, who became an evangelical Christian, told Terry in a
televised interview in 1993 that there were other Sons of Sam out
there. But FBI profiler John Douglas, who interviewed the convicted
killer, concluded he had acted alone. And the FBI put out a statement
saying there was no evidence of organized satanic crimes anywhere in
the U.S. Even though he had raised many legitimate questions about
the way police handled the .44 caliber killings in New York, Terry's
conclusions about a widespread pattern of cult murders were largely
discredited. His participation with the ratings-driven Geraldo Rivera
in a questionable documentary about the ritual murder and abuse of
children did nothing to help his standing. Still, people across America embraced the idea of a cult of devil-worshippers. It was part of the
zeitgeist. In their reaction to the easy sex and murderous rampages
of the seventies, many evangelicals embraced the idea that a diabolical force was to blame.

Despite its flaws, Terry's book strengthened the hand of those convinced an outsider committed the murder. Over the years, enough
odd events occurred to sustain their faith. In the early nineties, Arlis's friends learned that a classmate of theirs from Bismarck High
School, Pam Eckert, had called Bruce's parents insisting that she
knew something significant about the murder. Pam was a free-spirit-
ed woman who had moved to the West Coast, rarely staying in one
job for very long. One of Arlis's friends called her to find out what
she knew. Crying on the phone, Pam said she had returned to Bis-

marck because her mother was dying. Could the classmate call back? Arlis's friend waited for several months. When she tried again, Pam herself had died, age forty. An obituary listed no cause of death.

With the coming of the internet, *The Ultimate Evil* provided the foundation for a whole set of crime buffs pursuing conspiracy in the murder. One prominent artist who embraced Terry's theory was the actor James Franco, a Palo Alto native born three and a half years after the killing at Stanford. In 2015, Franco released a five-part YouTube video, "The Ultimate Evil," that brought Terry's theories to the small screen. Franco opened his video with an actress playing Arlis—blond, cute, almost ethereal—confronting a hermit-like character in a setting that looked like the rural woods of North Dakota. "We are here to show you the Lord's light," the actress said. "God loves you, no matter the evils in your heart." The video then focused on the Maury Terry character, an intense young man who takes risks in getting information to solve the mystery. The Franco video did not seem to be deeply grounded in the facts of the Arlis case. But it drew a memorable portrait of a crusading journalist seeking to coax facts from a strange and distracted Son of Sam. "Your conviction was a rush to judgment," Terry tells Berkowitz. Portrayed by actor Gary Bairos, Maury Terry comes across as a haunted man seeking his own way despite warnings to avoid the truth.

The Ultimate Evil oozed with fear. Terry wrote that he was subjected to a "false, smear campaign" by New York police officials and that a well-known cult had devised intricate plans to discredit him. If anything happened to him, Terry vowed, "several people whose names are at the top of a special list" would come under intense scrutiny. For those both inside and outside law enforcement who wanted to solve the Arlis Perry case, Terry advanced the investigation by collecting a swath of facts about the context of the murder. A number of people accepted his thesis that Berkowitz did not act alone. A Netflix special in 2021 entitled *Sons of Sam: A Descent into Darkness* made the point convincingly. But Terry's conviction that Arlis was killed in a broad satanic conspiracy was wide of the mark. The truth was much closer to home.

CHAPTER 29

THE THIEF

Even though he disappeared from the church after reporting that he had found a stiff, Steve Crawford retained his job as a security guard at Stanford for another couple of years. He was not charged with a crime. The investigators had only vague suspicions, the unease prompted by his changing story and his refusal to take a lie detector test. The union representing Stanford's community service officers, led by his friend Wayne Warwick, stood ready to help him. Crawford invoked his legal rights to avoid taking the polygraph. At a university that proclaimed its allegiance to civil rights, his refusal was no firing offense. Crawford told investigators he did not murder people or rob safes, and no one could prove the contrary.

It was clear, however, that Crawford was going nowhere in the Stanford Department of Public Safety. His performance on the night of Arlis's murder eroded his already questionable reputation in law enforcement. He made no real attempt to redeem himself. A story about Crawford in the mid-seventies, after the Arlis Perry murder, revealed his contempt for the work. A respected senior guard, military veteran Leonard Screws, was giving a briefing to a group of community service officers one morning when an alarm clock erupted. The clock belonged to Crawford, who sheepishly turned it off. Although his colleagues laughed, the incident fooled no one. Crawford kept the clock because he slept on the job.

After he left Stanford in 1976, the thirty-year-old Crawford embarked on a series of gigs that fell short of a career, a ramble with stops for coffee and donuts every few miles. Crawford was not obsessed with ambition. His resume suggested he cared less about the prestige of a job than about exploiting the opportunities it offered. He was a security guard for an apartment complex, an office worker for a mental health agency, an insurance adjuster, a salesman for an internet service, and a scout for a travel agency. It was the arc of a grifter. Except for brief periods of living in Southern California, he stayed in Santa Clara County, making no attempt to hide from investigators. He drove a recognizable car, a prized, yellow 1965 Mustang.

At the same time, Crawford took risks that would baffle other people. His employers did not understand that giving Crawford a set of keys invited hazard. When he worked for Stanford, he brought home expensive books and artifacts, explaining that they were gifts from a deceased friend. His friends recalled that later that when he worked as a private security guard at an apartment complex, he would lift an item or two from the lost-and-found, once bringing home a ten-speed bike.

In the late seventies, Crawford worked as a CETA employee for two Santa Clara County social service agencies. In some ways, it was a gig of last resort. CETA, the Comprehensive Employment and Training Act, was a federal program that offered training and jobs to the disadvantaged or unemployed. Through CETA, Crawford had an office job with Community Companions, a service that matched modestly paid helpers with mentally troubled people. He also was employed by the county's Information and Referral Agency, which directed callers navigating county government. Although the jobs didn't pay much, he lived modestly.

His personal life was equally checkered. In the mid-seventies, after the Memorial Church murder, he and his wife, Joyce, separated amicably, although they remained married until November 1979. Between the late 1970s and early 2000s, Crawford had at least eight addresses. Meeting his second wife through Community Companions—she was then a college intern—Crawford seemed to settle into solidity after the couple married in 1982. For the rest of the decade, they lived in a mobile-home park off Monterey Road in San Jose and then in a house in north-central Gilroy, a town famed for its garlic. Crawford's second wife had a good job with the telephone company.

Though he was nearsighted, color-blind, and losing his hair, the middle-aged Crawford was still a decent-looking man whom women found attractive. A photo of Crawford remodeling his house in the eighties shows a man with a well-trimmed salt-and-pepper beard, aviator glasses, and a T-shirt that read, "The Human Heart." Sensitive about growing bald, he always donned a hat before going outdoors. His beard covered a narrow, pointed chin. In his pursuits—motorcycle riding, Scotch-drinking, military history—he came off as a mix of regular guy and would-be intellectual. A longtime smoker, he cleared his throat before delivering an opinion, a practice that loaned him gravitas. His favorite music—he played it again and again—was *Victory at Sea*, the 1952 orchestral suite composed by Richard Rodgers. With his wife, Crawford joined a square-dancing group called the Dixie Derbys, which convened regularly at a South San Jose school. His friends remember a congenial man who liked to talk about history, a decent dancer complemented by his genial wife.

Behind the facade, there were warning signs that Steve Crawford was not quite like any other middle-class homeowner who enjoyed square dancing. One was his involvement with pornography. In the eighties, before the internet, Crawford sent away for a porn video from Canada, paying for it with a personal check. Not long afterward, a gaggle of U.S. federal agents showed up with a search warrant at Crawford's front door at the Monterey Road mobile-home park. The officers found no porn inside, and Crawford was not arrested. Just what was in the video is not clear. But the arrival of federal officials suggested it was more disturbing than shots of nude women.

The people who knew Crawford then say he put no great store in fidelity to his wife. He seemed to enjoy exhibitionism. At one eighties Halloween party attended by drama students at San Jose State, he fastened a human skull on his shoulder with a rubber snake emerging from it. Crawford seemed amused at the reaction it evoked. According to Stanford authorities, the skull with the snake was one of the items stolen from campus during the time Crawford was a security guard.

Through the latter half of the eighties and the early nineties, Crawford worked as an insurance adjuster for the D.L. Glaze Company, a firm founded by a San Jose State graduate. Of all his jobs during this period, it was probably the most stable. An insurance adjuster is generally paid by the insurance company that holds the policy on a given property. After surveying the damage to a home, the adjuster submits an estimate, which the company uses to determine a settlement. It is a system that works well with ordinary damage—say, a garage fire. It is trickier in something as cataclysmic as an earthquake.

A story from those days—if it is true—says much about Crawford. When the Loma Prieta earthquake struck Northern California four minutes after 5:00 p.m. on October 17, 1989, Crawford turned to a colleague at his Campbell office and greeted him with a high five. No one knew at that point that the quake would cause sixty-three deaths and the collapse of the double-decked Cypress Freeway in Oakland. Few understood it would wreck the Marina District of San Francisco, injure more than thirty-seven hundred people, and reduce parts of downtown Santa Cruz to rubble. But the tremors of the 6.9-magnitude quake were so serious that the two adjusters sensed the damage would be profound—and that their business would flourish. As buildings toppled and roads bent, adjusters would determine how much the insurance companies would have to pay.

Steve Crawford relaxing at home (undated photo).

A person who knew Crawford in that era remembers that he coached a piano-playing friend in the arcane way of recovering money from insurance. The pianist was unhappy that the insurance company was offering him so little money to repair his home after the Loma Prieta earthquake. Miffed at the insurance company for his own reasons, Crawford coached his friend on how to threaten litigation—and the homeowner increased his payout from $20,000 to more than $350,000. If the account is accurate—I have not been

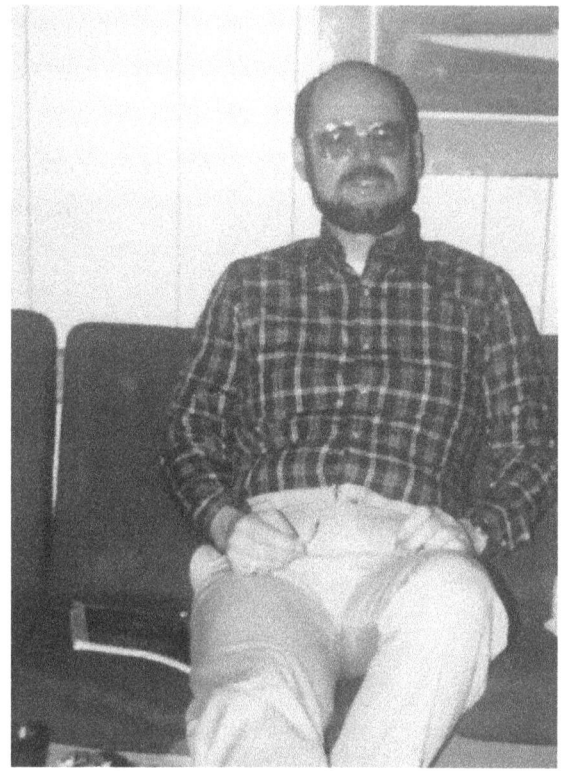

Crawford in the late 80s or early 90s.

able to verify it independently, although I believe it—Crawford was subverting a company he was supposed to be representing.

With the new decade of the nineties, Crawford's dance with the truth lost rhyme and meter. By early 1992, his wife had become increasingly worried about him. She later described him to officers as mentally unstable and drinking heavily. She knew he had girlfriends. It did not help that Crawford had a feud with his mother-in-law. In a letter written to the Gilroy police in March 1992, Crawford complained that his mother-in-law had taken his three guns to the police

Crawford on a motorcycle with a female friend.

department for safekeeping. In language that alternately sniveled and threatened, he thanked a Gilroy officer for meeting him and then warned him against returning the guns to his mother-in-law, saying she had a history of alcohol problems. "Over the past few weeks, she has called my employer, placed obscene and threatening phone calls and continually placed notes and letters in my mailbox of this same ilk," he said. Crawford concluded by saying, "In summary, I do not wish this individual to be in the possession of firearms, least of all, my own." He then listed his guns: a Colt Cobra .38 caliber revolver with a two-inch barrel; a Ruger Blackhawk .41 caliber with a six-inch barrel, and a Marlin .22 caliber long rifle.

Having determined the marriage had no future, Crawford's wife faced a potentially serious dilemma as divorce loomed. Although she was not married to Crawford while he worked for Stanford, she knew he possessed rare books and artifacts stolen from the university. And while she had urged Crawford to return the items, she worried about her own exposure to the law. Could she be a party to his theft? In the words of a probation officer, his wife was "concerned she would be held liable for possession of stolen property, especially since divorce proceedings were pending."

To safeguard her interests—and to get a record of what remained in the home after she moved out—Crawford's wife hired a private investigator. That turned out to be a less private decision than she expected. The private investigator sought to collect a reward by tipping the Stanford police to the theft. When he did so, the redoubtable Stanford Police Capt. Raoul Niemeyer rolled into action. In his memoir, Niemeyer recalled his conversation with the private investigator, who had sent one of the agents to inspect the home. "The lady (Crawford's wife) told the agent that her husband had a virtual museum in his house," the captain wrote. The agent had seen a number of black statues and carvings that he thought were priceless. When Niemeyer checked the files and found that a group of Haida Indian statues had disappeared in thefts from Stanford's archeology collection, he got a search warrant. At 6:52 a.m. on Saturday, April 25, 1992, more than seventeen years after Arlis was murdered, the Stanford police descended on Steve Crawford's Gilroy home.

PART THREE

CHAPTER 30

THE TOWN CRIER

In the decades that followed the murder, Stanford Police Capt. Raoul Niemeyer did as much as anyone to stoke interest in finding the killer. Although he was not the primary investigator—that job fell to sheriff's detectives—Niemeyer refused to let the case go. That was true in the trying weeks after the news broke. It was true in 1992, when he supervised the raid on Steve Crawford's Gilroy home. And it remained true after he retired from the university in 1999. From his home in California's Central Valley, where he lived with his wife and a pair of beloved bichons, the captain emerged as a one-man clearing house for reporters or investigators probing Santa Clara County's most famous unsolved murder. Long after he left Stanford, he pestered cold-case detectives with memos outlining leads. And he wrote an entertaining 2014 memoir, *War Stories Down on Stanford's Farm*, that began with the story of Arlis's murder.

As the case grew colder—it was in the freezer for much of the eighties and nineties—institutional memory mattered more. Inside the Stanford Department of Public Safety, a wave of hiring by Chief Marv Herrington meant most officers had no direct memory of the killing. At the sheriff's office, the evidence from the case was filed away in paper bags. New sheriffs won election, and veteran detectives were given new assignments. The old guard retired or moved on. On the Stanford campus, the churn of generations of students and junior faculty diminished memory. At *The Mercury News*, I had to remind friends what the case was about.

Throughout his quarter century at Stanford and beyond, Niemeyer served as the town crier, the man who demanded that the young victim in Memorial Church be remembered. Part of that reflected wounded professional pride, the shock of a boxer downed by an unexpected left hook. The captain detested the idea that such a big crime had gone unsolved on his turf. Part of it, too, reflected his outrage about the innocence of the victim and how she was murdered. Niemeyer himself had a daughter who later went to Stanford. "It was an awful thing," the captain said of the killing. "I became obsessed with trying to solve the murder."

That obsession was rooted in the way he was introduced to the case on Sunday, October 13, 1974, his third week on the job at Stanford. It started with a misunderstanding, the kind that can happen to anyone summoned from bed at 6:00 a.m. When dispatcher Charlie Papp reached the captain to tell him there had been a possible homicide at Stanford Memorial Church, Niemeyer exploded with characteristic language. "I knew it would happen, goddamn it," he told Papp. In truth, the captain had suicide on his mind. Having investigated three ugly suicides in his previous gig as a sheriff's sergeant, he had been given the nickname "Jonah." The misunderstanding was quickly straightened out. When he saw the body after racing up to the church from San Jose in his Ford Torino Cobra, Niemeyer knew it could not be suicide. "The sick SOB who did this wanted to shock God and everyone," he wrote in his memoir.

It was that smoldering outrage—and a deep familiarity with all the characters—that Niemeyer contributed most to the case. At Stanford on the morning of the murder, he interviewed Arlis's husband, Bruce Perry. In the sheriff's department, the captain had served with many of the investigators, including John Johnson and Dave Pascual, the two main detectives. As one of Chief Herrington's top people, he knew the weaknesses of the old guard at Stanford, particularly Steve Crawford. He had a good grasp of academic politics. Finally, he was unafraid to offend people by speaking candidly. Agree or disagree with Raoul Niemeyer, it was impossible to ignore him.

Several years after he retired, I sat down to discuss the case with the captain at a Central Valley restaurant. Niemeyer doubted that Crawford was the killer. Over lunch, he unveiled a theory that led back to a patient at the Menlo Park VA Hospital, a Vietnam War veteran who had claimed to be a surgeon. It was a theory that sheriff's investigators did not embrace, and one I did not have time to explore. (I was then working as a columnist.) What struck me, however, was how much Niemeyer cared about the case, how impatient he was with the bureaucracy, how unvarnished he was in his opinions. He believed the detectives had overlooked important avenues of investigation. Unlike cops who hoard clues, Niemeyer was convinced one of the best ways to solve the murder was to discuss it publicly. Although he would never have used the term, the captain believed in crowdsourcing.

Born of German and Portuguese ancestry in Berkeley but raised in Hawaii—his middle name is "Kalani," which means "heavenly one"— Niemeyer went to Punahou School in Honolulu, working summers and obtaining a partial scholarship. (Punahou was the same high school that Barack Obama attended a quarter century later.) The young Hawaiian then joined the air force and moved to the mainland, eventually entering law enforcement. At the peak of his career at Stanford, Niemeyer resembled Theodore Roosevelt—a square-jawed man with thick glasses, a stocky frame, and an abundant mustache. He made fun of himself as a "pineapple," a man unused to cold weather. Brash, funny, a superb raconteur, he told stories that mocked traditions and revealed the savage humor of a cop's job. The nicknames he coined had a way of sticking: The old guard cops were "knuckle-draggers." The community service officers who patrolled the dorms and quad were "door-shakers." Steve Crawford, whom Niemeyer called "Crawdad" in his memoirs, was "the ultimate bottom-feeder." The students carried away from demonstrations on canvas stretchers looked like "big burritos." Memorial Church, which tended to attract crazies, was "a real dung magnet."

Eager to inject humor into police work where he could, Niemeyer savored a practical joke. When a group of Stanford students planned a "nude-in" at Lake Lagunita, he gave a written directive to a young officer to check it out in the buff. To lend the order credibility, Niemeyer offered to let the officer carry his credentials in a tote bag, promising him backup. The captain then let everyone in the office know the gag was on. "When our victim opened the envelope and read the memo, the guy went berserk and shouted, 'No Way! No FN way," Niemeyer wrote. With a straight face, Niemeyer insisted that the order came directly from Chief Marv Herrington. The outraged officer demanded to see Herrington, who played it straight before disclosing the prank. (The young cop vowed revenge on Niemeyer, who insists the payback never arrived.)

The jokes masked Niemeyer's keen sense of public relations and his commitment to precision in a police operation. When he was hired by Herrington, one of the thirty-six-year-old captain's first moves was to order that the old khaki-colored police cars be painted white, featuring Stanford's red logo, a cleaner and more emphatic look. He trained cops with a zeal that pleased the chief but offended the old guard. And he established a good working relationship with reporters, who revered his "Book 'em, Danno" style. When he turned over a copy of Stanford's communications recordings from the night Arlis was killed, Niemeyer sought and received written acknowledgment from sheriff's investigators. "In law enforcement, a lot operates on trust," said Doug Williams, the former chief dispatcher for Stanford police and fire. "But Kalani wanted a *receipt*."

Niemeyer's own memories of the murder were based on firsthand experience of the crime scene and its aftermath. On Sunday morning, October 13, the lead investigator, Sgt. John Johnson, assigned Niemeyer to accompany detective Dave Pascual to the Stanford police annex to interview Bruce Perry. The captain ordered dispatcher Charlie Papp to send an officer to Quillen Highrise to pick up the distraught husband. "Advise him (the officer) not to say anything," Niemeyer told Papp. "Just pick him (Bruce) up. We'd like to talk to him down at the annex about his wife's disappearance." After grilling Bruce intensively, Niemeyer came away convinced the young man from Bismarck had not killed his wife.

In his 2014 memoir, Niemeyer wrote that the California Department of Justice had compiled information about a series of unsolved murders of young women in Northern California. He noted that most of the victims had been sixteen to twenty-five years old with slight builds and blond or light hair—not unlike Arlis. The captain also raised the possibility that the placement of the jeans over Arlis's body was the sign of a pentagram, a potentially diabolical symbol. "My view is that the killer(s) had incredible disdain and anger toward women," he wrote. It was an obvious point—but worth repeating.

In the years that followed, Niemeyer never forgot Crawford. But however much he detested Crawford's record in law enforcement, the captain thought the security guard lacked the fortitude for murder. In his view, Crawford was a "wuss," a man who feared the church at night. Like the sheriff's investigators, Niemeyer acknowledged he was troubled by Crawford's refusal to take a lie detector test—but he chalked it up to inexperience, a lack of training, and a sense of guilt about not checking the church more carefully. "He didn't want to screw up," Niemeyer told me. "I think he was trying to cover his ass because he was incompetent."

Not everyone liked Niemeyer's outspoken style. A few veteran cops grumbled that his memoir made him more central to the story than he really was. Others argued that his facts were not infallible. But no one could question his commitment to solving the murder. In 2004, he met with two sheriff's cold-case investigators who wanted to take a fresh look at the evidence. Two years later, he sat down with reporters trying to research the case. He cooperated with television producers examining potential national links to the murder. He investigated suspects dredged from the past. Ironically, the man who had worked so hard to find the killer emerged as one of the chief doubters about how the sheriff's department resolved the case.

CHAPTER 31

THE CIVIL LIBERTARIAN

When Captain Niemeyer encountered Steve Crawford on that Saturday morning in 1992, he found a man he described as "clad in a robe, shaking like a leaf, and acting as if he didn't know whether he should defecate or go blind." The cops had prepared for the confrontation carefully. With his usual thoroughness, Niemeyer assigned a task to each officer. Every artifact or book taken from the home would have a number, a record of who handled it. While the captain doubted Crawford had killed Arlis—he still thought the ex-security guard was too wimpish for murder—he searched for a pair of eyeglasses and an ice pick handle, two items missing from the murder scene.

The house echoed Crawford's pretenses of intellectual respectability. Near the front door, police spotted a foot-thick dictionary on a podium, a tome from Stanford's rare-books collection. They also found carvings, paintings, and antique furniture along with a plastic container holding eighty-one grams of cannabis. Nearby was a Stanford community service officer's badge and a set of campus keys that Crawford had kept when he left in 1976. Underneath a pillow, the police found a sexy purple negligee stained with semen. What irked Niemeyer particularly was an official Stanford diploma stolen from a university office. By taking the blank diploma to a printer and ordering his name engraved, Crawford conferred upon himself a Stanford degree.

The rest of the haul verged on the stupendous. The cops seized 280 rare books, including a few several centuries old. Among them were the Latin editions of *Consillia* (1536) and *Passerati* (1637) as well as a copy of John James Blunt's *History of the Christian Church during the First Three Centuries*, which first appeared in England in 1856. (Written by a Cambridge professor of divinity, it was an unusual choice for the unbeliever Crawford.) The searchers recovered seven Haida Indian argillite sculptures from the Pacific Northwest, said to be among Jane Stanford's favorites. Also seized were clocks, beads, an eight-by-four-foot tapestry, and medallions believed to have been taken from the Hoover Institution. Among the oddest items was a human skull with a rubber snake attached and a snake-shaped cane given to Leland Stanford by the Chinese ambassador to the United States more than a century before. Niemeyer estimated the value of the stolen items to be between $150,000 and $200,000. An enterprising thief but a lackluster curator, Crawford selected items he liked rather than the most expensive artifacts. "I don't think he was discriminating about picking certain materials of value," Maggie Kimball, head of special collections at Stanford, told the Associated Press.

Crawford was taken to Santa Clara County jail, where he spent two nights before he was released on $25,000 bail with the help of his brother, Bill. "He was hysterical about being locked up," Bill told me much later. A booking photo shows a baldish man with symmetrical features, a faintly derisive smile on his face. Open and shut as the case seemed, the statute of limitations prevented the police from bringing a theft charge against Crawford. The cops did not know precisely *when* most of the items were stolen. Instead, he was accused of possession of stolen property, a charge to which he pleaded no contest. It could at least be proven that he *possessed* the stolen goods.

Crawford's prosecutors confronted two unexpected problems. The first arose during the search, when one of the Stanford cops assigned to the raid was seen taking a portable Sony Watchman mini-TV and a posse box—a hybrid of container and clipboard—from the home and loading it into his car trunk. Invited by Niemeyer to observe the raid, Crawford's wife sounded the alarm, saying the TV belonged to Crawford and the posse box was hers. "That guy there just stole my stuff!" Niemeyer recalled her saying.

The Stanford cop insisted he was trying to safeguard evidence, a story that did not convince his superiors. He was suspended, relieved of his badge, and charged with stealing the TV set. Although his case ended in acquittal, the damage was done. The prosecution saw the Watchman affair as a snag in the charges against Crawford. A trial would allow Crawford's attorney to contend that the police were no

Steve Crawford at the time he was arrested in 1992
in connection with thefts from Stanford.

better than their suspect. Niemeyer called the incident "a debacle." Furious about the way the raid had unfolded, the captain dictated the details into a recorder on the way home. "Other motorists must have thought I was a nut job, as I was so pissed off, hollering into the recorder and gesticulating wildly," Niemeyer wrote later.

The second problem for the prosecution was that it was surprisingly difficult to prove that all of the precious items in the Gilroy home came from Stanford. Few of the books had nameplates inside the cover. A probation report concluded, "Ownership of the books cannot be established in most cases, although it is assumed that they were taken from the offices of professors and other locations throughout the university campus." The passage of time didn't help the prosecution's case. Many of the new officials at the university weren't familiar with the thefts. It's hard to read the details without concluding that Stanford had such a bounty of goods that theft didn't register in the same way it might at a poorer institution.

By arguing that his thefts were motivated by curiosity rather than greed, Crawford performed a masterful job of creating sympathy. He had never sold anything for profit, or so he said. A probation report said that "on one particular day, he came across a number of artifacts," adding that he had been exposed to these objects "due to his mother's ethnic background." That seemed like a bold-faced exaggeration. Steve's mother, Maxine Rosselle, was born in Seattle of English, Scottish, and French Canadian ancestry. It was true that Maxine's father, Barney Rosselle, had once lived in Juneau, Alaska, not far from the Haida Indian homeland on the former Queen Charlotte Islands, but it seemed far-fetched that such an elusive connection would matter. Why steal the books? "Personal interest in the subject matter was the primary reason, although admittedly, the volume was such that he was unable to read them in their entirety," the probation report concluded.

The probation officer seemed swayed by Crawford's plight. His report said Crawford claimed to have been in a "quandary" once the crimes were committed. He had thought about returning the stolen items, but he "never had the right opportunity." Once he left Stanford, the report continued, Crawford saw no alternative other than

A native Indian artifact discovered stolen from Stanford's collection.

to use the items as decorative pieces in his home. Some of the books belonged to him, and "most of the artifacts seemed to be of little value." This was pure hokum—the idea that Crawford could not find a chance to return stolen items was laughable—but the ex-security guard impressed the probation officer as accepting "full and complete" responsibility. The probation report recommended Crawford be held accountable by receiving a "maximum county jail sentence," which could have been up to a year. With credit for good behavior, that typically meant six months. (Many years later, I talked to the probation officer, who told me he did not remember the case.)

If Crawford put on a dance for the probation officer, it paled compared to the opera he staged for the judge, David Leahy, an ex-labor lawyer and one of the more lenient judges on the Santa Clara County Superior Court. In a letter to the judge, Crawford began by trying to establish his credibility as a custodian of money. "In fixing the present sentence, I would ask the court to consider that in the intervening 17 years since my offense, I have handled and had access to millions of dollars in public funds as a CETA (Comprehensive Employment and Training Act) funds administrator and private funds in the insurance industry without incident." Then, in voluminous detail, Crawford told the judge how faithfully he had tried to "coopirate" with judicial demands. (Despite his liking for books, Crawford never learned to spell well.) With permission of the court, he had gotten an eighteen-hour-a-day insurance adjuster's job in Florida after Hurricane Andrew struck in 1992. Because of court postponements, Crawford had to delay taking a new job and was working temporarily in Southern California. "It was not my choice to relocate away from home or to incur the additional costs to work in Southern California," he wrote. He was a man who had bravely faced the slings and arrows others hurled his way. "I need your help in avoid (sic) becoming destitute," Crawford wrote to the judge.

Leahy bought it. The judge gave Crawford a suspended six-month jail sentence, levied a $100 fine plus $300 in court costs, and ordered him not to be on the Stanford campus or where books or artifacts were maintained. In all, Crawford did two nights in jail, which he had served immediately after his arrest. It was an astonishingly light sentence for a man who had taken at least $150,000 worth of items from a prominent university. For the items whose source could not be proved, Leahy ordered an auction. Half of the proceeds would go to Stanford, half to charity.

Even this generous conclusion didn't satisfy Crawford. After his conviction, he sent a letter to Stanford police via his friend Sandy Mize, a community services officer. Saying that Stanford campus security had "arbitrarily and capriciously seized property from my home" and that he could no longer afford lawyers to contest the matter, he declared he was designating the ACLU of Northern California as the nonprofit to receive 50 percent of the proceeds. "It is my presumption that all or part of this property will be purchased by Stanford, therefore allowing it to acquire this property at less than half the actual value," he wrote in a statement that made him out to be the victim. Whether Crawford even had the right to designate the charity was dubious. He had found a way to tweak Stanford one more time.[1]

The conviction, however, marked a turning point in Crawford's life. In a swift downward spin, he lost his marriage, his house, and his job with the insurance-adjustment company, D.L. Glaze. In that same letter to Leahy, he talked about what he called the "embarrassment" of having to accept counseling and medication from the Orange County (CA) mental health department because of suicidal problems and depression. "I have not sought or received any other public or private assistance," he wrote, apparently forgetting that the CETA jobs were a federal benefit. Vowing to make good on his debts to the IRS, he added, "I have always paid my own way and believe I can do so again."

That, too, was a questionable pledge. Around that time—the early nineties—Crawford's first cousin, Mickie McGowan, received a plea from Crawford asking to move in with her in Los Angeles. Crawford said he was being evicted from a motel and needed a place to live with his cat. "He would only call me or find me when there was trouble," McGowan remembered. "He was living in a motel that had allowed him to live there by the month. He needed to come stay with me because he didn't have any money. I asked him, *Aren't you working?* And he said, *Well, I just got fired.*" McGowan rejected him. Trying to put a career together with children, she had her own challenges.

Even Crawford's connections from the time of his marriage seemed to fray. Nothing illustrated that more clearly than the story of Greg and Kitty LaFavor, who were friends from his square-danc-ing group, the Dixie Derbys. When Greg and Kitty married in 1991, they pondered who should preside over the ceremony. Then an idea presented itself: Crawford had obtained a license as a Universal Life Minister and had done a handful of weddings for friends. He could do it for the LaFavors. (Crawford joked that he had paid $25 for his certificate, passing on the chance to pay more to become a bishop.) A photo of the moment shows Crawford standing between bride and groom, wearing a bolo tie, two red flowers in his lapels, and a black cowboy hat that he removed for the ceremony. The couple wrote their own vows.

"Because we used him, we didn't have any have-tos, musts, no shoulda-coulda-woulda," said Greg, who died in late 2018.

"He didn't carry the holy water," said Kitty.

The coda to the nuptials revealed how much Crawford changed in the ensuing years. In the late nineties, lured by a new job for Greg, the LaFavors moved to Colorado. Then, in 2006, they moved back to San Jose, where Kitty had relatives. Hearing that Crawford was living not far away on San Jose's south side, they thought of visiting the man who had officiated at their wedding. Though much had changed—the other Dixie Derby couples in their group had broken up—it would be good to catch up on old times. Then they got a message back from a mutual friend. Crawford did not remember them. Faulty memory? An excuse? A lie? "We never pursued it," said Kitty. "We would have gone to see him, but when we heard he doesn't remember you, we said, *Oh, okay.*"

Financially, Crawford forgot even more. His pledge to repay the IRS was no more credible than his other promises. In 1998, Crawford filed for Chapter 7 bankruptcy: His major creditors were the IRS (more than $51,000), a Shell credit card ($6,092) and a Wells Fargo Visa card (more than $6,400). Crawford listed no current income and claimed to have only $200 in ready funds. He put down expenses of $50 a month for food, a strangely low number. His only asset was a 1995 Saturn that he valued at $6,600. His relationship with state and federal taxing authorities turned stranger a few years later, when he started using the Social Security number of a Southern California woman who had died in 2002. It's not clear what benefit Crawford received from using the woman's number, a few digits off from his own. But he could have been trying to avoid the reach of the IRS. Although using a stolen Social Security number is a federal crime, he was never charged with the offense.

Public records show that for part of the nineties, Crawford lived in Irvine and Burbank. But he eventually returned to the Bay Area. By the middle or late part of the decade—the precise dates are unclear—Crawford was enlisting people for one of the first dial-up internet services, EarthLink. EarthLink had been cofounded in 1994 by Sky Dayton, a Pasadena entrepreneur who was having trouble configuring his own system. Its pitch was that it was one of the first internet service providers to offer unlimited service for a flat monthly rate—$19.95. Crawford recruited customers inside the Fry's Electronics stores, then-essential destinations for computer equipment in Silicon Valley.

Eventually, Crawford moved on from that gig too, a nomad to the end of his career. One of his last jobs was acting as a scout and salesman for Apple Vacations, a travel company unrelated to the better-known tech company. Apple Vacations specialized in the Caribbean and Mexico, offering deals for travelers. On the Web, it was not a well-reviewed company. People complained about the accommodations. But Apple did allow Crawford to travel to tropical destinations on scouting missions. It was at Apple where Crawford was working in 2006, when he was approached by cold-case sheriff's detective Ron Breuss, who wanted his DNA swab and fingerprints. If Crawford preferred to forget the past, history hadn't forgotten him.

CHAPTER 32
THE AMATEUR DETECTIVES

One day in 1998, as they cleaned their garage on Sweetbriar Drive in Campbell, California, Dave and Pam Larson came across a yellowing copy of the *San Jose Mercury News* featuring a long story about the murder of Arlis Perry. Dave had set the piece aside because he had an interest in the case. Recognizing that many readers were new to the tale, *The Mercury News* returned to the Perry killing for a retrospective every decade or so, sometimes combining it with other cold-case murders. This piece contained more detail than most, largely because the detectives, tired poker players in a marathon game, were willing to reveal more about their hand. Accompanying the story was a photo of Detective Ken Kahn pointing to the palm print left on one of the candles used on Arlis's body. The 1991 article even had the case number, IR-74-14949. I remember the piece well. With Maline Hazle, I was one of the writers. In the first sentence, I likened the mystery to a novel by P.D. James, the British detective writer. We thought the case number added a touch of realism to our story, part of a series we called "The Unsolved Crime File." The most heart-breaking quote in the story came from Marv Dykema, Arlis's father, who told us, "Every time we talk about it, it opens a lot of new wounds. We'd sure like to catch the guy. We don't need more tears."

Despite our modest reporting victories, the news had not changed. It was not encouraging. In poker terms, the detectives were holding no more than a pair of eights. Almost two decades after it occurred, the murder continued to defy an answer. The investigators still believed the killer had followed Arlis into the church and surprised her at closing time, kicking a door out to escape. Their theory pointed to an outsider, someone unfamiliar with the church. Only a couple of years before, Kahn had flown to Virginia to attend a conference of investigators parsing the last confessions of mass killer Ted Bundy, who teased the cops up until his 1989 death in the electric chair. Using gas receipts, the FBI proved Bundy bought gas in Utah on the day before Arlis was killed. Five days after Arlis's murder, he killed a seventeen-year-old Utah girl. With Bundy ruled out, Kahn acknowledged the cops had no hot leads.[1]

Well after our piece ran, however, the seeds of the "Unsolved Crime File" fell on fertile turf at the Larson household. A professional link fueled the interest of the Campbell couple. Dave Larson spent much of his career working for Stanford University Press, which was about 125 yards from Stanford Memorial Church. Like everyone else at Stanford in 1974, he remembered the murder vividly. His wife, Pam, a versatile researcher, was willing to join him in exploring why it remained a mystery. As they approached retirement, they decided to devote their time and resources to solving it. "We watched crime programs," Dave told me. "You say to yourself, *They're looking at old cases. Why isn't someone looking at the Stanford murder?*"

With the soberness of the husband and wife who stood with a pitchfork in Grant Wood's 1930 painting "American Gothic," the Larsons emerged as the most dedicated researchers amid a cadre of private citizens who tried to solve the case. The couple returned to the church, inspected the locks, and drew maps of the sanctuary. They walked between the Stanford post office where the Perrys posted their letters and the entrance to Memorial Church. They visited libraries and collected as many newspaper clippings as they could find. Hoping to uncover clues in lyrics, they listened to dozens of solemn musical compositions. They badgered investigators in longhand memos with the salient points underlined. Every year, on the anniversary of the murder, they made a pilgrimage to Trader Joe's and bought a bouquet of flowers that they left in the spot where Arlis's body had been found.

Next to former Stanford Police Captain Raoul Niemeyer, the Larsons did as much as anyone to keep interest in the Perry case alive, particularly in the lean years. In Sherlockian tradition, they called themselves "amateur detectives."

"They were really good at keeping me going on this," said retired sheriff's detective Randy Bynum, a cold-case investigator who handled the case in the late 1990s and early 2000s. "They'd do their own research. They'd say, *What about this, what about that?* They'd say,

You should check this person out." The Larsons could be demanding, impatient, and suspicious. But those qualities reflected the passion they brought to the case. They investigated and wrote with exclamation points.

Early in their investigation, the Larsons came close to narrowing the focus on Steve Crawford, posing questions that undercut the prevailing theory that an outsider committed the crime. Among their contributions was a remarkably accurate chronology of the crime. They also came up with a plausible theory about the source of the ice pick. Toward the end, they embarked on a more fanciful path, born more of conjecture than fact. It coincided with one of the stranger stories of the case, the alleged sighting of a young blond woman atop the Memorial Church altar.

Drawing on his experience at Stanford Press, Dave Larson focused his first research on the weapon, raising the possibility that it could have been a modified instrument used in the press's hot-metal printing operation. "The weapon was reported to be an ice pick," he wrote in one of his first summations. "Who walks around with an ice pick? Does the recovered weapon have any ink, lead or oil residue on it? Is it really an ice pick or a modified tool?" Dave raised the possibility that the killer could be a young man who worked in Stanford Press's sales department and lingered behind pallets of paper in the bindery area. The theory about the young man turned out to be wrong—and there was no oil left on the ice pick in Arlis's brain. But the queries about the weapon were apt. The professional detectives had asked the same questions.

Though some of their assumptions were mistaken—they had no access to sheriff's reports—the Larsons did their best work in defining the central issue of the crime. Was Arlis murdered by an outsider who hid in the church or by an insider like Crawford? Not bound by the weight of previous queries or the judgment that the security guard was a wimp, they dissected Crawford's behavior with rigorous logic. Why did he close up fifteen minutes early? (At 11:45 rather than midnight.) And why, when Bruce Perry called to report his wife missing at 3:00 a.m., did Crawford not check the church? If the times reported were accurate, the Larsons wrote, "Arlis and Crawford were in the church at exactly the same time!" The word "exactly" underscored their excitement. The couple theorized that Arlis entered a few minutes before Crawford closed the church. "Knowing that he was the security guard, Arlis would probably not have felt any apprehension," they wrote. "I think he approached her from behind and attacked and killed her," said their memo. "He then staged the cult-like scene to direct the police investigation in other directions."

A dozen years after they started their probe, with Crawford still unarrested and DNA producing no matches, the Larsons turned their focus in another direction. In Detective Randy Bynum, they found a man willing to listen to their ideas. This time, the amateur detectives departed from the close logic of their first memos. Basing their research on a story that sheriff's deputies belatedly received about a nude woman seen in the church—a story that felt preposterous—they became convinced that a likely suspect was a young man who had been a freshman at Stanford in 1974 and grew up to be a recognized composer based on the East Coast. While their argument stretched credulity—and some investigators thought it plain folly—it had an impact on the case.

In his first year at Stanford, the musician joined a variety of undergraduate musical groups, including the marching band. He also played the flute. As a composer years later, he became known for lugubrious choral music that could be startlingly beautiful or deeply mystifying, anthem or dirge. By comparing titles of his pieces with elements of the crime, the Larsons argued that the composer should be considered a suspect. One piece referred to a broken door, while others included the words "pierced" or "breathless." To the Larsons, these could be references to the murder. The breathless Arlis had been pierced by an ice pick, and her killer had broken open a door. The couple counted twenty-two song titles they believed were linked to the crime.

After I became a columnist at *The Mercury News* and was no longer writing the "Unsolved Crime File," I sat down with the Larsons at a Campbell restaurant to discuss their theory. I can remember their excitement at their findings, their sense of uncovering a solid suspect. They were intrigued by the composer's decision to stage a homecoming at Stanford with a piece whose title featured the word "death."

"It seems more than curious, considering the nature of (the music), that (the composer), a Stanford student at the very time that Arlis Perry was killed, would choose Stanford as the place to hold this premier performance. Was this just a very successful alumni wanting to showcase his new program, or is it another example of daring us to figure out the puzzle of Arlis' murder?" the Larsons wrote in a memo that went to investigators.

I can remember thinking this was dicey and expansive logic. If the composer murdered Arlis, it was unlikely that he would write music calling attention to the crime. Intriguing as they were, the bleak titles did not make him a killer. Nonetheless, the Larsons' theory was not dismissed out of hand by investigators. It coincided with one of the stranger stories of the case, an alleged sighting of a young, blond woman atop the altar.

That report came from a technical writer named Brian J. Mc-Cracken, whose memory came to the fore decades after the crime. McCracken said he was walking past Memorial Church around midnight on Saturday, October 12, 1974, when he heard "strange flute music" coming from inside the church. When he went inside to investigate, he saw a young, blond woman naked on the altar, flanked by two lit candles. Nearby was a skinny, young white man wearing an Afro wig and playing a flute. "As I walked down the aisle, he looked at me—he doesn't seem happy to see me, and then she is lying flat on the altar, and she is looking straight up to the top of the church," McCracken told the *New York Post* in 2016. "She turns her head to the left and smiles. By this time, I am within 20 feet of the flutist and her on the altar."

McCracken said he assumed the two were playing a "Black Mass" game, not unheard of in Memorial Church. Not wanting to intrude, he left the sanctuary. Claiming a hectic traveling schedule at the time, McCracken said it wasn't until 2011, when he was speaking with a retired police officer, that he realized he may have witnessed the prelude to murder. When he went online to search for pictures of the Stanford band in the era, he identified the skinny, young white man with the Afro wig as the composer the Larsons singled out. (Bynum recalls that McCracken's story surfaced before investigators received the Larsons' memo.)

McCracken's narrative posed obvious problems. For starters, his failure to call the police at the time raised questions about the solidity of his story. A man who saw a young woman naked on the altar on the night she was killed would have had more credibility in 1974 than he would decades later. The murder of Arlis Perry was a huge story at the time. The second problem was that anyone who knew Arlis would dismiss the idea that she would lie naked atop an altar and smile at a stranger. She was uncomfortable with exhibitionism. Finally, the notes of my fellow reporter Maline Hazle suggest that McCracken might have been wrong in his timing. In 1991, Hazle talked with a "Brian" who had exactly the same story McCracken gave later—a nude woman atop the altar, a guy with frizzy hair playing a flute, etc. Her notes reveal that Brian told her then that the incident occurred the night *before* Arlis was killed. (When I asked McCracken many years later whether he had talked with Hazle, he said, "It's a possibility.")

Yet one of the paradoxes of the Arlis Perry case was that even a potentially crackpot theory could have resonance. McCracken's story evoked enough interest among investigators that they felt they should eliminate it as a possibility. In December 2011, Sheriff's Sgt. Herman Leon and Randy Bynum, by this point a private investigator who had retired from the sheriff's department, met with McCracken at a Chili's restaurant in Morgan Hill. The following February, Bynum and McCracken traveled without sheriff's detectives to confront the composer at a performance of his music at a college in Thousand Oaks, northwest of Los Angeles. As a private eye, Bynum still hungered to solve the case. And he described it as a chance to take a road trip to Southern California. Their cover was that they were journalists, which bent the truth. "I said, *How do you want to do this?*" Bynum remembered later. "He (McCracken) said, *We'll have to use a ruse. I got this affiliation with the news media. I called them; they said they would take the story.*" In 2018, McCracken told the online Opperman Report that he had called the Associated Press and volunteered to provide pictures and details of the performance. At best, it was a shaky way to get an interview.

Prepared with recording equipment that made the interview look professional, McCracken and Bynum met the composer in the greenroom of the college auditorium. Bynum remembers that he and McCracken agreed it was to be an interview, not an interrogation. At first, according to Bynum, the conversation proceeded cordially. The composer was cooperative and relaxed, willing to talk about his career and his time at Stanford. Then McCracken began asking pointed questions, making the composer uneasy. McCracken said he became very suspicious when the composer acknowledged having an Afro wig. "McCracken wasn't patient enough," Bynum recalled. "He got a little antsy and started a line of questioning that was very accusatory." Thanking the composer for his time, Bynum ended the interview.

When McCracken said he was ready to make a citizen's arrest, Bynum confronted him outside the greenroom. "I said, *Dude, you can't do that. You can't start accusing people. You can't interrogate this guy. Interview is one thing, interrogation is another thing. If he said something that's a form of confession, what are you going to do? It's a mess, dude.* He wasn't too happy about that, but that's how it was."

Years later, McCracken told me that he reluctantly acceded to Bynum's directive. "I was under the authority of someone (Bynum) who was a professional investigator," he told me. "I felt he didn't quite understand where I was going. He wanted to control what was going on."

The composer-as-killer idea, however, remained front and center for the amateur detectives. Bynum remembered that he talked with the Larsons about the possibility of getting DNA from the composer. As always, they were persistent, asking whether the private investigator would consider taking a trip East himself. "I said, *I'd be happy to go back if you wanna pay.* So that kind of went to the wayside," Bynum recalled. McCracken, who puts great stock in the Afro wig ("It's the linchpin of my theory"), is still convinced the composer was the likely killer. Cold-case investigators have dismissed this idea. As I look back on the Thousand Oaks interrogation, my sympathy grows for the composer, questioned as a murder suspect because of a late tip and several odd song titles. I've chosen not to use his name in this account. The notion that the Arlis Perry murder could be explained in lyrics—or the sighting of a young flutist wearing an Afro—remains one of the case's strangest cul-de-sacs.

CHAPTER 33

THE SOUND GUY

In some ways, the probable weapon in the murder of Arlis Perry can be traced back to the voice of B. Davie Napier, the revered Yale scholar who became dean of the chapel at Stanford in 1966. It was not that Napier had anything to do with the killing. By 1974, he had moved on from Stanford to become the head of the Pacific School of Religion in Berkeley. And it was not that Napier was a poor preacher. He was renowned for his ability to translate the humor and pathos of the Old Testament. Unlike many of his predecessors, however, Napier did not command a voice that reached easily to the remotest pews at Memorial Church. He spoke in quieter, more contemplative tones. So Stanford authorities decided to install a sound system, the church's first. Memorial Church was in the midst of change any-way—the church was embarking on allowing traditional services for Catholics and Jews. When Napier delivered a sermon that invoked the Beatles, saying institutions that insulated themselves from injustice were living in a "yellow submarine," the famous song was piped into the church.

The job of installing the system was given to an Oakland company, but the young man who laid the lines and placed the microphones by climbing around the church was a technically minded undergraduate named Mark Dalrymple. Dalrymple knew Memorial Church well. As a freshman in 1963–64, he set up the feed from the church to KZSU, the campus radio station, broadcasting Sunday morning services live "in case anyone was awake," as he remembered it. When someone was needed to run the sound system, he was the obvious choice. It became his part-time job, paying $1.50 per hour at first (a little more than $11 today). The money was useful. After getting his first undergraduate degree in biological sciences, Dalrymple returned for a second in geology. The church assignment helped open a career. Dalrymple became a technical expert at the university, responsible for many of its new audio and recording systems. Years later, his profile on the Stanford Department of Music website described Dalrymple as "techie, and chief schlepper, emeritus." An industrious, genial man with a gentle wit and a well-trimmed beard, Dalrymple grew fruit at home and took an interest in steam engines. When I caught up with him at his Los Altos home in 2018, the seventy-three-year-old was near the end of his life, on an oxygen machine. But nothing was askew with his superb memory. In all senses of the word, he was a sound man.

Primitive compared to versions available today, the sound system at Memorial Church had its nerve center in the small, rectangular room between the sanctuary and the Round Room, the church office. Dalrymple kept tools and equipment in a stained-pine cabinet about three feet high and three-and-a-half feet wide. The cabinet had two drawers above two lower cabinets, a standard configuration for inexpensive furniture. In the upper-left drawer were microphones, matches to light the candles, and a few other odds and ends, including an ice pick, the cheap kind with a square, wooden handle. Despite its throwback image, it was a useful instrument. Dalrymple deployed the ice pick in hard-to-reach places that eluded a screwdriver. "I'd use the pick on parts of the sound system when I needed a fine point," he told me. "An example would be teasing a wire strand into place in a cable to make a connection."

In the days after Arlis was killed, Dalrymple and nearly everyone else involved with the church endured repeated interviews with sheriff's deputies. "I got fingerprinted up to my elbows," he remembered. He had an airtight alibi. On the weekend of the murder, the soundman had been on the same geology field trip as Bill Aaron, the backup sexton of the church. Dalrymple was able to describe the pepperwood tree that offered him shade at Humboldt Redwoods State Park, 250 miles up the coast off Highway 101. Decades later, in an interview with a cold-case detective, he insisted that he had mentioned the ice pick to investigators in 1974—and given Dalrymple's phenomenal memory, it's more than probable he did.

The ice pick in the cabinet went undocumented in the original report, although Sgt. Johnson's notes mention a "hidden panel" in the church office that contained various tools. Old-timers at the church theorized that an ice pick might have been kept in the room to chip the ice used to keep soft drinks cold during church functions. It wasn't until Dalrymple was re-interviewed in 2016 by a sheriff's cold-case investigator, however, that the significance of the ice pick he used came into focus. The investigator asked him about the cabinet, inquiring what was inside. Dalrymple replied with specificity, listing the tools. For the cold-case detectives, Dalrymple's response was a revelation. It offered the best answer, though maybe not an indisputable one, to a mystifying question: Where had the killer obtained the weapon?

As a lethal tool, the ice pick boasts a notorious resume. An ice pick is commonly associated with the murder of Leon Trotsky by one of Joseph Stalin's henchmen in Mexico City in 1940, although the murder was committed with an ice ax, a heavier and more brutish cousin. In the American gang wars of the 1930s and 1940s, an ice pick was often the weapon of choice, frequently inserted through the ear. It was cheap and available, and its narrow shaft could puncture organs. Even better, an ice pick could terrorize foes. The threat of execution by ice pick was often deployed to bring a gangster in line. One of the most infamous ice pick killings occurred in July 1937, when two hired killers accompanied one of their friends, gambling boss Walter Sage, on a not-so-friendly ride in New York's Catskill Mountains. According to accounts at the time, the two killers leaned forward from the back seat to chat with Sage. One of them grabbed Sage by the neck, pinning him to the seat while his confederate rained down more than thirty puncture wounds on Sage's torso. The killers hog-tied Sage's body and attached it to the frame of a slot machine before dumping it into nearby Swan Lake.

On the Stanford campus in the late sixties and the seventies, the ugly potential of the ice pick provided the grist of laughs. In 1967, a *Stanford Daily* columnist suggested that victory in the Big Game between Stanford and Cal should be honored by a different symbol than the ceremonial ax, which had been stolen from the campus by conspirators from UC Berkeley. The answer from one female student: A Big Game ice pick. "I can hear the yell now," she told the columnist. "Give 'em the ice pick, give 'em the ice pick, give 'em the ice pick. Where? Right in the…" Perhaps mercifully, the anatomical target was left out of the column. (In the original cheer, Stanford fans cheered for the ax to be delivered to the neck.)

In the Memorial Church murder, the effort to explain the source of the ice pick produced a deluge of theories. It was not a tool most people would carry around, even if they were handy. One idea detectives considered was that the killer carried the weapon in his boot, perhaps in a sheath. That raised the possibility that the murderer could be a security guard, perhaps one who sought protection from the strange characters who visited the sanctuary. It was no secret that the security guards who had been full-fledged Stanford police officers were unhappy at losing their weapons. Could the ice pick have been a replacement for a gun?

Dalrymple's memory refracted the light on these questions. The investigators had thought about a killer who would bring an ice pick with him into the church. It was one of the elements that drew them to mass murderer Ted Bundy, who carried an ice pick in a tool bag. But what if the weapon was *already* in the church? An outsider who followed Arlis into the church would not have known where such a weapon was stored. Just as the time demanded to lay out the body suggested a killer familiar with the rhythms of the church, so, too, did an ice pick plucked from a cabinet suggest a murderer knowledgeable about its contents. If the killer had seen Arlis praying, he would have time to enter the small room, retrieve the ice pick from the drawer, and circle around behind her. The sound cabinet was located in the heavily trafficked corridor between the Round Room and the sanctuary, a path a security guard would know well.

Like so much else in the Arlis Perry case, this was a long way from conclusive. There was no proof the ice pick Dalrymple remembered was the lethal weapon. Dalrymple was not sure of the last time he had seen the tool—though the search after the murder in 1974 did not uncover an ice pick, which suggests it was gone from the church. What's more, the shaft in Arlis's brain could not be traced to a particular ice pick. Dalrymple described a cheap vintage model with a square handle and advertising on at least one side. (Ted Bundy's model, by contrast, had a bulb-shaped handle.) The square-handled ice picks with advertising were given out by the hundreds of thousands after the first patent for them was awarded in 1914. It was common to deliver a block of ice and throw in the ice pick for free. A vending machine would offer them for a quarter. Nonetheless, Dalrymple's memory filled a crucial gap. It went a long way toward clarifying at least two legs of the crime: means and opportunity.

In the latter part of the new century's first decade, before the critical interview with Dalrymple, investigators examined whether the killer had used a *second* implement to hammer the ice pick deeper into Arlis's brain after she was dead. No part of the ice pick was visible when sheriff's deputies first viewed the body. Around the entry wound on the back of Arlis's neck was a scrape that measured one half inch by one quarter inch. Just behind the point of entry, the coroner, John Hauser, had found a "mass palpable." I've looked at Hauser's original notes, and they do not say how deep the shaft went under the surface. Hauser simply wrote that it was "beneath the skin." The cold-case investigators pursued the idea that a killer who ripped away the handle must have hammered the shaft deeper into her head to make it invisible. I'm not sure I buy this theory. Using a hammer or another implement feels too complicated. One scenario is that the killer tried unsuccessfully to remove the shaft by hand and finally decided it was better to push it manually deeper into the brain, perhaps using the butt of the ice pick handle.

There was one more test left. Just how might a killer have wielded an ice pick? A friend of mine, Rod Diridon Jr., got interested in the crime when I explained what had happened. One day in early 2020, he invited me to his house in Santa Clara, where he had assembled a collection of ice picks and a coconut meant as a substitute for the human skull. We agreed this was far from scientific. My guess was that a coconut rind was softer than the bone that protects the brain. And yet there were enough similarities—the hard shell, the soft inside, the shape of the coconut—to make the test intriguing. The shaft of

Rod's square-handled ice pick matched the length of the shaft found in Arlis's brain. We found that it was possible to pierce the coconut at its stem with a vigorous blow. We also learned that the handle of an old ice pick—the square kind with lettering on the side—could break off if we wiggled it back and forth. The coconut acted like a vise. If the ice pick was old, it seemed more vulnerable. It pointed to the long-lost tool in the cabinet.

CHAPTER 34
THE BARNACLE SCRAPER

In his first decade as a Santa Clara County sheriff's deputy, Sgt. Rick Alanis earned a reputation as a hardworking cop who paid attention to detail. In a department where favoritism sometimes played an outsized role in promotions—it helped to be on the good side of longtime Sheriff Laurie Smith—Alanis had climbed to his position as detective on merit, keeping his head down when the politics swirled around him. A baldish, good-looking man in his mid-thirties, Alanis had a gift for putting a reluctant witness at ease. As a property-crimes investigator, he impressed his bosses by generating leads and solving crimes. So it was no surprise when Alanis was given the job of cold-case investigator, assigned to breathe life into cases judged comatose. The young detective thrived in the tough, frustrating business of sifting through fading memories and misinterpreted evidence. Willing to challenge conventional wisdom, Alanis made his biggest contribution to solving the murder of Arlis Perry by understanding the waistband sizes of one of the most famous labels in the world.

When he was handed the Memorial Church case in 2014, Alanis did not know who Arlis Perry was, an ignorance that left him sheepish later. But the assignment came at a critical time in his life. Not too long before, his young son had been diagnosed with autism. Because of the unrest and challenges of his home life, Alanis had declined an offer to join the homicide team. His bosses suggested instead that he look at the Perry case. Perhaps a few things could be done on a timetable that fit the detective. When Alanis interviewed Arlis's parents, Marv and Jean Dykema, as well as her sister, Karen, he got a sense of who Arlis was. Oddly, the investigation became a godsend. It gave him an outlet and a purpose as he was trying to manage issues at home.

In the new century's second decade, the Arlis Perry case stood as the biggest unsolved case in the department's history. True, a cluster of unsolved murders remained from the Stanford area in the early and mid-seventies—Leslie Perlov, David Levine, and, in San Mateo County, Janet Taylor. But the Perry case had occurred in sacred space, with a victim who had been praying, a young bride who left behind a bewildered husband and extended family. It had a defined crime scene, bundles of physical evidence, and a killer who left a cruel signature. The case seemed like one that could be solved. Yet it was far from straightforward, and the passage of four decades made it more difficult. The Arlis Perry case consumed more than four years of Alanis's life. As encouragement and goad, the detective carried around a picture of Arlis in his wallet. For him, just as for the original investigators, the quest was personal.

In reopening the case, Alanis had to scrape barnacles from an old hull, a vessel battered by time and misfortune and forgetfulness. The physical evidence from the 1974 probe was not preserved as carefully as the Bulldog, Tom Beck, had predicted in his 1980 interview with Maline Hazle. The evidence had been moved several times. It wasn't even all in the same place. The coroner's office had remnants of the case. The vaginal wash from the "rape kit" used to examine the body was missing. The thicket of tracking numbers made things worse. Each piece of evidence had been packaged and labeled in paper bags (plastic tended to disturb the evidence, particularly in the heat). Each was given a sheriff's tracking number. A duffel bag of items was sent to the FBI, which had its own numbers. Finally, many pieces were sent to the Santa Clara County crime lab, which had yet a third numbering system. An investigator seeking to master the evidence had to learn three languages of bureaucratic labeling.

Undeterred, Alanis sifted through the bags of evidence. When he got to Arlis's Levi's, which had been draped across her body, he realized something did not fit. The county crime lab, which had tested what were thought to be Arlis's pants for evidence of blood and semen, had described the item as "one pair of blue jeans, Levi's brand, 505, W36, L32 collected from Arlis Perry" (Item #2, FBI Item #17). The waist designation came from the Levi's label, which depicted two horses hitched to a pair of jeans and pulling in opposite directions. Known as the "two-horse patch" since it was introduced in

The Santa Clara County Board of Supervisors honored detectives
Rick Alanis (third from left) and Noe Cortez (fifth from left).

1886, it was one of the world's most instantly recognizable brands,
designed to show the strength of Levi's jeans.

It might have been easy to read past the description. What struck
Alanis, however, were the numbers on the patch. Arlis was five-foot-
five and a half and weighed 125 pounds. She was not fat. The chances
of her wearing jeans with a thirty-six-inch waist were minimal. As he
checked further, the reason became clear. The thirty-six-inch-waist
jeans belonged to Bruce Perry, whose Levi's had also been collected
by investigators in 1974. At some point, Arlis's and Bruce's jeans had
been switched and mislabeled.[1] The tests that deputies thought had
been done on Arlis's pants were actually done on Bruce's pants. The

jeans Arlis wore had not been tested for forty years. Alanis does not like to swear. But his reaction was succinct: "Oh, shit."

This was no minor error that could be dismissed as a housekeeping mistake. Draped upside down over her half-nude body, Arlis's jeans were always a central piece of evidence. There was always a chance the killer's DNA was on those Levi's. It was no surprise that earlier tests on Bruce's thirty-six-inch-waist jeans came up with nothing useful. (The last test by the crime lab was done in February 2010.) It was the equivalent of relying on a witness who insisted a criminal was bearded and portly—when he was beardless and skinny. Knowing that he had to have Arlis's jeans tested, Alanis sent them back to the crime lab. What the lab found changed the contours of the investigation. From that moment in October 2015, the barnacle-encrusted hull suddenly looked like it could be made seaworthy.

With newfound purpose, Alanis went back to re-interview witnesses, including Bruce Perry and Crawford. Alanis took DNA samples from people who had been in the church, collecting buccal swabs in the same way his predecessors had dusted for fingerprints. The genetic puzzle was never going to be neatly solved—the state of the evidence was not that clean—but the detective was trying to narrow the possibilities. Almost apologetically, he asked witnesses for patience as he blew on the coals of old memories. He had a line of conversation that filled in the gaps. Unlike most cops, he knew how to flatter.

Born in 1978, four years after Arlis's death, Richard Michael Alanis was part of a large extended family in Gilroy, California, a modest-sized town half an hour south of San Jose. At the time of his grandfather Norberto's death in 2004, there were eleven grandchildren and eight great-grandchildren in the Alanis clan. Alanis liked to tell people that he grew up in the shadow of St. Mary's Catholic Church, the premiere Catholic Church in Gilroy. In his senior yearbook at Gilroy High School, where he played varsity baseball and soccer, he wrote: "In life, there will always be people who criticize your every action. In order to succeed, you must be able to look past them."

A fit man who wore glasses with heavy, black upper rims that made him look faintly like a buff Groucho Marx, Alanis worked out at Orangetheory Fitness, followed country music, and coached youth soccer. His way into law enforcement was led by his older brother, Fred, who was hired by the sheriff's office after a stint with a smaller force. The brothers did the standard lower-level assignments before moving up the ranks. Fred worked in internal affairs and eventually became a lieutenant. Rick, eight years younger, joined the department in 2001 and served in court security and patrol before becoming a detective. It was an auspicious time for a deputy with ambition. With a wave of retirements, important jobs were opening up in the department, which had seen a hiatus in hiring and promotions in the nineties because of the creation of a separate Department of Correction.

Assigned to solving crimes in southern Santa Clara County, Alanis played a role in investigating one of the sheriff's most challenging cases, the 2012 murder of Sierra LaMar. The fifteen-year-old

Sierra disappeared when she left her Morgan Hill home for her bus to school on March 26, 2012, prompting a massive search by volunteers. Six days later, crews found Sierra's pink bag with a folded T-shirt and pants inside. Her body was never found. With the help of DNA, sheriff's investigators arrested Antolin Garcia-Torres, who was convicted in 2017 of her murder. It was a high-profile case that demanded careful weighing of evidence and treatment of witnesses.

The same skills counted in the Arlis Perry case. As he reworked the original investigation, Alanis distanced himself from the approach of a previous generation of cops. In one of his first telephone interviews with Bruce Perry, by this time an eminent child psychiatrist based in Houston, the detective showed sympathy for what Perry had endured. When Bruce explained how rough the original interview had been—the detectives in search of a husband's motive had not told him Arlis was dead until after questioning started—Alanis responded, "I listened to it. It was tough to listen to. The older philosophy was to play hardball. That was persistent for years. Personally, I don't take that approach." Alanis apologized to Bruce for having to seek new fingerprints. Subtly, too, Alanis tried to bring Bruce into the investigation, letting him know that the sheriff's department was committed to solving the case. "I feel like everybody deserves to be kept in the loop, and the fact that our office has not given up on the investigation," Alanis told Bruce.

The time granted to Alanis was no small thing. Under pressure to solve cases, cold-case detectives perform triage, focusing on crimes with promising leads. The advent of DNA turned the terrain of cold cases upside down, offering avenues that had been blocked before. But that did not mean that the new Perry evidence promised certainty. The case still demanded a fresh dedication of shoe leather. The reinvestigation of the murder received a big boost from Alanis's boss, Sheriff Laurie Smith, who was with the department when the murder occurred four decades before. After Alanis discovered the switched jeans, Smith made it possible for him to have free rein, the equivalent of a producer green-lighting a movie.

Inevitably, the witnesses' loss of memory confounded the task. When he visited Crawford's first wife, Joyce, Alanis began by explaining that the investigation was still ongoing and asked Joyce whether anything had come to mind. "I haven't even thought about it," she replied. Alanis then explained he wanted to get a little more information about how Steve prepared for work in 1974.

"Do you remember his work uniform, what it looked like?" he asked.

"It was a uniform; I don't even know the color," Joyce replied.

"Did he wear a belt?" Alanis prodded.

"I can't recall from forty years ago," Joyce said. "I know he had a belt. I don't know what was on it."

When Alanis asked Joyce whether Steve felt bitter about being demoted by then-Chief Marv Herrington from policeman to a community service officer, Joyce did not remember. For a detective, it was like trying to climb a vertical rock wall without handholds.

In other interviews, Alanis was more successful in revisiting details. He got Bruce to confirm that he and Arlis had had unprotected sex on the day of her murder. The detective also pursued a pivotal angle that had not been in the original reports: Was it possible that Crawford had seen Arlis on an earlier occasion? Bruce said it would have been very unusual for Arlis to have been at the church at night, though there were times that Bruce tutored students in math in the early evening and Arlis was alone. (Crawford typically worked a late-night shift, though his schedule varied.) The young couple generally visited the church together. Finally, Alanis persuaded Bruce to talk in more detail about why he believed that Arlis might have been locked in the church.

"I had a roommate as a freshman who used to go to the church all the time, and one night, he fell asleep at the church," Bruce explained. " He had OCD, he would stay up and get exhausted. One night, he went to the church and fell asleep, and got locked in. That's the only way I even knew the church was locked."

"Oh, wow," Alanis responded. "Locked in the church." It was hard to imagine an old-time detective saying that.

Yet for all the time that Alanis spent filling in the gaps of the case—and persuading people to talk candidly—his most significant finding came in the matter of the misplaced Levi's. The import of that discovery rested on a quiet drama unfolding in the county's crime lab. To understand it, you needed a rudimentary understanding of betting odds. The results were a long way from winning the trifecta at the racetrack. It helped to know that DNA was not always a magical tool. But the lab test was potentially the first big breakthrough after forty years.

CHAPTER 35
THE CRIMINALIST

When Kevin Kellogg attended high school in the mid-nineties in Roseville, California, a fast-growing suburb northeast of Sacramento, one of television's biggest hits was *The X-Files*, a science-fiction drama featuring two FBI agents, played by David Duchovny and Gillian Anderson, who investigated unsolved cases touched by the paranormal. Kellogg was hooked. "I was a big fan," he said. "Growing up, middle school and high school, that's all I watched." At Woodcreek High School, Kellogg was the quarterback for the football team, winning praise for his passing and running as the new school reached gridiron respectability in his senior year. *The X-Files*, however, shaped his future. By the time Kellogg was studying cell biology as an undergraduate at the University of California, Santa Barbara, he knew he wanted a career that melded science and law enforcement. After studying DNA in graduate school, he did stints with the California Department of Justice and the San Francisco

Police crime lab before joining the Santa Clara County lab in 2010. He had never heard of Arlis Perry or Steve Crawford. But all his experience, including watching *The X-Files*, prepared him for a critical role in the Memorial Church case.

A handsome man with a beard, dark hair, and an unmistakable enthusiasm for the job, Kellogg had not been with the crime lab for long before he was assigned as a criminalist attached to District Attorney Jeff Rosen's cold-case unit. Elected over the incumbent Dolores Carr in a narrow race in 2010, Rosen was reshaping the office—and one of his early moves was to reestablish the cold-case unit, which had suffered a hiatus during budget cuts. It consisted of a prosecutor, a DA's investigator, and a criminalist. The DA's investigators worked with local police and sheriff's detectives, though an edge of competition appeared with Sheriff Laurie Smith, who was anxious to claim her share of the credit. (In Santa Clara County, both the DA and sheriff are elected positions.) In the sheriff's office, the traditional view was that an outside intruder committed the Perry murder. By the middle years of the century's second decade, however, that view had changed. And the DA's cold-case unit, which came to include Deputy DA Steve Dal Porto and investigator Mike Brown as well as Kellogg, joined in pushing for a fresh look at the evidence. All of them had a sense of unfinished business.

Under Rosen, the DA's cold-case unit took aim at some of the county's highest-profile cases. One of their probes resulted in the conviction of Gary Swierski, a fifty-one-year-old Sunnyvale wallpaper hanger who was found guilty in 2012 of strangling and burying his wife seven years before. In another big cold case, the DA's office suffered an embarrassment in 2014 when it was forced to dismiss murder charges against two men accused of the 1989 murder of Cathy Zimmer, a thirty-eight-year-old mother whose body was discovered under a quilt in the back seat of a car parked at the San Jose airport. The office acknowledged that the attorney who previously led the cold-case unit had been having an affair with a crime-lab technician who would be called to testify—although top prosecutors said there was no linkage between the affair and the dismissal of charges. Nonetheless, the DA's office could boast an enviable record overall with old cases. Between 2007 and 2020, it convicted fifteen killers in cold cases. Rosen remained keenly interested in the Arlis Perry case. After the Zimmer fiasco, Deputy DA Dal Porto, a respected veteran, was brought in as the prosecutor. At the lab, Kellogg's job was to handle cold-case tests in expedited fashion.

Their most important tool was DNA, the modern era's version of fingerprints. Although virtually all DNA sequences are shared in humans, there is enough variation, in the best of circumstances, to identify individuals. Modern DNA testing relies on something called "short tandem repeats" (STRs), sequences of DNA analyzed through a process that mimics biological replication. By examining what they call "regions" of DNA, crime-lab technicians can match evidence from a crime scene to a sample given by a person. In particular, they are looking at alleles, gene markers responsible for characteristics like height or eye color. The more closely the patterns of alleles match, the more certain the identification. Given an uncorroded sample of DNA from the crime scene and a buccal swab from a suspect, investigators can reach a quintillion-to-one certainty that the DNA matches that of a particular person. Or, more correctly, that the probability that a random person will have the same DNA profile is one in a quintillion. (A quintillion is one followed by eighteen zeros.)

Through the nineties and into the new century, cold-case units flourished with rapid advances in DNA technology. It was akin to the evolution of mobile devices from the brick-like models of the early nineties to sleek smartphones fifteen years later. DNA measurements had become much more acute, the databases more extensive, the possibilities enhanced. It did not take as much material to perform a test. Criminalists like Kellogg could now also test so-called "touch samples" of DNA—DNA that did not come from bodily fluids. While that technique was controversial, it could point detectives in the right direction. The lab could also generate *partial* DNA profiles, which were less than conclusive but could help narrow the hunt. Because the Perry murder was committed before DNA testing became prevalent, pieces of evidence in the case remained unexamined with the latest equipment. Before 2015, the only significant DNA from the church came from a semen deposit left on a kneeling cushion, which some investigators doubted was central to the murder. That result had been entered years before in law enforcement's Combined DNA Index System (CODIS) without producing a match.

The chances for DNA testing in the Arlis Perry case expanded dramatically when investigator Rick Alanis discovered the mix-up of

Bruce and Arlis's jeans. Bruce's jeans, with the thirty-six-inch waist, had yielded no usable DNA results. But Arlis's jeans, which had been labeled as Bruce's, were a different matter. Suddenly, the crime lab had a whole new horizon to explore with more sophisticated gear.

Kellogg began by exposing Arlis's jeans to fluorescent light to pick up stains that were not easily visible, like semen, breast milk, or sweat. "I look at those stains that fluoresce," he remembered later. "So there are lots of stains. But there was one stain that gave me a result." It was on the exterior of the left leg of her jeans, near the back of the knee. He also found a stain inside the jeans, in the crotch. Under a microscope, he identified both as semen. After so many years, it had degraded. But for the first time since Arlis's murder four decades before, it gave investigators something to work with.

The stain in the crotch was the more explainable of the two. Kellogg's test indicated that the semen likely came from Bruce. Since the Stanford sophomore had told deputies that he and Arlis had unprotected sex on the day she went to the church, no one in the crime lab was surprised at the finding. The stain on the back exterior of the knee, however, required more elaboration. In his first effort to tease out DNA clues, in August of 2015, Kellogg concluded that it was a mixture of semen—and because of its complexity, he could not identify the contributors. Then he performed a second test using a bigger sample from the stain. In October 2015, he reached a qualified conclusion. The stain could have at least two contributors. One was Bruce Perry—again, no surprise. The second was security guard

Steve Crawford, who was listed as a possible contributor to a minor component of the mixture.

That careful language suggested the numbers were less than commanding. It was only a partial DNA profile based on the YSTR chromosome, which is identical down through the male line. In a game of bingo, it would be like filling four or five noncontiguous squares on a twenty-five-square card. It advances the chances of winning but does not allow a contestant to yell "bingo." Kellogg placed the number on Crawford's DNA at 1:714, which meant there was a one in 714 chance of the partial match occurring by chance. (The criminalist put Bruce's number at 1:781.) Put another way, one out of every 714 men would be expected to match the partial profile in a random selection. If that sounded conclusive, it was not. In rough terms, it could mean that it would fit two dozen or so male students and staff on the Stanford campus. In all of California, it might match more than twenty thousand men. Of course, there were only a handful of men in the church that night, including Crawford. But compared to DNA that placed odds in the billions, the number pointing to the security guard was very weak. The crime lab once employed a standard of one to 300 billion before making a definitive match with DNA. (It now simply reports the numbers.) A prosecutor who looked at the case for the DA's office said the partial profile wasn't enough by itself to bring charges.

"It's like a ten-point physical description from a witness," says Tiffany Roy, a DNA forensic analyst in Florida. "Let's say you have a witness who can describe a suspect's hair color, their height and weight, their scars, their tattoos. That information is extremely useful." Roy says a partial profile that produces numbers in the hundreds is much less compelling. "It's as if we're told it was a six-foot-tall Black male," she continued. "When you say this information matches the defendant, that is true, but it's not a clear picture of the whole story."

That wasn't the only problem with the partial profile. It was unusual—though not impossible—to find a *mixture* of semen at the same spot on the jeans. That required complex thinking about the order of events. Bruce's semen would have been explainable. But did the killer masturbate and leave semen where it could be picked up by the jeans? Could the mixture have come from a candle that was thrust into Arlis's body and then removed? The partial match did not allow for a conclusive answer.

In other jurisdictions, DNA mixtures have posed pitfalls. In a study by the National Institute of Standards and Technology, the same DNA mixture was given to 105 American crime labs and three Canadian labs. They were asked to compare it with DNA from three suspects in a mock bank robbery. Most of the labs correctly matched two of the suspects to the evidence. But seventy-four of them, roughly two-thirds, wrongly concluded the sample included DNA from the third suspect, who should have been "cleared" in the test. In other words, the labs showed a tendency to clump their findings. Even reputable criminalists display a tendency to reach an expected conclusion.

Nonetheless, Kellogg's finding on the stain helped deputies and the DA's cold-case team. For the first time, DNA evidence pointing to Crawford, however tentatively, had been found on Arlis's clothing. Alanis sought to bolster the case by testing other men known to be in the church that night. "They went with the approach of getting everybody who was in that church and excluding them," Kellogg explained to me. "I think it was best explained by saying he (Crawford) was a contributor. But like I say, it's not the best stat."

If the jeans yielded a debatable finding, another part of Kellogg's testing produced a clear-cut result. It came about through what he recalls as an unprecedented offering from a law enforcement agency. On the afternoon of Wednesday, November 16, 2016, a week after Donald Trump was elected president, Kellogg met with prosecutor Dal Porto and sheriff's cold-case investigator Rick Alanis at the county offices at Berger Drive in San Jose. After a lot of patient searching, the investigators had pulled together all the remaining evidence from the Arlis Perry case and displayed it on a series of tables. For a crime-lab analyst, it was like being offered an all-you-can-eat buffet at a Las Vegas casino. "Rarely will I go to the sheriff's office and have all the evidence laid out on different tables, brought out one by one, to see whether we should look at it," Kellogg told me later. " I had never really done that before."

Kellogg searched for DNA on a variety of items, including Arlis's sweater and jewelry. Three rags found in the dumpster to the west of the church in 1974 held particular interest. The rags appeared to have been washed many times, giving them a bleached appearance. They also bore iron-brown stains that suggested blood. Surprisingly, they had never been tested in the forty-two years since the murder.

Why had they not set off more alarm bells at the time? The cold-case team theorized that deputies in 1974 might have thought the blood had come from Rich Karlgaard, who had a bicycle accident nearby. But that was strictly speculation, quickly disproved. The source of the rags was unclear, although prosecutors later said the church kept a supply of rags in its sub-basement. Kellogg guessed that one of the rectangular rags might have come from a bedsheet, another from a T-shirt, and a third from a pillowcase.

Using a chemical known as O-TOL plus a touch of hydrogen peroxide, the criminalist then tested for blood. Though the stains had degraded over the years, they produced the characteristic blue-green reaction that suggested blood. "It looked like something that you'd wipe your hands with," Kellogg remembered. "It wasn't clumpy. It had more irregular stains." This time, he reached a result that met the crime lab's "source attribution" DNA policy of one to 300 billion. The blood belonged to Arlis. It was not just her blood type—O— but *her blood*. A potentially critical piece of evidence had rested in the locker for more than four decades without being identified.

Kellogg hoped to take it further. He ran tests known as "contact DNA" sampling to try to find out if the killer might have left traces on the rags. But contact DNA testing is difficult in the best of circumstances, and this was very old material. So the hope for a swift, compelling answer from the rags was dashed. From an investigatory point of view, nonetheless, the matching of Arlis's blood helped fill in the contours of the crime. The killer had cleaned up after killing Arlis, perhaps using the rags to wipe his hands. That pointed to an insider rather than a slash-and-run outsider, who would be less concerned with neatness. Among other things, an insider would know where to find rags to clean himself with and where to dispose of them—in a dumpster sitting a few yards from Memorial Church.

CHAPTER 36

THE FORGETFUL SEPTUAGENARIAN

The Del Coronado apartment complex at 5273 Camden Avenue in San Jose is a collection of nondescript 1970s-style buildings with a big flagpole, a motel-style entrance, and banners on the second-floor balcony that proclaim rental openings. It was here that Steve Crawford lived in a studio apartment for the last 15 years of his life, a span in which he evolved from middle-aged salesman to memory-challenged old man. Age treated him harshly. A driver's license picture from his late sixties showed a shrunken, bald man with deep lines on his face, smiling in an exaggerated way. Crawford's neighbors remembered that he rarely left the apartment before 7:00 p.m.—he was not a recluse but a late riser, a guy who wore a cowboy hat and walked with a cane. "He's a good guy, never had any problems," his apartment manager said. His relatives said he suffered a slight stroke and had a cancerous growth removed from his leg. It was hard to think of him as a killer. He seemed more like a candidate for assisted living.

About 10:00 a.m. on Thursday, August 18, 2016, a bright, cloudless day with temperatures in the low eighties, Sheriff's Detective Rick Alanis and his colleague Sgt. Noe Cortez arrived at the apartment complex with a search warrant to collect Crawford's fingerprints. A haze of forensic confusion preceded their visit. In going through the evidence, the investigators found that they did not have a usable set of fingerprints for Crawford. In the early phase of the case, the sheriff's office did have a palm print from Crawford, which had not matched the print found on the candle. Then, in 1992, Crawford's fingerprints were taken when he was arrested in connection with the theft of valuable artifacts from Stanford. In 2006, a cold-case detective, Ron Breuss, made a fresh attempt to obtain Crawford's fingerprints. A report from Breuss said that Crawford gave up a buccal swab for DNA and promised to come to the office to give a full set of prints. When Alanis looked for those prints, he couldn't find them. It was another barnacle. "I was not certain whether or not Crawford ever came to provide his prints," Alanis wrote, avoiding any blame of his predecessors. Alanis had no trouble getting a search warrant for fingerprints from Santa Clara County Superior Court Judge Nona Klippen.

In truth, the investigators wanted more than fingerprints. Alanis and Cortez hoped to talk with Crawford, prodding him to recall details of a crime that had occurred forty-two years before. By this point, they had a strong conviction that Crawford was the killer.

When they arrived at Del Coronado, the manager offered to knock on the door for them. Alanis and Cortez were happy to accept the offer. If he could, Alanis preferred to treat suspects politely. He wore plainclothes that day.

"Hi, Stephen," he said, using Crawford's full first name, a usage almost no one else adopted. "It's Rick Alanis. How are you?"

"Pretty good," Crawford replied in a raspy voice. When the detective asked to come in, Crawford apologized for the apartment. "I'm sorry for the disarray," he said.

A driver's license shot of Crawford in later years.

Alanis reacted with exaggerated politeness. In his way of interviewing, a detective got more by acting like a social worker than a cop, befriending a suspect rather than berating him. "No, I understand," he said. "You got your bed right here, it's nice. Do you want to have a seat?" (A studio at the Del Coronado apartments was typically fourteen by thirty feet, with the kitchen at the rear.) Before he got down to the events of 1974, Alanis offered to bring Crawford a glass of water. Then he struck a chord of empathy. "I know it's been a long time, but back when you were working as a Stanford security guard, you were the unfortunate person who had the misfortune of finding the Arlis Perry murder. Do you recall that?"

Crawford replied warily: "Somewhat."

The detective then explained his efforts to revisit the murder, as if he were recruiting Crawford to join him as a cold-case investigator. Alanis made it sound as if the sheriff's records division was much like the ordinary homeowner's garage. "Obviously, with a forty-one-year-old file (it was actually closer to forty-two), some things aren't available to us anymore; they get mixed up, some shuffling and moving," he explained. Then Alanis invited Crawford to come with him to the sheriff's office for fingerprints.

"Can I get a ride back?" Crawford asked.

"Of course, of course," Alanis replied. "We have our fingerprint guy, and he gets what he needs fairly rapidly. And we'll get you back as soon as we can."

Although he remembered giving up both a buccal swab and fingerprints to Breuss years before, Crawford agreed to go along. As they left, Alanis complimented Crawford on his hat from the SS Jeremiah O'Brien, the 1943 Liberty ship that came to rest in San Francisco, a rare survivor of the Normandy invasion. Always solicitous, the detective offered to bring along any bags or inhalers Crawford needed. "I'm not due for medication until about two," Crawford said.

The ride to the station featured more of the same—lavish politeness from Alanis, terse answers from Crawford. He did not seem to grasp that he had emerged as the prime suspect in the Arlis Perry murder. Alanis chatted about the problems of Ryan Lochte, an American swimmer in the 2016 Olympics. Though he knew the basics already, Alanis asked his suspect about his military service. Crawford told the detective that he was based in Korea during the Vietnam War, serving thirteen months at an air base there, four years overall. Did he have a specialty? Alanis asked.

"I was a sergeant," Crawford replied, not giving much away.

"I know it's been a long time, but if no one ever said it, thank you for your service," Alanis told him. It pushed the limits of flattery, but the cold-case investigator wanted to keep his man talking.

"Thank you," Crawford replied. "It wasn't a very popular war."

At the sheriff's office on Younger Avenue, the sheriff's fingerprint expert, Tim Fayle, took Crawford's fingerprints and palm print swiftly. Then, in interview room number one, Alanis got down to the business of persuading Crawford to talk about the Perry murder. First, he went through an elaborate effort to put his suspect at ease. Crawford wasn't under arrest or detention. If he wanted to go home, all he had to do was say so. The door to the interview room was unlocked. Yes, the interview would be recorded by video and audio. That was just for purposes of accuracy. For the moment, the charade that Crawford was helping the cops in their probe was intact. Using a cane with a lumpy, pronged tip, Crawford shuffled into the room and sat down.

The investigator began sympathetically, asking Crawford if it was difficult to remember the night at Memorial Church. "It was troubling at the time, but I kind of blocked it out of my mind," Crawford replied. "It's like I've forgotten about it." Even for an ailing seventy-year-old, it was a preposterous response, but it was a passive opening in the chess match between an aging man claiming ignorance and a young detective marshaling the pawns of an assault. Alanis did not confront Crawford on the statement. Instead, the detective lauded him. The ex-security guard was an important witness, and any details he could remember would help. Alanis commended him for attempting first aid on Arlis. This was a detail that was not in the initial sheriff's reports, but as the interview made clear, Crawford had told deputies that he had attempted "close chest massage" on Arlis's body. Alanis explored the point, asking Crawford whether he had ever had first-aid training in the military. Crawford thought he had, but he said he could not remember details.

Alanis wasn't ready to surrender the guise of helpful listener. Asking Crawford if he remembered where he had been interviewed by sheriff's deputies, he obtained a nugget not in previous reports. Crawford correctly recalled that he had spoken to detectives at his home and at the Stanford police station. Then he added that he remembered watching as cars started showing up at the church after he found the body. Trusting Crawford's version of events was always risky. But if that statement was near the truth, it suggested he had not ventured far from the crime scene before the dispatcher struggled to find him. Alanis pressed him on what he could remember when he found Arlis's body. Crawford said he could only remember seeing her on the ground and then calling for help. For the moment, his leaving the scene was left alone. When Alanis said it was understandable that the guard would ask for help, Crawford replied, "Well, what are you going to do?"

Then Alanis's questions sharpened, and Crawford's answers dulled. The detective reminded Crawford that he had told investigators that he had noticed a candle sticking out of Arlis's shirt. Crawford said he couldn't remember that detail because he "wasn't there very long." As Alanis pressed him again about seeing Arlis on the floor, Crawford looked at his wristwatch as if to check the time, signaling that he was impatient with this line of inquiry. When the detective asked whether he remembered anything else about the layout of Arlis's body—her coat, her sweater, the candles—Crawford paused and said, "Hmm, not really." Suggesting that the details would be in the crime-scene photos, Crawford was still playing the passive role of forgetful witness.

That answer was hard to fathom. Many people who reach seventy—as Crawford had six months before—lose mental dexterity. But Crawford's wry response to Alanis's flattery about his military service was evidence that his wit could still be sharp. This was an extraordinary murder, an event that sticks in memory for a lifetime. It was an experience that friends and colleagues say rattled Crawford for years. And while Crawford had received only rudimentary police training, he understood the importance of a crime scene. Now he was telling Alanis he couldn't remember the layout of the body.

The detective kept plugging away at Crawford's recall. After reminding him again that his memory mattered, Alanis told him that in attempting first aid on Arlis, he might have changed her body position. Crawford then apologized if he had moved the body, saying he hadn't been sure it was a crime scene. When Alanis asked him whether he had followed the Maury Terry book that detailed an occult theory of the case, Crawford said he "did not pay attention to that." That was unlikely: People who knew him say Crawford did read parts of the Terry book, published in 1987. And deputies years later found a dust jacket from the book inside his apartment. Crawford was a crime aficionado. He enjoyed talking about crime and investigations with his brother, Bill, a Mountain View cop. Now, in the biggest case of his life, he was displaying studied ignorance. He told Alanis that he might need "hypnosis therapy" to remember. Not once in the interview—nor in his many years of dealing with the cops—did Crawford use the name "Arlis."

Alanis now started moving his pieces into open attack. Did Crawford remember seeing any candles other than the one protruding from her blouse? No. Was it reasonable to think his fingerprints would be on the candle on her chest because he touched it? Yes. Would his fingerprints be on any other candle? Crawford doubted it.

Did he recall touching Arlis's blue jeans? Crawford did not remember. What about her sandals or underwear? Again, Crawford couldn't recall. Did he see a candle between her legs? Crawford paused and said, "Mmmm, no. I remember she was on the ground and didn't respond to me, and I got the hell out."

The talk then shifted to DNA. The cold-case detective had a partial DNA profile on Arlis's jeans that pointed to Crawford. It was weak—not enough grounds alone for prosecution—but Alanis did not explain that. Instead, he asked Crawford if there was any reason his DNA would be transferred to Arlis's body. Crawford said it was possible: he was there. "Well, I was touching everything," he said. Pressed by Alanis to explain what he meant by "everything," Crawford said he touched the walls, the furniture, and "her, obviously." Then Alanis ran through the pieces of Arlis's clothing once more, the litany more accusative. He probed whether Crawford's DNA could have been on the sandals, the blue jeans, the underwear. Underwear? Crawford said he didn't think so. But he conceded that his DNA was likely to have been everywhere. Would he answer the same for other pieces of clothing? "Well, back in those days, uh, you know, you weren't, you didn't worry about that kind of contact," Crawford said. He added five words: "Since nobody knew about DNA."

Because it could be read two ways, that was an intriguing response. One explanation is that Crawford was simply stating the obvious. He had touched the body and left his DNA. In that sense, he was offering an apology for disturbing the crime scene. But the phrase "worry about that kind of contact" could be read as an acknowledgment of the risk of an assailant. Crawford was not a dumb man. His statement left open the possibility that his "worry" was that DNA could identify him.

Alanis coaxed one more significant statement from his suspect. The detective asked Crawford if he had ever met Arlis before the night at Memorial Church. "No, well, I suppose I'd seen her around the grounds, but I don't recall ever meeting her," Crawford said. That could have been the foggy recollection of a forgetful old man. But as Alanis noted later, Crawford had never acknowledged seeing Arlis before. This was something new. Bruce Perry had told investigators that he was typically home with Arlis at nights, when Crawford worked his night shift. But Bruce told the *Palo Alto Times* that the two occasionally went to the church at night. Just when Crawford might have seen her remained unclear. Alanis tried to clarify this point without much success, asking if Crawford had ever talked with Arlis. "Not that I recall," Crawford said. "I don't think that was the case." Pressed one more time, he said, "No, I didn't know who she was."

With all pretense of teamwork gone, Alanis embarked on one final line of questioning. He asked Crawford again whether it would be surprising to him if his DNA was found on Arlis, and Crawford answered, "Well, no, because I was there. I was actually touching her at the time." Then Alanis asked the critical question: Had Crawford had any sexual contact with Arlis? Crawford paused and said, "Mmm, well, the first time I saw her she was on the floor...on the ground." It wasn't an answer, so the detective tried once again.

Was there a reason for his semen DNA profile to be found on Arlis? "Umm, no," Crawford replied. Would his saliva DNA be on Arlis if he had spoken to her? "Well, yeah, but I don't recall saying anything to her," Crawford said.

For a homicide detective, a lie is as good as the truth, sometimes better. But like almost everything about the ex-security guard, a fog of ambiguity remained. Alanis told Crawford that his statement did not match the evidence he had gathered: it was, in the detective's understated words, "not a favorable position to be in." Crawford understood this for the accusation it was, telling the detective that he was sounding more like an interrogator than an interviewer. He asked to end the talk. Good to his word and not possessing enough for an arrest, Alanis honored his pledge to give Crawford a ride home. But it was not the last time Alanis visited the Del Coronado apartments. Two years later, he returned with an entourage.

CHAPTER 37

FAMILY SKELETONS

Two months before the Arlis Perry case reached its crescendo, an undercover Sacramento County law enforcement officer ambled into the front yard of a suburban Sacramento home with a dark-tiled roof, an imposing garage, and a neatly trimmed lawn. The Citrus Heights home belonged to seventy-two-year-old Joseph James DeAngelo, a retired mechanic and former small-town cop whom investigators believed was the Golden State Killer, one of the most notorious serial murderers in California history. In his middle-class neighborhood of wide, curving streets, DeAngelo was known as a gruff man who could flash a temper as he puttered in the yard. "Crazy Joe," his neighbors called him.

On that Tuesday, April 24, 2018, the agent employed a ruse that echoed the Golden State Killer's approach four decades before. The officer pretended to be lost, needing directions (the Golden State Killer told victims that he was "looking for a friend"). Following the expected script, DeAngelo bellowed at the intruder to leave. The distraction allowed other officers to slip behind DeAngelo and overwhelm the older man. When DeAngelo protested that he had a roast in the oven, his captors promised they would take care of it. Then they whisked him away to jail.

In truth, DeAngelo's goose was well and truly cooked. At a press conference the next day, Sacramento County authorities announced they had solved the Golden State Killer case, saying there was a DNA match between DeAngelo and the murderer. Sacramento County DA Anne Marie Schubert declared that "we found the needle in the haystack, and it was right here in Sacramento." Two years later, DeAngelo pleaded guilty to thirteen murders and admitted to dozens of rapes up and down the state.

Even with that litany, DeAngelo was not a suspect in the killing of Arlis Perry. His DNA did not match the evidence collected in the Stanford case. And the Golden State Killer's method differed from that of Arlis's murderer. DeAngelo's arrest, however, highlighted the reach of DNA—and a new way of deploying it through genetic databases. It came at the same time as the emergence of a law enforcement-friendly DNA firm in Reston, Virginia, called Parabon NanoLabs, which *did* have a role in the Arlis Perry case, albeit in a way no one expected.

The capture of the Golden State Killer raised the stakes for Santa Clara County deputies trying to build the case against Steve Crawford. The comparisons were inevitable. In both cases, the suspect was an aging ex-cop living out life in obscurity. In both cases, investigators were relying on DNA. But if the Golden State Killer's DNA introduced a high-definition television picture, the results in the Memorial Church murder resembled the fuzz and snow of early 1950s broadcasts.

The spree of attacks east of Sacramento in the mid-seventies haunted investigators for four decades. Originally called the "East Area Rapist," or "EAR," and later "the Original Night Stalker," the killer initially preyed on single women. Selecting homes near open spaces or creek beds, he used a bicycle to escape. As his tally climbed, he grew bolder, attacking couples and murdering as well as raping. Typically, he entered through a sliding glass door and forced the woman to tie the man up. Placing a set of dishes on the man's back, he threatened to kill the woman if he heard a rattle. He would then rape the female, occasionally taking a break to raid the refrigerator. As he shifted operations southward to Ventura and Orange counties, he sometimes ended the evening by killing both man and woman.

Through the inspiration of a Southern California author, Michelle McNamara, who died two years before DeAngelo's arrest, the attacker earned a lasting new nickname that broadened the geography of his crimes: "The Golden State Killer." In an ugly prequel, he is also believed to have been the "Visalia Ransacker" before he moved to Sacramento. The abundance of monikers underscored how prolific the killer was—and how slow law enforcement was to link his crimes across the state.

The ability to uncover the Golden State Killer was rooted in a strange and tangled case that developed a decade after Arlis Perry's murder. In the early eighties, a fortyish man was living with his five-year-old daughter at the Holiday Host RV Park in Scotts Valley, about forty miles south of Memorial Church. Calling himself Gordon Jenson, he made himself useful around the park by performing small repairs. His neighbors, however, suspected something was wrong. The little girl, named Lisa, was heard crying at night.

When a friendly woman at the park remarked that her childless daughter would love to have a girl like Lisa, Jenson made a remarkable offer. Why not take Lisa on a trial basis? If it worked out, an adoption would follow. The woman took Jenson up on his offer, and her daughter was overjoyed. But when the daughter and her husband began adoption proceedings, they found Jenson had disappeared. As investigators learned later, he was Lisa's kidnapper, not her father. His real name was Terry Peder Rasmussen, a navy veteran and Denver native born in 1943. Under various aliases, including "Robert Evans," he compiled a lengthy criminal résumé in several states. Convicted in 2002 of murdering his wife in Richmond, California, and burying her in the basement, he died in High Desert State Prison in Susanville in 2010.

Decades after she was adopted by a different family in Southern California—she had a happy childhood—Lisa tried to find her birth parents. She enlisted the help of a San Bernardino County sheriff's deputy, Pete Headley, who in turn sought the assistance of a genetic genealogist, Barbara Rae-Venter. With Lisa's DNA and profiles the public had uploaded to a website called GEDmatch (pronounced Jed-Match), they were able to locate Lisa's second or third cousins on the East Coast. (Such a search is helped by the fact that the Y chromosome is passed down through the male line.) From there, it was a matter of triangulation until they were able to identify Lisa's original family. Her real name was Dawn Beaudin, and she was last seen in Manchester, New Hampshire, around Thanksgiving in 1981, when she was six months old. Her mother, Denise Beaudin, disappeared at the time after living with a man named Bob Evans. Authorities came to believe that Rasmussen, in his guise as Evans, was responsible for killing a woman and three girls whose bodies were stuffed into metal drums near Allenstown, New Hampshire. They became known as the "Bear Brook" murders.

The Beaudin story evoked fresh hope from detectives across the country. If DNA could be used to identify a woman who did not know her roots, could it be employed to find unknown killers, thus rekindling thousands of cold cases? Until that point, investigators had matched DNA left at a crime scene with a law enforcement database known as CODIS, a bulky and time-consuming process. For starters, it relied on finding an offender who had been arrested and given up his DNA. In many cold cases, including daunting ones like the Golden State Killer, authorities had no point of comparison.

The Bear Brook case seemed to promise that DNA left at a crime scene would allow investigators to work backward, finding the killer through publicly available genealogy databases. It was a mélange of science, birth notices, obituaries, and family trees. The new technique was not infallible, and it generated controversy from people who had uploaded their DNA without expecting that it would be used by police. But matched against traditional DNA tests, it launched investigators into fertile new territory.

Like Pete Headley in his search for Lisa's parents, Pete Holes, a Contra Costa County investigator in the GSK case, sought the help of Rae-Venter, a retired patent attorney who practiced genealogy from her home on the Monterey Peninsula. A friendly man with a ready smile, Holes became the Golden State Killer's Javert, a persistent adversary. Initially, Holes and his team had no idea who the killer was, though they estimated he was born between 1940 and 1960. Their most significant evidence was his semen, including a deposit collected for a rape kit by the Ventura County coroner's office. Through a tedious process of elimination—they once dispatched a New York sheriff's deputy to check a gravestone—the GSK investigators constructed a large family tree that pointed to DeAngelo. Using DNA found on the door handle of his car and more from a tissue in his garbage can, they matched his DNA with the sample from the Ventura County rape kit.

Meanwhile, Parabon was pursuing genealogical searching with its own methods. Parabon hired a personable genealogist, CeCe Moore, to mine the growing databases kept by GEDmatch and other sites. Because law enforcement already had a good relationship with Parabon, the firm was known to the Santa Clara County cold-case investigators. Their most fruitful collaboration came in the investigation of the murder of Leslie Perlov in the Stanford foothills. Before she was killed in February 1973, Perlov fought her assailant, leaving scrapings from his skin under her fingernails.

While Parabon was unable to help the cold-case detectives with the partial DNA profile from Arlis's jeans—it was not conclusive enough—the Reston firm could assist with the semen deposit on the kneeling cushion. The DNA from that deposit had never found a match in the law enforcement database, CODIS, which suggested that whoever left it had not been arrested subsequently. With access to genetic databases, Parabon could sample a far broader universe, including profiles of relatives of the man who had left the deposit. And that unearthed a surprising coda in the Arlis Perry murder.

CHAPTER 38

THE SHOOTER

On Thursday, June 28, 2018, a cool day by the standards of a San Jose summer, Deputy DA Matt Braker knew a big morning could await him. He also understood it might produce little of value, the flotsam of an old case with an aging suspect. A lithe, baldish man with a smile that hinted at a keen mind, Braker was the head of the Santa Clara County DA's cold-case unit. He was also one of the office's top homicide prosecutors. The year before, the fifty-one-year-old Braker successfully prosecuted three jail guards for the murder of a mentally disturbed inmate in a trial that exposed a pattern of abuse by correction officials. As a prosecutor, Braker knew how to summon the outrage of a jury. He won the conviction by describing the blows the inmate suffered and the sneers the guards used.

On that summer morning, Braker was awaiting the results of a search of Steve Crawford's apartment on Camden Avenue. It had been nearly two years since Sheriff's Detective Rick Alanis had visited Crawford and escorted him to the sheriff's office—two years in which investigators took DNA from the witnesses in the church, tested the clothing and fabric in evidence, and refocused attention on the chronology of the crime. A group of investigators and prosecutors met at Memorial Church to walk through the steps of the murder. They explored tunnels linking the church with other parts of campus. Early in his review, Braker came to believe Crawford was the likely killer. Painstakingly, he and Alanis prepared a search warrant for Crawford's ground-floor studio.

Alanis's statement of facts recited the basics of the law enforcement case without dwelling on its shortcomings. A partial DNA profile pointing to Crawford had been found on the back of Arlis's jeans, and there was no credible reason why it should be there. The ex-security guard had offered conflicting versions of what happened on the night of the murder. His story of seeing Arlis slipping in behind him at around 11:15 p.m. was untrue, according to three witnesses at the church. It might not have been enough by itself to convict Crawford, but it was enough for a search warrant. The investigators sought anything taken from the crime scene, including Arlis's glasses. They intended to search Crawford's belongings, including his computer. If this was not officially a fishing expedition, the deputies were bringing along their rods, tackle, and waders.

Knowing the detectives planned to descend on Crawford's apartment early, Braker stopped to buy a chocolate croissant and a cup of coffee. Then he parked his car on the street outside the Del Coronado apartment complex and waited for the call from the deputies. Above all, he wanted to know the results of the search. But his presence also served as an insurance policy. If the DA's office were to prosecute Crawford, Braker wanted to know the search went smoothly. After all, there was a bad history with searching Crawford's home. Although an argument that a search was defective was hard for defense attorneys to sustain, a good prosecutor left nothing to chance.

Suddenly, Braker heard a brace of patrol cars and emergency vehicles racing past him, sirens at full blare. They seemed headed for the Del Coronado apartments. While Camden Avenue is a wide and busy street— a broad carpet runner leading south from Highway 85 toward the foothills—it was an unusual cacophony for a summer morning. "I thought, *Why the hell would they do such a song and dance for a search warrant?*" the prosecutor recalled. "*What the hell is going on?*"

The short answer was plenty. "Hell" might have fit events too. The sirens were sounding because of an unexpected finale to the murder. Backed by other deputies, Alanis and Sgt. Noe Cortez had knocked on Crawford's teal-colored door and announced themselves. After a long wait, Crawford came to the window of his studio and made eye contact with Alanis. In a high-pitched, raspy voice, he said he needed time to get dressed. Prepared to show patience, the detectives waited. The minutes ticked by. At one point, Crawford seemed to open one of the vertical blinds of his apartment, which hung near his bed. "I'm moving kind of slow, sorry," he said. It was an extraordinary lull, like the long prelude to a medieval battle.

Concluding that Crawford was stalling, Alanis used a key from the apartment manager to open the door to the studio a crack. "Mr. Crawford, we're going to help you out," Alanis said. In front of him, he saw Crawford sitting on the bed with his neck tilted down, a large gun in his lap. Crawford seemed startled when the door opened. Alanis quickly retreated, seeking cover behind a window air-conditioning unit near the ground. "Gun, gun, gun," he announced. "Mr. Crawford, put the gun away. Put the gun away." It was a sign of Alanis's approach that he used polite address even to a man who pulled a gun. As the investigators retreated, they heard a ringing gunshot. Crawford had lifted the gun and fired one bullet into his temple. From a spot in the courtyard, Alanis's partner, Cortez, could see the action. Later, the detectives theorized that Crawford intended to fire at them, ready to commit suicide by cop and happy to take a deputy with him. During the long wait, the heavy weapon had slumped into his lap. For Alanis, it was too close a brush with death. That air-conditioning unit was not much of a shield.

The inside of the studio was a gory mess. The bullet pierced Crawford's temple, traversed a metal fan above a kitchen range, and buried itself in an apartment wall. None of the deputies was hurt, although one tripped in the retreat. Crawford had fired a serious weapon—a Ruger .41 Blackhawk revolver, a gun he had owned for at least a quarter century. It was one of the guns he petitioned the Gilroy police to return to him during the unraveling of his marriage in 1992. Weighing forty-two ounces, not quite three pounds, the gun was meant as a modern-day answer to the Colt revolver. Called a "bear gun," it had done the damage the words implied. The paramedics could do nothing to save the ex-security guard. Crawford was dead at age seventy-two. The suspect in Santa Clara County's most famous unsolved murder had departed life without answering more questions. It was his final invocation of his Miranda rights.

When the detectives replayed the body-cam recording taken of the event, they deciphered Crawford's final words, uttered in a soft voice just before he pulled the trigger. "Why are you doing this to me?" he said. The obvious explanation for the question was that Crawford believed he was being hounded by investigators. Suicide was a way of evading the final indignity of jail. Later, the detectives also considered a chilling notion: Could those words have been Arlis Perry's final words as well? There is no way of knowing for sure. Would Crawford have had the self-knowledge—and yes, the gall— to repeat the words of the woman he was suspected of killing? The journalist in me wants to believe it's true. If she had a moment to understand what was happening to her, Arlis might have said those words. But ultimately, I'm a skeptic. In his lifetime, Crawford rarely took responsibility for anything he did wrong. It seems more likely that the words reflected his animosity toward the detectives.

In the ensuing weeks, a healthy debate arose about whether the detectives handled the knock and entry as skillfully as they should have. A few law enforcement critics argued that the team was not in the right tactical position to enforce a search against a man known to have guns. Others said the detectives should not have given Crawford so much time. In their view, it would have been safer to rush the apartment. In fairness, the detectives did not expect Crawford to commit suicide. Stall, yes. Lie, certainly. But suicide came as a surprise. More important, the investigators wanted to talk once more with Crawford. If they broke down the door, any chance of speaking to him was gone. In his interview two years before, Alanis had gotten a few nuggets from Crawford, notably the suggestion that he had seen Arlis before. Might there be more?

When Crawford's body was removed, a search did not uncover Arlis's glasses or the ice pick handle or a bracelet. But it did produce several intriguing items. In a box in Crawford's closet, the detectives found the dust cover of Maury Terry's book, *The Ultimate Evil*. The detectives also found what seemed like a suicide note apparently dated two years earlier, when Alanis had visited Crawford.

Written on the stationery of Hawaiian Hotels & Resorts, a legacy from his time at Apple Vacations, the note was scrawled in Crawford's habitual block letters, containing his usual misspellings. Over the years, his writing had edged toward the illegible, as if he could scarcely hold pen to paper. The note did not mention the murder. Under the headings "2016" and "Suicidal," he wrote, "When you can't get around anymore, take care of yourself, speak intelit (g?)aby, or even control a pen, it's time to check out. Can't even remember my address anymore. The DR (doctor) said the medulla degeneration would progress and require hospice. Can't afford. I've lived too indepently (sic) to put up with being a basket case."

The diagnosis hinted at the severity of Crawford's medical problems. Medulla degeneration is an irreversible process that afflicts nerve cells that control the respiratory system or involuntary reflexes like gagging or sneezing. It can be shaped by several factors, including inherited gene mutations or alcohol abuse. Alcohol abuse ran in Crawford's family: both of his parents were heavy drinkers, as was Crawford himself. The ex-security guard, however, was premature in his judgment that he could not afford hospice. For an air force veteran eligible for Medicare, it would probably be free. A more likely explanation was his fear of being "a basket case."

In the pocket of a jacket in the closet, the detectives found $7,500 in cash. The source of that money has never been explained, but it suggested Crawford wanted a mobile insurance policy if he needed to leave swiftly. Steve had told his brother, Bill, that if anything happened to him, he would leave cash in one of his slippers. In hindsight, the most significant piece of their conversation was Crawford's implicit belief that something might happen to him. Pursued by sheriff's detectives for years, he had never forgotten he was a suspect in Arlis Perry's murder.

After sweeping through the apartment, the deputies confiscated his gun, his important papers, and his 1995 Saturn, the same car Crawford had driven for more than twenty years. The investigators left several items behind, including—oddly—a box of bullets for the Ruger. The detectives did not need them, and they were given to Bill's family, who told investigators they did not want the gun.

Did the dust cover of the Maury Terry book mean anything? It was the one explicit reference to Arlis's murder found in Crawford's apartment. It could have been an odd trophy. But the jacket might also have meant less than it seemed. Terry never tried to pin responsibility for the murder on Crawford. The New York-based author had tied Arlis's killing to the Son of Sam, David Berkowitz. However terrifying the cover, Crawford could have enjoyed a reminder of a book that implicitly absolved him.[1]

The more significant question was what the suicide meant. If Crawford was innocent, why would he shoot himself? There was plenty of precedent for a murder suspect committing suicide. In a famous 1830 case in Salem, Massachusetts, which involved the murder of an elderly sea captain, the chief suspect, Richard Crowninshield, hung himself from two silk handkerchiefs looped through the bars of his jail-cell window. The great orator, Massachusetts Senator Daniel Webster, was called upon to prosecute the case against Crowninshield's co-conspirators. His remark about Crowninshield went down in history. "There is no refuge from confession but suicide, and suicide is confession," Webster declared. For Sheriff Laurie Smith and the later generation of investigators, Crawford's suicide was tantamount to confession.

Nonetheless, a cadre of people who knew the case well doubted Crawford's guilt. A few of the doubters were officials who knew Crawford well. Acknowledging his shortcomings as a cop, they did not see him as a killer. Retired Sheriff's Sgt. Ken Kahn, who handled the case for years, said he wasn't convinced Crawford was the killer.

"Until they can convince me with some new evidence, I doubt it," he told me. "I just don't feel right in my gut or my heart that Crawford is the right guy."

Months after Crawford shot himself, one of the Stanford community service officers who knew him best, Sandra Mize, told me, "How would you feel if you were hounded for most of your life for something you didn't do?"

Crawford's first cousin, Mickie McGowan, who had no particular love for Steve but had known him since he was a child, seconded the thought. "I don't imagine him doing anything like that," she said of Steve's chances of being the killer. "He was just a misfit."

The doubters centered their argument on what they saw as Crawford's "wimpy" nature. Confronted by another person's anger, he had been known to freeze, arms at his side, retreating emotionally. "He was afraid of that church," said Stanford Police Capt. Raoul Niemeyer, who counts himself as one of the chief doubters. "He was a frickin' wimp."

That point of view was underscored by a former Stanford police detective sergeant, John McMullen, who arrested Crawford in 1992 in connection with the theft of artifacts from Stanford. "He's the kind of guy, from thirty feet away, he's a blabbermouth," McMullen remembered. "When you approached him, he'd say, *You're not gonna hurt me, are you? Oh my God.*"

To be sure, being a wimp does not foreclose being a murderer. The history of murder is punctuated with wimps. One of the more infamous serial killers of the 1980s was Paul Michael Stephani, the so-called "Weepy Voiced Killer" in the twin cities of Minneapolis and St. Paul. After killing or assaulting a young woman, the killer would call police in a high-pitched tone, apologizing and asking that he be stopped. After the murder of his last victim, a forty-year-old nurse, he called the police and said, "Please don't talk; just listen. I'm sorry I killed that girl. I stabbed her forty times."

For the cops, the real questions in the Arlis Perry murder had always focused on the trail of evidence rather than the thorny switchbacks of motive. Even for those who thought suicide answered the question of guilt, the puzzle of *why* remained. In his landmark book *The Mask of Sanity*, psychiatrist Hervey Cleckley famously explored what he called the psychopathic personality. Discussing the case of a young woman who was a chronic truant and runaway, Cleckley quoted her father saying, "I wouldn't exactly say she's like a hypocrite. When she's caught and confronted with her lies and other misbehavior, she doesn't seem to appreciate the inconsistency of her position. Her conscience seems still untouched. Even when she says how badly she's acted and promises to do better, *her feelings just must not be what you take them for.*" (My italics added.) They were words that a number of people believed could apply to Crawford. And that was before the investigators learned what was on his computer.

CHAPTER 39

THE POLITICIAN

Nine hours after Steve Crawford pulled the trigger of his bear gun, Santa Clara County Sheriff Laurie Smith convened a late-afternoon press conference at the sheriff's headquarters on Younger Avenue in San Jose, a former social-services building refitted for the security needs of law enforcement. Attended by a gaggle of thirty or so reporters and camera operators, her remarks were aimed at prime-time local television. Earlier in the day, the sheriff had been at the Camden Avenue scene, but her comments were circumscribed, largely because she declined to identify Crawford. As a politician with a stormy relationship with the media, Smith wanted to reclaim the narrative. Fighting for reelection, she had drawn a serious opponent in former Undersheriff John Hirokawa, a onetime ally. An end to one of the county's most celebrated murder cases could only help her with voters.

A tall, imposing woman with a shock of blond hair and narrow, pursed lips, the sixty-six-year-old sheriff had a stare with an edge of hardness in her eyes. She had served as sheriff for more than nineteen years, the best part of five terms, an extraordinary tenure in local politics. A Michigan native who had joined the department in 1973 as a matron, or female jail guard, Smith boasted that she was the first female sheriff in California.[1] She once nurtured ambitions to become the chief of the California Highway Patrol, a goal thwarted by Republican Gov. Arnold Schwarzenegger. On this day, she wore her uniform: a khaki tunic, olive-green pants, and a blue patch on her right sleeve that said "Sheriff." Flanking her was a blown-up 1992 booking photo of Steve Crawford. On the other side was a photo of Arlis Perry wearing a brown-checkered top over a brown sweater. For such a veteran politician, Smith seemed uncomfortable in the glare of the cameras, nervous as she read her script.

"In 1974, there was a callous and cold-hearted murder of an exceptional young woman," Smith began. "My heart goes out to the family…A mother and father lost a daughter. A husband lost a wife…It comes with great honor for me to announce we solved a forty-three-year-old cold case." Smith went on to laud her detectives and talk about her personal connection to the case. She was only three years older than Arlis and shared her Midwestern roots. This day's news, she said, had brought closure to Arlis's family. "We were able recently to link Crawford's DNA to the crime scene," she announced. It was not a very informative press conference—it oversimplified the case—but it was a triumphant moment for the sheriff.

Arlis in an informal photo.

The next day, Friday, June 29, the sheriff met with the media for a second time at Younger Avenue, taking reporters in clusters of three or four rather than a big scrum. No one who knew Smith's discomfort with the media was surprised. For the sheriff, talking to small groups was far easier than handling a horde of questioners. This time, she enlarged upon the deputies' mission when they knocked on Crawford's door.

"We went there to serve a search warrant with the intent to arrest him," she said. A little later, she added. "We look on this as closure. We believed we had solid evidence to arrest and even convict Stephen Crawford." This statement seemed to bolster the sheriff's argument that her investigators had solved the case. It was one thing to serve a search warrant on a prime suspect. Putting him away for good sounded far more authoritative.

Of all the sheriff's assertions that day, the promise of arrest stirred the most controversy inside the law enforcement establishment. It irked top attorneys in the DA's office, which was still not ready to charge Crawford. The search warrant affidavit prepared by investigator Rick Alanis identified Crawford as the likely killer, but the purpose of the search was to find items that linked him to the murder. It was not an arrest warrant. Inside the DA's office, Deputy DA Matt Braker favored charging Crawford, but a long conversation with top prosecutors would have had to take place first. The sheriff had the power to arrest Crawford "on view," as immediate arrest is known. In a case of this magnitude, however, no one wanted to see Crawford taken into custody—and then released a few days later. That would have been a huge embarrassment, another stumble in an already haunted case. In county law enforcement, no one had forgotten the saga of Maurice Nasmeh, an architect accused of killing Jeanine Harms, a forty-two-year-old woman who disappeared after returning to her home with a man she met at a Campbell brewpub in 2001. Because of inconsistencies in the way a crime specialist worked on fibers, Nasmeh was released from jail only to be killed by Harms's brother in a spectacular murder-suicide in 2011.

Among those who doubted Crawford's guilt, and even among those who accepted him as the killer, the sheriff's statement raised the question of whether she embroidered the purpose of the mission on Camden Avenue in the interests of her reelection. A few weeks before Crawford's suicide, her challenger, Hirokawa, had finished strongly in the June primary, denying the sheriff an outright primary victory for the first time since she was elected two decades before. The suspicions gained credence when the sheriff described the tasks remaining on a case she proclaimed as solved. The deputies were examining Crawford's Saturn and the 2016 suicide note. "I know there's a lot more work to do on this case, even though the suspect I believe is the killer is dead," Smith said.

In truth, Crawford's suicide was convenient in many ways. It allowed a sheriff running for reelection to claim that the department's biggest unsolved murder now had an ending. It saved the district attorney's office from having to try a case that still had holes. It let detectives put the finishing touches on their probe without having to reveal the mistakes storing evidence. It rescued the crime lab from having to explain the fragility of its DNA numbers. It gave Stanford an explanation for a brutal crime. And it permitted reporters to write with freedom about Steve Crawford's apparent guilt. Yes, a motive was elusive. No one understood the demons in Steve Crawford's past. But suicide seemed to supply an answer: If Crawford was innocent, why would he end it all?

In her mini-press conferences on Friday, the sheriff said deputies had found "his DNA" on "her items" without being specific about either term. "After that, we had to re-interview people," she said. "We contacted everyone who had been in the church that night. We took their DNA and fingerprints. We wanted to rule them out." If the DNA had unquestionably identified Crawford—as opposed to being a partial profile—it was legitimate to ask why investigators needed to obtain DNA from other witnesses. But the sheriff hovered in the fuzzy reaches of science. Asked how the sheriff's department had gotten Crawford's DNA, she was even vaguer. "It seems like years ago we got his DNA off something he discarded," she said. "I don't know if we had a search warrant to get his DNA or got it another way." In homicides, she explained, "going back many years, we have a storehouse of evidence. We have a tremendous amount of evidence. Even where there's been a conviction, we keep the evidence for life."

To the surprise of few who had followed her career, Smith's presentation was littered with factual errors and misleading statements. She told reporters that detectives had recovered a copy of the Maury Terry book, *The Ultimate Evil*. In truth, it was only a dust jacket, a mistake the sheriff's office corrected quickly. On other points, Smith displayed stunning ignorance, saying she did not know why Crawford had been arrested in 1992 (in connection with thefts from Stanford) or whether he had declined a lie detector test. (He refused a polygraph in 1974.) While investigators had followed Crawford to try to get a discarded cup or utensil—and reported finding a cigarette butt—the sheriff omitted that Crawford had given a buccal swab to cold-case detective Ron Breuss in 2006. Finally, the sheriff overstated the care with which the evidence was preserved. In truth, county investigators had lost a major part of the rape kit, the "vaginal wash." And for many years, the sheriff's department had mistakenly switched the jeans of Arlis and Bruce Perry. If the case had gone to trial, the handling of evidence would have been a vulnerability for the prosecution.

In her long tenure, Smith had proved herself to be an indifferent administrator who often seemed like she had only a hazy grasp of what was happening inside her department. Having taken back control of the jails in 2010 from the former Department of Correction, she inherited a host of problems that crested with the 2015 beating death by jail guards of Michael Tyree. Even earlier, she was accused of showing favoritism to San Francisco 49ers linebacker Aldon Smith, letting him ride in the sheriff's helicopter and shoot guns at the sheriff's range while he was under investigation on weapons charges. Two years before the sheriff claimed victory in the Perry case, a blue-ribbon commission headed by former Superior Court Judge LaDoris Cordell recommended that Smith be replaced.

Until that point, broad discontent among her troops had failed to dislodge Smith. Her longevity reflected the power of incumbency and a busy electorate that did not pay close attention to the sheriff's operations. (In the late seventies, I covered county government as a full-time beat. But at the time of Crawford's suicide, *The Mercury News* no longer had a dedicated county reporter.) As a Republican in a liberal county, Smith forged alliances with Democratic politicians and labor leaders. And because she had access to internal records, she knew the foibles of any in-house opponent. Of all the political advantages she possessed, however, her status as a woman in law enforcement might have been the most significant, one that she invoked with deft political jujitsu. In 2018, when the San Jose *Mercury News* ran a story about a twenty-six-year-old allegation that Smith had sexually harassed a male deputy, she denounced it as a perversion of the Me Too movement—and an attack on her as a woman. There was no story there, her people insisted. It was all absurd, ridiculous.

All of this meant that Smith's legion of critics paused before taking on the sheriff frontally. Frequently at odds with her brethren in law enforcement and other officials in county government, Smith remained a potent and ambitious politician who remembered the people who crossed her. The vulnerability she showed in public masked a vigorous ego. On the department's helicopter, the tail number corresponded with her birthday: N621LS. (June 21 was her birthday, and her staff assumed that the "LS" stood for Laurie Smith.)

Linked to her political agility was Smith's most dumbfounding talent, an ability to show empathy on behalf of people victimized by her department. When the worst occurred, Smith could sympathize with the victims. After Tyree was killed by jail guards, Smith commiserated publicly with the Tyree family, which did no favors to the county's legal position. The county agreed to pay $3.6 million to Tyree's survivors to settle the case, and the Tyree family lawyer, Paula Canny, later emerged as a full-throated defender of the sheriff. In her

2018 reelection campaign, Smith turned a potential pitfall—racist and sexist texts sent by correction officers —into a way of clobbering her opponent, John Hirokawa.

After Smith's press conferences on the Arlis Perry case, the sheriff seemed to have seized control of the narrative once again. But one obvious question remained. Was Crawford involved in the other sensational murders connected to Stanford—with victims Leslie Perlov, Janet Taylor, and David Levine? Investigators had always doubted that the Memorial Church killer had committed the other crimes. The church killing involved a time-consuming layout of the body—a presentation, a show—that the other murders did not have. In the Perlov and Taylor murders, the killer had used a car, a tool missing at Memorial Church. Initially, Smith's department seemed to discount the possibility of Crawford's larger involvement. Robert Salonga, a reporter for the San Jose *Mercury News*, wrote a story saying that sheriff's officials believed Crawford was not connected to any of the three other killings.

In her Friday talks with reporters, however, the sheriff opened the door to speculation. "We have a chart of unsolved homicide cases from when he was living in the area versus when he was not living in the area," she said, explaining that detectives were trying to see whether there was any correlation. In terms of the three other Stanford murders, the department had known the answer to that question for more than forty years. Crawford had been employed by Stanford between 1971 and 1976. And while he had spent time in Southern California, he had lived primarily in Santa Clara County.

That did not make him a stronger suspect in the three other killings. But Smith's statement left the impression that the sheriff's department was refusing to rule anything out.

In November 2018, less than five months after Crawford committed suicide, Smith beat Hirokawa handily to win a sixth term. The controversy that accompanied Smith's administration, however, did not disappear. In the summer of 2020, the sheriff faced the most serious problem of her more than two decades in office. Five men, including a sheriff's captain, were charged with taking part in a plot to exchange official concealed-weapons permits for a $90,000 contribution to a committee supporting her 2018 reelection. In politics, this is known as a classic "pay to play" proposition. (Only $45,000 was paid down by a security firm based in Washington state before a DA's investigation started.) In November that same year, DA Jeff Rosen upped the ante by announcing that a grand jury had indicted Undersheriff Rick Sung in a plot to exchange sheriff's weapons permits for two hundred Apple iPads. In a related case, an insurance broker was alleged to have given Smith's campaign the use of a luxury box at a San Jose Sharks hockey game in exchange for a gun permit. On Valentine's Day in 2019, the campaign used the suite to celebrate her reelection.

The cases stirred interest partly because the coveted weapons permits were designed for private security agents protecting leading executives like Facebook CEO Mark Zuckerberg or Apple CEO Tim Cook. For the sheriff, the biggest political damage unfolded when it was revealed that she and Sung invoked the Fifth Amendment before a grand jury. It raised the logical question: If the sheriff had done nothing wrong, why had she invoked her right not to incriminate herself? The DA's office pledged that it was not done investigating, though charges were eventually dismissed against a couple of the defendants outside the department. In the end, the sheriff's many problems caught up with her politically. Facing civil charges of misconduct, she resigned in October 2022 before her term expired. Her long tenure was capped at twenty-four years.

CHAPTER 40

THE OLD MAN IN A WHEELCHAIR

On a November afternoon in 2018 outside the gray mausoleum known as the Hall of Justice on Hedding Street in San Jose, Santa Clara County District Attorney Jeff Rosen reached for the words of the Talmud as he stood before the cameras. In his nearly eight years as DA, Rosen had become well-versed in dealing with the media, often using his platform to impart an ethical lesson. "There's an expression that if you take one life, it's like you've taken the whole world," said Rosen, a slender man who prosecuted homicides before his election in 2010. The DA went on to laud sheriff's deputies and his cold-case unit for bringing a seventy-four-year-old Hayward man, John Arthur Getreu, to justice. Now bald and in a wheelchair, wearing Clark Kent-style glasses and an orange jumpsuit, Getreu had just appeared in court on charges of the 1973 murder and attempted rape of Leslie Marie Perlov in the Stanford foothills.

The Talmudic saying fit the moment. The 1973 Perlov homicide, which occurred twenty months before Arlis was killed, lingered as one of two sister cases to the Memorial Church murder. It was investigated by many of the same Santa Clara County sheriff's deputies, including Sgts. John Johnson and Dave Pascual. There were obvious similarities. Both Perlov and Arlis were strangled, though the coroner ruled that Arlis died from the thrust of an ice pick. Arlis had worked in a law firm, Perlov in a law library. Arlis was married to a Stanford premed student in 1974. Perlov had graduated from Stanford in 1972 and was engaged to a former Stanford premed student. Because of disparities in method, investigators came to believe the two women were killed by different men. But there was still a shred of doubt. A few months before, Sheriff Laurie Smith had said that deputies were looking at Crawford as a potential suspect in the Perlov case. That possibility seemed foreclosed by the new charges. But the appearance of the old man in the wheelchair renewed questions in the opposite direction. Was there a chance that Getreu killed Arlis?

What united the cases, as Rosen noted, was their impact. Each murder cut a wide swath, destroying hopes and changing lives forever. For the families, the cases were never cold, never forgotten, never shelved. When the district attorney finished on that November day, a slim woman wearing a gray top and black leggings stepped up to explain in rich and heartbreaking detail just how much a murder had altered her life. She was Diane Perlov, the younger sister ("by fourteen months") of Leslie. Clearly a woman of pluck and humor, she traced the landscape of a survivor's emotion with sensitivity and grace.

"Over forty-five years, we have been in touch with the many detectives who worked on this case," she said, repeating a statement she had read out in court. "But the call I'll never forget was the call last Tuesday from Lt. (Noe) Cortez, who simply said, *Diane, we got him. I was stunned and still am.*"

The Getreu arrest served as the counterpoint to the suicide of Steve Crawford, highlighting the kind of evidence that was missing or botched in the Perry case. When the old man was arraigned on that November day, the investigators could feel the certainty they had been denied in Arlis's murder. More than four months before, when Crawford killed himself, Arlis's relatives had responded with cautious thanks that the case was concluded. They were true to their Midwestern roots—short, direct, clipped. In the eloquence of Diane Perlov, I could see just how deeply and how long a family could suffer. "Closure" is a pernicious word. It implies that sorrow can be tidied up and stuffed in a closet next to the brooms and bleach. But at least the Perlovs could see a man brought to justice, an event that forced an explanation for the rupture in their lives. In the murder at Memorial Church, the presumed killer played with the cops until the end of his life. In the murder of Leslie Perlov, the accused flashed a scowl as he listened to charges that promised life behind bars.

By the fall of 2018, John Getreu had reached the stage in life at which his violent past had almost receded. His career testified to the ability of serious young offenders to escape the judicial system with light punishment in the 1960s and 1970s. And it illustrated a phenomenon that seemed to be missing in the Crawford case: a sexually motivated killer could murder again, perhaps was *driven* to murder again. Born in 1944, the son of a man who became an army master sergeant, Getreu was convicted in Germany of the 1963 rape and murder of Margaret L. Williams, the sixteen-year-old daughter of an army chaplain. The young man acknowledged meeting his victim outside a dance at an American youth club in Bad Kreuznach, a town not far from the Rhine River. Her body, strangled and sexually assaulted, was found on a baseball diamond behind the club. Eighteen at the time of the murder, Getreu was tried as a juvenile in a German civilian court and served a relatively short sentence before returning to the U.S. on parole. Getreu acknowledged raping the girl but said he did not mean to kill her. "I am deeply sorry for her parents," Getreu told the German court. "And if I could do something to bring her back, I would do it."

Back in the United States in the early seventies, Getreu worked as a surgical orderly at San Jose Hospital and earned $500 a month as an orthopedic technician at Kaiser Hospital in Redwood City. He also served as a research technician at Stanford Hospital and performed a stint as a commercial security guard on the Peninsula at roughly the same time that Steve Crawford served as a security guard at Stanford. As the disclosures of DNA suggested four decades later, a common thread among the accused in these cold cases seemed to be a background in the lower ranks of law enforcement. The Golden State Killer, Joseph James DeAngelo, who was charged with a series of murders based on DNA, was a former police officer in Auburn, California.

In August 1972, six months before Perlov was killed, Getreu was working as a security guard when he reported an odd break-in at a computer-tape manufacturing company in Redwood City. As Getreu told the story, he drove up to the company's workplace on Second Avenue and found three young teenagers standing near an open door. The kids scattered, but inside Getreu found a can of kerosene that had been poured over a pile of paper and trailed to the door, where there were several wooden matches. The fire inspector reported that several cabinets inside the building had been rifled. The authorities praised Getreu for foiling an arson. But given his record before and after, questions arose about the accuracy of his account. For his report to be true, he would have had to arrive just before a match was struck, a lucky bit of timing. The kids he described were never found—and later, when he listed his work history for a probation officer, Getreu did not mention the stint as a security guard.

When Perlov was killed the following February and Janet Taylor was murdered a year later, Getreu did not immediately appear on the radar of investigators. That did not mean he stopped breaking the law or assaulting women. In January 1975, Getreu was arrested on charges of raping a seventeen-year-old Palo Alto girl. Police said the assault happened at the girl's house after a late-night movie and pizza evening with several Explorer Scouts. (Getreu's wife was advising the group.) Though the girl testified that Getreu had put his hands on her neck and threatened to strangle her, the familiarity between victim and the defendant and a more forgiving judicial view toward sexual assault worked against prosecutors. It was his word against hers. Getreu pleaded guilty to statutory rape, known as "illegal intercourse with a minor." He served a month in county jail, checking in on weekends. Even then, he was given a break one weekend when his mother fell ill in Vacaville. (In February 2020, the assault victim, then sixty-two, came back to court to testify against Getreu in his murder case. "This is the nightmare that has lasted for years," she said.)

From the perspective of more than four decades later, when a simple Google search might have changed the equation, it was stunning that the probation officer assigned to the case mentioned nothing about the murder and rape in Germany. The report described Getreu as a man of "above average intelligence with no prior legal referrals." To be fair, investigators were hampered because the German case was tried in a juvenile court. Some of the events might—literally—have been lost in translation. But the crime had been covered intently by newspapers in Ohio, where Getreu's family came from. At the very least, an understanding of Getreu's past might have focused interest on him as a suspect in the Perlov and Taylor murders. It's hard to imagine Getreu's history being overlooked today.[1]

What had not changed was the DNA under Leslie Perlov's fingernails—the scrapings of skin from her killer. Leslie fought her assailant. When she was killed, the deputies did not have DNA as a tool. And intermittent attempts to revive the case never produced a suspect. Then, forty-five years later, the DA's office and the county crime lab turned to Parabon NanoLabs, a law enforcement-friendly Virginia company that matches DNA samples. Using a genetic database, Parabon produced a list of names that led authorities to John Arthur Getreu. After following him around, deputies quietly obtained a sample of the Hayward man's DNA. When it was compared with the DNA under Perlov's fingers, authorities concluded that it was a one-in-65-septillion match.

The genetic match led to Getreu's appearance on that November day inside Department 23 of the Hall of Justice, as well as the statement that Diane Perlov read in court. Looking directly at Getreu, Diane began by talking about how close she was to her sister. "We were sometimes mistaken for twins, but you could always tell us apart because I was an inch taller, as long as I can remember," she began. "We shared a room, we shared clothes, we shared secrets." Diane remembered that her sister had introduced her to poetry, philosophy, and antiwar demonstrations. When Leslie left for Stanford, even though it was just a few miles away, Diane cried because of what she would miss. "With Leslie, we laughed so hard our sides would ache," she said. "And no one else could make me laugh so hard." (When I interviewed Arlis Perry's sister, Karen, in 2018, I caught a glimpse of that same filial love: Karen laughed as she talked about Arlis's misadventures as a baker of cakes.)

In court, Diane tolled the effects of murder, noting that she had owned the scarf the killer used to kill Leslie. "For me, I cannot walk alone in the woods. After work, I will not walk through a deserted parking garage wearing a scarf," she said. "I won't let anyone touch my neck." She explained how her son had never known Leslie—but cherished an oil painting of his aunt that had been commissioned by his grandmother after the murder. When Diane's son and his wife had to evacuate their home after the Woolsey fire struck Southern California in early November 2018, they carried away the portrait of Leslie in their small car.

In their pathos and humor, those details drove a spike into the side of anyone who believed an arrest would repair the havoc of murder. Diane lauded the detectives. Then, staring at Getreu, she added the words that Arlis Perry's family could have echoed. "I'm telling you all this because I want you to know that murder does not just affect the deceased," she said. "It changes many lives. And it impacts a family forever. And while justice doesn't heal all wounds, it is the least we can do."

It was a searing indictment, as damning as the charges themselves. DA Rosen was right: a murder had taken a whole world. But it was not the end of the story for Getreu. He was accused of destroying yet another world. Six months later, San Mateo County authorities announced that they were charging him in the 1974 murder of Janet Taylor, the daughter of the Stanford athletic director. While investigators had long assumed the two killings were linked—they occurred just a year apart, in similar conditions—the assumption in law enforcement circles was that the DNA in the Taylor case was not as compelling as that in the Perlov murder. Then, in a preliminary hearing in November 2019, authorities announced that they had recovered DNA from Taylor's torn, green corduroy pants. They put the probability that it belonged to anyone other than Getreu at one to 102 billion, a convincing number. Meanwhile, investigators dismissed the idea that Getreu might have been involved in the murder in the church. None of the evidence, including the DNA found on Arlis's jeans, matched the Hayward man.

Yet the belief that Getreu could have killed Arlis never vanished among the original Memorial Church investigators. Among those who watched Getreu's appearance in court was John Johnson, the original detective in the Stanford case. Even after Crawford's suicide, Johnson retained doubts about the security guard's guilt. In an email he sent me in 2020, he wrote that his view of the murder in the church pointed to Getreu more than Crawford, particularly given Getreu's record. "Putting Crawford and Getreu against a wall, I would now pick Getreu as a likely killer of Perry, a possible suspect," he wrote.

Meanwhile, as the COVID-19 pandemic reshaped court schedules, time was pressing for prosecutors in both the Perlov and Taylor cases. The window for prosecuting Getreu would not last forever. "The clock is ticking," San Mateo County Deputy DA Sean Gallagher explained to reporters. Gallagher was prescient: before Getreu was scheduled to go to trial at the end of September 2020, he was hospitalized with what authorities described as a brain aneurysm.

In the end, however, Getreu lived long enough for the justice system to deal with his crimes. In November 2021, he was sentenced to life in prison for the murder of Janet Taylor. In early January, 2023, Getreu pleaded guilty to murdering Leslie Perlov. There was never any evidence that he was involved in the murder of Arlis Perry. But the old man in the wheelchair was never going to see freedom again.

CHAPTER 41

AN AUTHOR ASTRAY

In any unsolved case as sensational as the Arlis Perry murder, newspaper stories follow a script of futility. First are the screaming headlines, the lurid descriptions, the vow by cops to find the perpetrators. Next come the attempts to keep the narrative alive: sometimes investigators judge that they can disclose a clue, a promising lead that could use the public's help. Sooner or later, these stories dribble away. Then newspapers seize on anniversaries to revisit the crime. After all, subscribers change and have never heard of the tragedy. If an anniversary doesn't fit, reporters ditch the calendar and write stories about cold cases. The Arlis Perry case stood at the top of my list. The unsolved murder poked at my fiber as a reporter. Confident in my judgment as a pastor's kid, I did not realize the quest would take me too far.

When Maline Hazle and I did our retrospective on the case in 1991, we wrote under the accurate but cursory headline "Murder in Stanford church remains a mystery." We had a less than flattering photo of Arlis, one without her glasses. We ran a picture of the candle that had been inserted into Arlis's body, and we identified Guy Blase, a partner in the Palo Alto law firm who had seen a husky young man visit the law firm thirty-six hours before her murder. Overall, however, our conclusion was what the headline said. Because the partial palm print taken from the candle was not judged a match with Crawford, the investigators did not consider him a suspect. (In the story, we said "eliminated," which events proved wrong.) Hooked on the mystery, I vowed I would take a leave from my day job and write a book if the case was ever solved.

I came to understand the case better when Sheriff Laurie Smith let me read through the initial crime file in early 2008. By that time, I was writing a local column, my own pulpit on crime and politics. While it was never spelled out, I think the sheriff believed it would not hurt to cultivate my goodwill. We set ground rules. I would not do anything that would undermine the marquee case. If it was still unresolved, I would check with her before writing. (When the sheriff announced the case was solved, I felt relieved from that pledge.) After absorbing the reports, I was convinced that Crawford was the likely killer.

Not long afterward, I sent the sheriff an email summarizing my reasons. First was his strange behavior the night of the killing—calling to report that he had found a "stiff" and then disappearing from the scene. Second was the logic of the inside job. It took the killer a while to lay her body out, and few people were familiar with the church's schedule. Third was the inconsistency of his story—telling detectives he had visited the church twice and then changing his story to include a third visit. The fourth dealt with his access to tools, including an ice pick.

My final reason focused on the strange story from May 1973, when Crawford reported he had several talks with an unidentified man in the quad about how "eerie" a place Memorial Church would be for murder. That thought seemed to lack a predicate, a reason for the topic to arise. The sheriff wrote back to say she agreed with my thinking but wanted to check further about whether the church's west doors were locked, as Crawford said. This, too, was a critical point to explore—and I give Smith and her detectives credit for pinpointing it.

Had my theory stopped there, I could have claimed prescience. But like many people who followed the murder, I was driven to explain motive. After I saw the crime-scene photos, I drew a sketch from memory of how the body was laid out. More a stick figure than anything else, my sketch erred in one significant detail. I drew the upside-down jeans in a higher position on the body than the killer had left them. Instead of the waistband extending below her knees— as it was at the crime scene—I placed it at her waist. I had also drawn the jeans stretched out: they were actually draped loosely over the body. It might not have seemed significant at the time, but the error led me in the wrong direction for six months.

Well before Steve Crawford committed suicide, I showed that sketch to a source who specializes in reading the psychology of crime scenes. He asked a few questions and then suggested that my sketch resembled the Chi Rho, the Christian symbol used by the Roman Emperor Constantine. Described as "Christ's monogram," the Chi Rho combines the first two letters for "Christ" in the Greek alphabet. It looks like a large "P" intersected by an "X." As it happened, the Chi Rho appears repeatedly inside Memorial Church: in the vestibule to the church, it forms part of the wallpaper, alternating with the "Alpha and Omega" medallion. As my friend reminded me, it is also on the caps of priests. My source asked me whether Crawford had been raised Catholic—and I said yes, he had gone to Catholic elementary school and a prestigious Catholic boys' high school in the San Fernando Valley. His brother, Bill, had served as a brother in the Holy Cross order.

It struck me then that I had arrived at a persuasive reason for murder. If the killer had left the Chi Rho as his signature, he might well have an animus against the Catholic Church or Stanford. If it was the church, what might have ignited his rage? What if Crawford had been molested by a priest as a schoolboy? Would it account for the brutality inflicted upon Arlis? Given Crawford's exposure to Catholic schools and the Holy Cross brotherhood—and his status as a suspect in a murder that seemed to have ritual connotations—it wasn't an illegitimate question. While the odds were against it, I had to explore the possibility.

According to legend, the Chi Rho played a role in the Battle of the Milvian Bridge, fought by Constantine outside Rome in 312. His standard, or labarum, showed a wreathed Chi Rho, a symbol of the Christianity he was bringing to the top reaches of the Roman

Empire. The symbol even made its way into Britain with the Romans. In 1963, a fourth-century Chi Rho was dug up in the Dorset countryside of England. Beneath a blacksmith's clothesline lay a glorious mosaic that belonged to a Roman villa. Prevalent in European churches, the symbol was embraced by Jane Stanford. In the reconstruction of the Stanford Memorial Church after the 1989 Loma Prieta earthquake, a piece of the original mosaic wall depicting a Chi Rho was discovered in the foundation and incorporated into the communion table.

It's almost impossible to identify a victim of priestly abuse unless he or she steps forward. But that didn't stop me. On the second-hand market, I bought a well-thumbed copy of *The Official Catholic Directory*, a compendium of priestly assignments. My research took me deep into the underbelly of the Catholic Church in Los Angeles during the 1950s and 1960s. Long after his death in 1989, the founder of Our Lady of the Valley Church was accused of one count of sexual molestation in the years just before Crawford had gone to school there. So was another priest who had been at the church between 1961 and 1963, years when Crawford had been attending Notre Dame High School. Perhaps most terrifying of all was the saga of Rev. Benjamin Hawkes, the second-in-command to Cardinal McIntyre, who had visited Crawford's high school in the 1962–63 school year. Hawkes used his position to abuse many young boys. In those years, the church had a *Chinatown* feel to it, deeply corrupt and wielding untold damage.

Crawford as a freshman at Notre Dame High School in Sherman Oaks (center of picture, underneath boy at the middle top).

My theory of priestly abuse, however, had a mountain of flaws. Most of the accusations in Los Angeles had never been proven, though the church's awful record in policing itself suggested they were largely true. Just the proximity of an errant priest did not make Crawford a victim. Crawford did not like the church or religion in general, but I never found evidence that he was abused. His brother, Bill, told me that Steve was never an altar boy. Crawford once told a girlfriend that a man had tried to seduce him when he was in his late teens or early twenties. He said he had dinner with the man and followed him to his hotel room, where he rejected the older man's advances. There's no sign that the older man was a priest or a brother. In fact, there's no proof the incident occurred.

Still, the possibility of the Chi Rho symbol at the murder wouldn't quit my mind. When Crawford committed suicide in June 2018, I went to his apartment building and explained the possible Chi Rho connection to television reporters. While I put it conditionally—it was, after all, only a theory—my comments suggested a motive for a murder that had stymied investigators. Because I was willing to talk about the case when the sheriff was not, my comments got wide coverage.

It wasn't until I looked at the crime scene photos one more time that I realized the Chi Rho was a stretch. The fact that the jeans were so much lower on the body than in my sketch made the "X" part of the symbol much less clear. The symbol seemed more like a diamond than a Chi Rho. That meant I had to dispatch my own brainchild, one of the hardest things to do in reporting. The killer could still have meant something by the way the body was laid out. But the theory that it was designed as a denunciation of the Roman Catholic Church seemed harder to prove, a bridge too far. As I looked harder at the background of Steve Crawford, another possibility arose: What if he staged the whole scene to make it *look* like it had religious or occult meaning?

Ultimately, several things convinced me the answer to that question was a conditional yes. Crawford was a habitual liar. Acting out of pure rage against the church would have required someone more dedicated to the truth than Crawford. That someone was playing with the cops felt closer to reality. When he stole artifacts from Stanford during his time as a security guard, he invented stories of their origins for his wife, Joyce. In his square-dancing days, a fellow dancer nicknamed him "the Prodigious Prevaricator" for the inconsistencies in his stories. It all suggested a man unafraid to manipulate the scene.

My quest did teach me how a conspiracy theory is born. Take a fallible premise (my sketch), stir in a believable reason (hatred of the church), mix it with explosive headlines (priests accused of molestation), and you suddenly have something Trumpian, a volatile brew fitted for the new century. I was not that different from anyone else who wanted to interpret the facts—maybe bend the facts—to reach a conclusion. I wanted so badly to find a motive that I deserted my best skeptical instincts. The Chi Rho was an intriguing theory but no more. Anybody who studies the Perry case is better off accepting a dose of ambiguity, acknowledging that the motive is shrouded in a broken past.

CHAPTER 42

THE HEALER

In the end, it was fitting, a ledger balanced by grief and hope. The chief survivor of the crime thought most deeply about its causes. In the trying decades after the murder, the most uplifting thread of the narrative followed the life of Arlis's husband, Bruce Perry. The widower and former suspect reached international renown as a child psychiatrist by explaining traumas not so different from the one he endured at Stanford. And he did it with the help of the most famous talk show host in America.

In the fall of 1974, the murder hurled Bruce into a wilderness of grief. Resisting advice to return to his studies swiftly, he wandered the country, staying with friends in Grand Forks, Colorado, Atlanta, and Chicago. Sometimes he had only a few dollars in his pocket. The best explanation of his ordeal came in a twelve-thousand-word piece by Steve Bogira in the weekly *Chicago Reader* in 1992, when Bruce was working with troubled children as a doctor at the University of

Chicago. "I had to get control of what happened, instead of having the event control me," he told Bogira. "Something had happened that was completely out of my control. I had to get away from the feeling that because unpredictable, uncontrollable things happen, I might as well not do anything."

Bruce acknowledged that he'd had to deal with reservoirs of anger. It was traumatic enough to lose a spouse two months after a wedding, unimaginable to a young man on the cusp of career and family. But murder—a brutal, sensational murder—compounded the blow, thrusting his marriage into the klieg lights of the curious. A bruising interview with the cops made the experience worse. Bruce didn't know where to direct his anger. And his undirected rage made it harder to emerge from his emotional cul-de-sac. "When I accepted the fact that death was a part of life, it did not matter that much anymore what the person who killed her looked like or was like," he said. Instead, Bruce tried to draw strength from the experience, telling Bogira that because he couldn't imagine anything worse, it made him "free to be whatever I wanted to be."

One omission from the *Reader* story might have been revealing. In recounting what happened late Saturday, Bruce told Bogira that he and Arlis went for a walk. When he was ready to return home for more studying, he said, she wanted to walk more. That was true. His version, however, did not mention the tiff that preceded their parting. It was the second time Bruce apparently left that fact out of the story. When he talked to the *Palo Alto Times* in 1974, he said his wife walked toward the church when he returned to Quillen. The *Times* added the background of the argument, attributing it to investigators. While any number of reasons might explain the omission, it's hard to think a husband in Bruce's situation would escape all guilt, all second-guessing.

Although he returned to Stanford for the spring quarter in 1975, Bruce was unable to escape the shadow of the murder. The pity of his friends and classmates was suffocating. So he transferred to Amherst College in Massachusetts, where he was when detective Tom Beck reached him to talk about Arlis's missing glasses in 1976. At Amherst, Bruce took the courses he wanted, resuming the behavioral research he had begun with Stanford professor Seymour Levine. Leaving Amherst without an undergraduate degree, he was accepted to medical school in 1977 at Northwestern, his father's alma mater.

After getting a joint MD and PhD from Northwestern in 1984, Bruce completed a three-year residency in psychiatry at Yale, where he studied the brain chemistry of veterans who had been diagnosed with PTSD, or posttraumatic stress disorder. It was work that pointed him toward the trajectory of his career. He came to be intensely interested in early childhood experiences—particularly physical or sexual abuse by parents or others—that made children vulnerable to PTSD.

Some of his fellow students assumed that he was attracted to the field by what he had gone through in the murder. In Bruce's view, that was not really fair. His first work with Levine at Stanford came before Arlis's death. Nonetheless, Bruce said it was probably no coincidence that he remained in the field of PTSD and its impact on kids. Rejecting the easy premise that "children are resilient," Bruce delivered the message that trauma in children lingered because their brains had been changed in chaotic experiences. They were *wired* differently. To control self-destructive impulses, he believed in using drugs to treat kids. But it wasn't unusual to see the young doctor down on the floor with a child, coloring in a book. Above all, he tried to bring empathy to the job.

By the early eighties, Bruce had remarried—this time to a woman two years older than he—and started a family that came to include five children. For a while, the Perrys lived in the old-line Chicago suburb of Oak Park. Not long after Bruce gave the interview to the *Chicago Reader*, the family moved to Houston, where Bruce took the positions of chief of psychiatry at the Texas Children's Hospital and research professor at the Baylor School of Medicine. He founded the ChildTrauma Academy, a nonprofit that focused on the lives of abused children, a field that burgeoned in the nineties. When the law enforcement siege of the Branch Davidian compound unfolded in Waco, Texas, in 1993, Bruce was summoned to the scene to explain the impact on the children.

Then and later, Bruce displayed an audacious way of bending authority toward his purposes. One of the first people he met in Waco was a commanding Texas Ranger, a man skeptical of psychiatrists. Needing to find a way of making the man an ally, Bruce made a bet with the ranger. It was routine for a doctor to take the pulses of children as a test of stress. The normal rate is eighty beats per minute. Bruce told the ranger that if the pulse of a sleeping girl was below one hundred beats per minute, he would leave. The skeptical law enforcement officer would no longer have to deal with the shrink.

For anyone other than Bruce, it would have been a chancy wager. One hundred beats per minute would already be very fast. For a sleeping child, it would reveal heavy stress. The girl's actual pulse was 160, twice as fast as normal. Bruce stayed, and he and the ranger became collaborators. Rather than subjecting the kids to standard therapy, he focused first on creating a stable, predictable environment. He warned the FBI against storming the Branch Davidian fortress, advice that was not taken.

In a 2006 book he wrote with Maia Szalavitz called *The Boy Who Was Raised as a Dog*, Bruce described dealing with cases that gnawed at the soul, including the story of Justin, a boy raised in a dog cage by the boyfriend of his dead grandmother. Having grown up with dogs as his companions, Justin was throwing food and feces at nurses by the time Bruce saw him. Even more harrowing was the story of Sandy, a three-year-old girl whose throat was slit after she witnessed the murder of her mother. Bruce described how the little girl picked up a stuffed rabbit, slashed at the neck, and repeated, "It's for your own good, dude," the words her assailant used as he cut her throat. The girl survived in the apartment for eleven hours, alone, drinking milk that then leaked out through the cut in her throat. Bruce called the incident an example of the loss of control and sense of powerlessness that trauma can inflict on a child. As a psychiatrist, Bruce sought to return that pawned sense of command to kids. A reader senses his compassion and impatience with convention.

Bruce regularly appeared on television to talk about mistreated children, giving interviews to CNN, MSNBC, and CBS News. But it was his collaboration with Oprah Winfrey that made him a rock star in the field of child trauma. The two had known each other since 1989, when Oprah invited Bruce to a conference on child abuse at her Indiana farm. The alliance deepened with Bruce's involvement with the Oprah Winfrey Leadership Academy for Girls in South Africa. On a 2018 *60 Minutes* broadcast with Oprah, he sounded deeply knowledgeable about the perils facing children who grow up with violence or chaos. A big man with an edge of sadness around his blue-gray eyes, Bruce understood the call-and-response of an Oprah interview. Speaking with his hands, he parried Oprah's questions with plain answers.

"And if you're a child who's raised in an environment of chaos, of uncertainty, of violence, of neglect, you are being wired?" Oprah asked at one point.

"Differently," Bruce said. "And typically in a way that makes you more vulnerable. Kids that grow up like that have much higher rates of risk for mental health problems, much higher rates of risk for doing poorly in school."

In 2021, Bruce and Oprah collaborated on a book entitled *What Happened to You?*—a slender volume that explored the impact of trauma on the brain, particularly in the first two months of life. The title shifted the ground from a conversation that began with the question, "What's wrong with you?" Organized as a series of question-and-answer sessions between Oprah and Bruce, the book explored how abuse and neglect shaped the developing brain. Balancing Bruce's scientific insight with Oprah's storytelling, the book did not mention Arlis's murder. Here and there, however, Bruce's answers seemed informed by his experience.

In a video that preceded the book's release, Oprah asked Bruce to explain something he called "posttraumatic wisdom."

"That's referring to the experience where you've been able to get through adversity and you're now at a safe place in your life and can look back and reflect," he said, holding his hand up as if he were a school crossing guard. "You use your pain and transform it to power and help other people. I think of the most transformative people I've ever known; every single one of them had personal pain and traumatic experience that was a core element of who they became." Then he added words that could have applied to himself. "It's not like it goes away," he said. "It's not like you're free of distress or depression or anxiety. It's just that it didn't destroy them. Those people tend to have tremendous empathy for others who are struggling. They also tend to have wisdom. They're wise about the ability to live with pain."

As I listened to Bruce's responses, I could sense a man who did not shirk from the power he described—a man whose ambition to help was spurred by pain. With Oprah's prodding, he delved into how his research touched topics like racism, police brutality, and the pandemic. Although his language veered toward the arcane, Bruce had a ready way of using analogies that were understandable. He could interpret the hardship in the life of Oprah, who brought emotion and narrative fire to their talks. Because the duo extended hope to the suffering, they were an effective team. One of them had been beaten and abused as a girl. The other had lost his wife in a sensational murder. Now they were at the crest of an idea that offered empathy rather than judgment. It wasn't that something was wrong with you. It was that something had happened to you.

For Bruce, this was well-plowed turf. Throughout his career, he wrote about how childhood trauma could manifest itself in adulthood, leading to a predilection for drugs, alcohol, and porn and to alternating patterns of persuasive lying and body-shaking failure to control threatening situations. Bruce suggested people in this circumstance tended to do well in solitary professions such as a night watchman. That had an uncanny ring. According to Arlis's friends, Bruce had always suspected that the security guard at Stanford— Steve Crawford—had been involved with his wife's murder in some way. At the least, his description of a wayward adult seemed to fit Crawford, who *did* alternate between moments of persuasive lying and utter failure to control situations. Curling up in a fetal position, Bruce told Oprah, was "essentially an act of remembering" by the lower brain.

In a 2016 interview with writer Jeanne Supin in *The Sun Magazine*, Bruce talked about why a kid might fall into isolation or addiction, speaking generally but coming close to the basics we know of Crawford's youth. Bruce suggested that such a kid would not be part of the in-group: he sat by himself at lunch and went home after classes. Mom and Dad worked. So the kid would turn on the TV and eat Doritos even though he wasn't hungry. As he got older, he might learn about online porn. He would learn that if he drank, he might feel less anxious.

Supin asked Bruce about someone who committed a heinous, violent act: What did he think of the notion that someone was born bad? Bruce said he did not believe that people were born bad, though genetic components might make it difficult for someone to develop empathy for others. The best way to understand people, he explained, was to uncover their stories—where they came from, what their family was like, what had happened in their surroundings. Mentioning his visits to death row, he said, "I can't always put my finger on a single event, but it's rare that, after hearing an inmate's story, I don't have a clue why he's there. Frequently, I'll see multiple experiences that might have contributed to it. Almost always, the inmate's story includes being marginalized by a group he wanted to be a part of. Many of the worst serial killers were humiliated, degraded, and marginalized by a parent."

Steve Crawford never talked about his childhood. We know only shreds. His parents, Ed and Maxine, drank heavily, and Maxine had a fierce temper when she was drunk. Steve was not the musical star that his older brother was. In a family picture from the early fifties, Ed, Maxine, and Bill are all holding instruments, a jolly trio. Steve, who would have been four or five, is not present. In some ways, Crawford's refusal to talk about childhood might have been telling in itself. Crawford was never part of the in-group at Our Lady of the Valley School or Notre Dame High School in Sherman Oaks. After his high school classes, he headed home to Venice. While he wasn't dumb, he scraped through academically. It's hard to escape the feeling that something happened to him at home, something that made him feel marginalized. Without knowing the specifics, Bruce might well have identified the core of the problem.

Though I tried several times, I was never able to persuade Bruce to sit down for an interview. Arlis's friends say that when he was told that the deputies had fastened on Crawford as the killer after the 2018 suicide, Bruce wanted to know only that they were certain. He could never put the murder completely behind him. At best, he could try to draw strength from a terrible event. His 2006 book, *The Boy Who Was Raised as a Dog*, was dedicated to Arlis Dykema Perry.

CHAPTER 43

THE DEPOSITOR

Even after Sheriff Laurie Smith announced that the case was solved, a couple of surprises awaited her detectives. One of them came from the semen stain on the kneeling cushion inside Stanford Memorial Church. As repugnant as the evidence was—the "yuck" factor was inescapable—the issue of masturbation, sometimes called "the shameful vice" in theological history, remained critical. At the core of the controversy was a kneeling cushion sometimes known as a "hassock." Each was the size of a thick pillow—21.5 inches long, 9.5 inches wide, and 7 inches tall. Stuffed with sawdust and covered in red corduroy, they were comfortable, sturdy accessories for worshipers who prayed on their knees at the front of the chapel. Dean Hamerton-Kelly considered the cushions archaic. But a handful of older parishioners preferred them. The hassocks injected one more piece of color into the church's glorious decor.

No one knew what kind of strange ceremony the killer conducted next to Arlis's body. For decades, however, the possibility lingered that her killer used the kneeling cushion to masturbate. Between the first and second rows, a dozen pews from Arlis's body, investigators spotted the worn cushion on the floor. On its surface was a semen stain from a man with "O" blood type, the most common. (Slightly less than 40 percent of people have the O-positive blood type.) The deputies' reports did not describe how fresh the stain was, though the cushion was discolored in a photo taken by crime scene investigators. Also found on the cushion was a hair, described as "blond to brown," that had been forcibly removed from the scalp. Lab tests concluded that the hair had no bleach or dye and came from Caucasian origin. It did not come from Arlis. In the years before DNA, that was the limit of the technology.

Without proof that the semen was left on the night of the murder, investigators had a difficult task gauging its relevance. Too many strange events occurred inside the church. Because the cushion was found a good distance from the body—thirty-five feet or so—some investigators doubted whether it offered any significant evidence. It would not have been unheard-of for a man to have ejaculated at another time or for a couple to have had sex atop the cushion. Even hair-pulling could be part of a strange ritual. Stanford Police Capt. Raoul Niemeyer said police once treated the sanctuary with a black light to pinpoint stains like semen. "It lit up like the Milky Way," Niemeyer recalled.

In truth, masturbation was a problem all over campus. In his memoir, *War Stories Down on Stanford's Farm*, the captain wrote of a well-respected Palo Alto urologist who masturbated in the library when coeds were nearby. He was known to bend down beneath a table and look up the girls' skirts as he pretended to collect his books. Another offender, labeled "The Mad Masturbator" by Niemeyer, performed his vice at Meyer Memorial Library, nicknamed UGLY by undergraduates. This man waited until women fell asleep and then masturbated onto their hair. The practice of quasi-public masturbation was so prevalent, Niemeyer says, that a well-known Stanford professor once began research on how often the phenomenon was reported at universities.

All this might have been consigned to the dustbin of the squalid if the kneeling cushion could be ruled out as a meaningful piece of evidence. Instead, it remained a central part of the legend. The assailant could have killed Arlis and then masturbated on the cushion. Or he could have masturbated near the body and put the cushion back in its ordinary spot. If investigators accepted that the murder was sexual in nature—and it was that, among other things—then the cushion might explain how the killer satisfied himself. Before the crime lab produced the weak DNA profile from Arlis's jeans, the hassock was the focus of the DNA search.

Nonetheless, it was a tricky piece of evidence that worked in one direction, a turnstile that permitted forward motion but blocked retreat. It might mean something if the semen could be linked to a suspect. The absence of a match, however, offered no exoneration.

The assailant could have killed Arlis *without* masturbating on the cushion. It could be argued that a murderer who cleaned up blood—as Arlis's killer did—might have avoided the kneeling cushion altogether.

Years later, when the DNA from the stain was entered into the law enforcement database, CODIS, authorities hoped that it would lead to an arrest. No matches were found. When Steve Crawford gave a buccal swab to detective Ron Breuss in 2006—after initial resistance—there was no match reported between semen on the kneeling cushion and his DNA. That seemed to strengthen the case of investigators who believed the murder was committed by an out-

A kneeling pillow of the type found near
the chancel of Memorial Church

sider. While the absence of a match did not eliminate Crawford as a suspect, it complicated the efforts of those who considered him the killer. They were obliged to argue that the stain on the cushion came from someone else. But from whom?

For an answer, Santa Clara County authorities turned to Parabon NanoLabs in Reston, Virginia, the genetic-testing company also involved in tracking down John Getreu, the man charged in the murders of Leslie Perlov and Janet Taylor. Parabon used a DNA database and genealogical research to find a relative of a man who had been a twenty-six-year-old librarian at Stanford at the time of the murder. While the librarian had not submitted his DNA to a publicly available database, his relative had. Reasonably certain that the librarian deposited the semen on the kneeling cushion, the detectives obtained a youthful picture of the man on social media. Suddenly, a seventy-year-old man was being called to account for ugly behavior more than four decades earlier.

The detectives established that the librarian came to Stanford after receiving an undergraduate degree from UC-Berkeley in 1970. What stirred their interest was a subsequent stop in his career. In early 1981, when he was in his early thirties, he worked as a librarian at Oklahoma University in Norman, Oklahoma. He was there when a twenty-one-year-old coed named Tracey Neilson was stabbed to death in her apartment in circumstances not very different from Arlis's murder. The possibility that the man who had left his semen on a Stanford kneeling cushion in 1974 was also in Oklahoma at the time of the Neilson murder threatened to upheave the established theories of the Perry case. What if Crawford really was *not* the killer, despite his suicide in June of 2018? At the very least, the lead demanded more investigation.

Apart from the geographical setting, the similarities between the murders of Arlis Perry and Tracey Neilson were striking. The two young women were blond Midwesterners with similar smiles. Each had married a high school sweetheart who was studying for a medical career. Each had been stabbed to death. In each case, the killer was believed to have taken a souvenir—in Arlis's case, her glasses, and in Tracey's case, her keychain. Both cases flummoxed detectives for decades.

An OU junior who had been the salutatorian of her high school class in Canadian, a small town in Texas, Tracey Neilson was a funny and smart woman who loved to cook. On January 5, 1981, her twenty-first birthday, she had returned before noon to her apartment in nearby Moore, Oklahoma. According to state police, she had been seen running errands at a local grocery store that morning. When she didn't answer phone calls for the rest of the day, her friends and family became concerned. A little before 5:00 p.m., her husband, Jeff, returned to their apartment with an expensive bottle of perfume for her birthday. On their bed, he found Tracey lying face up, her throat slashed and her chest stabbed multiple times. Two neighbors provided slightly different descriptions of a man seen near her apartment that noon.

Fortunately, the Oklahoma investigators had a solid fingerprint that they were convinced was left by the killer. Authorities called it "one of the best pieces of evidence" in the case. (Jeff Neilson's family helped convince legislators in 1994 to pass a law funding the state's first automated fingerprint-identification system, which could scan an entire repertoire of prints.) At some point, the Santa Clara County detectives compared that print with one from the librarian and found no match. Whatever his other odd behavior, the librarian had not killed Tracey Neilson. As of the end of 2022, the Neilson case was still unsolved.

That left the question: How did the librarian's DNA—or what was thought to be his DNA—end up on the cushion inside Stanford Memorial Church in 1974? Even if he did not commit the Oklahoma murder, could he still be guilty of killing Arlis? Solving that question demanded an interview in person. One day in the fall of 2018, the investigators knocked on the door of the librarian's home in Oregon. When they explained why they were there, he lost his composure. The shock of being associated with a murder case rattled him. But the shame of how he had left that deposit haunted him. When he was young, he told the investigators, he had a problem. He liked to masturbate in quasi-public places like Stanford Memorial Church. To back up his word, he produced medical records showing that he had sought treatment for his behavior. His wife vouched for him. The deputies were able to establish to their satisfaction that he had not killed Arlis. The long grab of DNA proved he had been a strange young man with a shameful vice. It did not show he was a murderer.

CHAPTER 44

THE CODA WRITERS

Four decades marks an eternity for a murder to remain unsolved. Though we are used to seeing old men wheeled into court on DNA evidence, time recalibrates the scales of judgment. Justice isn't blind. It's covered by cataracts. In the coldest of cases, including the murder of Arlis Perry, the killers essentially have gotten away with the crime, spending the bulk of a lifetime free. Knowing mortality will trump the punishment of the law, prosecutors jail them with an eye on the intensive care unit. The effort to explain old crimes resembles a truth commission more than a trial. In the Perry case, the attempt was marred by fading memories, incomplete evidence, official secrecy, and the death of witnesses. Yet the dimensions of loss, like a tattoo on the wrist, could not be disguised.

When I began my research, I set out to find as many figures in the story as I could. Their memories added texture and grit to the narrative. I was also curious to know what had become of them—

and how they regarded the case decades later. A few, like Bruce Perry, preferred not to talk with me. A few others departed life early, well before the sheriff's office reopened the case. Still others, already in bad health, died during my research. In the diaspora spurred by retirement and the Bay Area's high cost of living, many had moved to the Central Valley or the Sierra foothills. None had forgotten Arlis Perry. In some way, the murder marked them all, a tattoo on the back of the wrist. On an online page meant to memorialize Steve Crawford, an anonymous contributor wrote, "May you forever rot in purgatory."

Crawford's suicide failed to bring a sense of finality to everyone. Among investigators who had spent their careers exploring other suspects and pursuing the "outsider" theory, there was a reluctance to believe Crawford was the killer. A new generation could embrace the principle of Occam's razor—that the most likely explanation for a crime is probably the correct one. It was harder for detectives who had dismissed Crawford as a suspect early on. When they talked about the case, they would bring up the weakness of the DNA evidence and the lack of a match to the palm print on the candle. To the doubters, Crawford was too much of a coward to commit murder. "I don't think this will ever be solved," said former Stanford police captain Raoul Niemeyer.

Even among Arlis's friends and relatives, wariness lingered. They were relieved that the long puzzle had an answer. Yet like everyone else, they had trouble understanding the *why* of the murder. When I spent a week in Bismarck researching Arlis's early life, several people

asked me whether I thought there was anything to the occult conspiracy theories of the killing. It had been part of the discussion for
so long in Bismarck that it was almost a disappointment to think
the murder was committed by a lone security guard, a man in full
view of investigators. Finally—and this is hard to say—I occasionally
sensed polite exhaustion with the case. It happened so long ago that
the shock and outrage of the 1970s was hard to renew.

After Crawford's suicide, when a reporter from my old newspaper, the San Jose *Mercury News*, reached Arlis's eighty-eight-year-old
mother, Jean Dykema, she talked about how sad she was that her
husband, Marvin, had not lived to hear the news. (He died in March
2018). She said Marvin was obsessed with wanting to know who had
killed their daughter. "It's been horrible, and my husband wanted to
know so badly, and he died three months ago," she said. As a Christian woman, Jean told the reporter, "I know there is someone far
greater that will punish this person. I don't have to do that." I wanted
to talk to Jean myself, but her relatives persuaded me that it would
only burden her more.

The doubters were right on one key point. The murder left a trail
of unanswered questions. Not the least is why Crawford apparently
did not kill again. True, FBI profiler Howard Teten had predicted
back in 1979 that the killer might well not repeat the crime. Since
then, however, we have been exposed to any number of sexually motivated serial killers, their crimes magnified on the internet. "You
have to ask why he would *not* do it again," said Dr. David Arredon-
do, a Menlo Park psychiatrist who has testified in criminal cases. It

was a fair question that my interviews did not answer. But in tracing the people who played a role in the story, I came up with several footnotes that cast more light on the mystery.

One of the people I talked to early in my research was Steve Crawford's first wife, Joyce, who divorced Steve amicably in 1979 and eventually remarried, moving to the Central Valley with her husband. I was intrigued by that phone call from dispatcher Charlie Papp to Joyce early on Sunday, October 13, 1974, when Crawford went missing from the crime scene. I was particularly interested in one word.

Papp asked Joyce whether her husband was home.

"No, he's not," Joyce said.

"Did he call earlier or something?" asked Papp.

"Uh," Joyce said, hesitating.

"I know I called your line a little earlier and it was busy," Papp said. Too busy tending other fires, the dispatcher never followed up his question.

I wanted to know what the "uh" meant. It might have been an extraneous detail. My chances of getting her to remember it forty-four years later were remote. But to me, it stood out like an exclamation-point emoji. It raised the question of whom a young wife was talking to at 6:30 or 6:45 a.m. on a Sunday. If Papp was right about the busy signal, the chances were good it was her husband. Did Steve call her after he found the body? If so, what did he say? If the "uh" meant she was talking with someone else, might Joyce remember whom?

So on a spring day in 2018, I drove to Joyce's home in the Central Valley, a ramshackle green house near a school. It was not the best of neighborhoods. While I was there, the police conducted a raid on the house across the street, apparently for drugs. Joyce, a serious smoker in her late sixties, had aged markedly. Her blond hair had turned gray, her complexion pallid. She came outside to talk to me, but it was clear that she wasn't overjoyed to see a reporter on her doorstep. She wasn't impolite. But between puffs on a cigarette, her answers veered toward the vague and uninformative.

A San Bernardino resident who had moved to Palo Alto for what she called "the friendlier air," the onetime waitress remembered in some detail what she had been doing on the night of the murder. After her shift at the San Jose airport had ended at midnight, she had gone out with friends from work to the Coleman Still, a watering hole not far away. She said she got home around 2:00 a.m. and went to sleep. But her memory of the rest of that Sunday had faded more severely than a pair of jeans left in the sun for decades. She remembered nothing unusual about Steve's return from work, though she acknowledged that he felt depressed in the following weeks after being criticized for leaving the scene. Most significantly, Joyce did not remember getting the call from Papp. The "uh" question wasn't about to get an answer.

Joyce did, however, recall what led up to their separation and eventual divorce. In the years that followed, she said, Steve brought home various old and expensive-looking books, hiding them beneath the incoming mail. He explained that they came from a friend who had died. Joyce tired of his explanations—and in truth, the volumes had come from Stanford. "That didn't seem like a matter of trust," she told me. "He went his way; I went my way." Later, after Crawford committed suicide, she acknowledged there was another reason. In reply to a query I sent her, she replied, "After the Stanford murder, and about that time, our sex life went bust." Apart from what happened at Memorial Church, there seemed to be no ready explanation for that. Crawford was twenty-eight, Joyce twenty-two. The loss of libido is often attributed to medications, depression, or stress. Could it have something to do with Crawford's status as a suspect in the murder of a young woman who looked, at least on the surface, much like his wife? Joyce told me she would refer any further questions to her attorney.

At least Joyce was still alive and willing to talk to me. The tally of the departed I searched for could have filled an obituary page. Dispatcher Charlie Papp, who had such a terrible shift on the night Arlis was killed, died in 1984 near Paradise, California. Walt Konar, the Stanford investigator who was stopped by a CHP officer for speeding to Memorial Church, died of multiple sclerosis in early 2005 at the age of fifty-eight. Konar rose to become a captain with the Stanford police—and continued to enjoy fast sports cars. Attorney Guy Blase, who had spotted Arlis talking to the husky man at the law firm, died of cancer in 2003, raising money for good causes almost up to his death.

Mark Dalrymple, the genial soundman who used an ice pick in wiring the church, died in early 2019, several months after talking with me. Writer Maury Terry, who wrote the book on occult theories of the Perry murder, died in 2015 at the age of sixty-nine, his reputation for probity tarnished by an over-the-top TV collaboration with Geraldo Rivera. Robert Hamerton-Kelly, the charismatic but controversial dean of Memorial Church, died in Oregon in 2013, having published two dense books on religion and violence.[1]

A number of alumni from the case went on to significant careers. Wes Bowling, who had dusted for fingerprints on the western doors of the church, had a ten-year tenure as chief of the East Palo Alto police, a force perpetually scraping for resources. His partner, Tom Sing, became an assistant sheriff and ran unsuccessfully for sheriff in 1998 against Laurie Smith before retiring in Hawaii. Most notably, Rich Karlgaard, the student who became a suspect because he tossed *The Bismarck Tribune* into the dumpster, became a prominent journalist. In 1989, he cofounded the magazine *Upside*. And in 1998, he was named the publisher of *Forbes*.

Steve Crawford's older brother, Bill, stayed on as a Mountain View cop well into the new century. In retirement, he drove a bus for youth outings before he died of heart disease in September 2018, three months after his brother committed suicide. He was seventy-eight. One of his friends told me that Steve's suicide wore on Bill's health. Before he died, Bill told me he had met Steve a little more than a week before the suicide at the Cup N Saucer, a middlebrow restaurant midway between their homes in south San Jose. (Motto: "Eat Good, Feel Good, It's All Good.") "We talked and yakked," Bill told me. The topic of Arlis Perry never came up.

The Rev. Don Dekok, who married Bruce and Arlis Perry and then presided over her funeral two months later, stayed with the Bismarck Reformed Church for another twenty-two years, becoming a deeply respected minister in town. He left for a job starting Reformed congregations in northwestern Iowa. Now in his mid-seventies, he lives in Iowa, a kind man who still ponders that first searing test of his ministry. Finally, the amateur detectives, Dave and Pam Larson, retired to a home in rural Northern California. Dave still keeps files of the case in his garage and has not given up his theory of the composer-as-killer. (See chapter thirty-two.) "There's more to this story than the sheriff's department has indicated," he told me.

Several of the retired deputies moved to the Central Valley but stayed close to the story. Among them were Ken Kahn and Tom Beck, the good cop-bad cop duo who inherited the case from the original investigators. Kahn died of cancer in 2021. Stanford Capt. Niemeyer and Sheriff's Sgt. Dave Pascual, who interviewed Bruce Perry, settled within fifteen miles of each other south of Sacramento. Detective Randy Bynum, who picked up the cold case in the late 1990s and early 2000s and later tracked the composer to a Thousand Oaks concert, became a private investigator and now lives in the Phoenix area. Bob Pulling, the deputy who helped clean out the dumpster next to Memorial Church, moved to a house next to a golf course in Hollister.

In all my interviews, the most poignant story came from John Johnson, the original investigator who took command of the crime scene. Promoted to lieutenant, John Johnson continued to hold the respect of his peers. When he retired in the late eighties, his fellow deputies gave him a fifty-six-centimeter Klein bicycle, which he used to ride across the country. The murder haunted the athletic detective. "I was there for thirty years, and nothing bothered me more than that," he told me. When Johnson bicycled past the Stanford campus in later years, he couldn't help thinking about Arlis Perry or Leslie Perlov. In the mordant way of cops, he told his bicycling companions not to look over the edge of the road. He didn't want to find another body.

CHAPTER 45
THE JOURNAL KEEPER

He always kept a journal, at least for the last four decades of his life. First it was handwritten, preserved in a black spiral volume. Then, in the early years of computers, he put it on floppy discs. Finally he used word-processing software to enter it on his computer. When sheriff's investigators confiscated Steve Crawford's computer and files after his suicide, they had little idea of the sheer volume of the contents. It took months of work to decipher the thousands of pages. Parts of the journal had a wistful or depressed tone. But the bulk revealed a man obsessed with satanism and violence toward women. FBI profiler Howard Teten had been right, uncanny in his prediction so many years before. The presumed killer *did* keep a journal. Detectives Rick Alanis and Noe Cortez, who did not have tender stomachs at the thought of crime, confided that it made them want to vomit.

I have not seen the Crawford journal. I am not sure I want to. But I have talked to someone who was briefed on its contents. And

I've confirmed its outlines with my law enforcement sources. It does not mention Arlis Perry or the murder in Memorial Church. Even in his dotage, Crawford was too cagey to be that blunt. But taken in total, the journal entries and videos from his apartment leave little doubt that Steve Crawford was the killer. To me, it offers stronger evidence of his guilt than the partial DNA profile found on Arlis's jeans. At its core, the writings describe how Crawford led a double life, a Jekyll and Hyde existence—glib travel agent or retiree by day and misogynist schemer of violence by night, a man who celebrated the torture of women. He was not just the wimp that some theorists thought. "This was Steve's innermost thoughts and plans to harm people, laid out in graphically explicit terms," said my source. "It was thousands of pages of disgusting porn and language, charged with demonic references."

Of all the ugly entries in the journal, one of the ugliest was his account of how he raped a woman he knew well—I will call her Cara—after rendering her unconscious. He kept a meticulous record. He described how he slipped sleeping pills into her wine, recording the time when she lost consciousness. Confident she had fallen asleep, he injected half a cup of Vaseline into her vagina. Then he raped her at length, without her regaining consciousness. Crawford confided in his journal that he thought of Cara as a disposable object.

His ramblings show that Crawford was consumed with female genitalia and assaults against women. He wrote about his one-night stands with other women, his visits to peep shows, his proud exhibitionism. In particular, the journal revealed an urge to insert objects into a woman's vagina. Because of the candle shoved into Arlis's body, this was of keen interest to investigators. Assuming Crawford was the killer, it showed that his interest in such behavior was lifelong. Rape has been understood as an effort at domination, at utter control, at debasement. But this went beyond that. Embedded in Crawford's ramblings was a yearning for revenge, played out on the stage of the sacred. "I think he deliberately chose to hate God, to hate women, to hate Stanford University," said my source. "The chapel was the perfect spot to take out all his targets."

The journal was complemented by an extensive video collection that focused on child pornography, rape, and snuff movies, all neatly labeled by subject and stored in library-collection format. I paused when I heard that. It's one thing to be consumed by the ugliest pornography. The image that comes to mind is an unathletic creep in his basement. To have it in library-collection format bespoke a man confident he would not be caught, a viewer almost blasé about the contents. Idly, I wondered whether the Dewey decimal system could accommodate a madman. The snuff films were reported to be particularly realistic. In one of them, a man appeared to insert a large, screw-like instrument into a woman as she sat on a bed with a child.

In almost all the videos, the victim was young, petite, and blond. That seemed to be no coincidence. Crawford had targeted blond women. Both his wives were blond. The women in the videos called to mind the most important victim of his life, the blond Arlis Perry. In a sense, Crawford was reenacting the crime. The cops never found the souvenirs from the murder that they hoped for—the handle of the ice pick, her eyeglasses, her Caravelle bracelet. Crawford may not have needed them. In his collection of violent porn and rape, he had a substitute.

The detectives encountered more surprises when they unpacked the search history on Crawford's computer. The former Stanford security guard returned repeatedly to satanic sites. At one of them, the user was given a chance to act as the "hero," a figure who ventures forth to prove male dominance by sexually torturing women. The conspiracy theorists in the Memorial Church murder had long theorized that the killing had some satanic or occult connection. Here, decades later, was proof that the suspected killer was intrigued by diabolical conspiracy.

The search history contained one more site that disturbed the detectives. After Rick Alanis had returned Crawford to his apartment following a trip to the sheriff's office in August 2016, Crawford had gone onto his computer and looked up a website that described how to make a bomb. As detectives reconstructed it later, Crawford wanted to rig his apartment so that he could bomb Alanis and Cortez—and himself—to smithereens if the cops returned to arrest him. It never happened—Crawford apparently abandoned the effort. But it played into theories that Crawford wanted to commit suicide by cop on his final day. (Although, oddly, the cops also found the business card of an out-of-state defense attorney in his apartment. Despite his pleas to poverty, Crawford may have toyed with the notion of legal resistance.)

What did it all add up to? First, the journal and videos and Web searches did more to provide the context for suicide. If nothing else, Crawford could have faced serious time behind bars for his possession of child pornography. He was not a man who would go lightly to jail. The two days he spent behind bars after his arrest by Stanford police in 1992 were traumatic enough. Beyond that, Crawford must have known that the contents of his journal would be introduced in court if he was ever charged with the murder of Arlis Perry. The link between his obsession with violence against women and what happened to Arlis would have been too damning. If sheriff's deputies did not have enough evidence to convict him when they knocked on his door, they would almost certainly have it once they searched the journal and videos. Crawford's tug on the trigger of his .41 caliber Ruger wasn't just a signal of exhaustion by a seventy-two-year-old afflicted with mental infirmity. It was the move of a man who wanted to avoid trial and prison. Crawford almost certainly realized that his four-decade long game of playing with the cops—FBI profiler Teten was right about that too—was approaching an emphatic checkmate.

As it happened, the journal was the elusive ghost in the story of Arlis Perry's murder. At least twice, it could have fallen into the hands of authorities. The first time occurred in the early eighties, when federal agents showed up at the Monterey Road trailer park where Crawford was living with his second wife. I have not been able to find the records of that visit: it resulted in no charges. When the agents came across the journal and asked if they could take it with them, Crawford's wife declined permission.

A similar missed chance occurred in 1992, when Stanford police swooped down on Crawford's house in Gilroy in their investigation of stolen university artifacts. Again, the cops asked Crawford's wife what they should do with the journal. Not having read it herself, she told them to put it back in its place. And in fairness, the Stanford police had more pressing problems that morning. One of their own was accused of taking a portable TV from the Crawford house. Crawford's spiral notebook journal did not hold the same weight as the graphic video evidence seized from his apartment after his death. But at the least, the description of drugging and raping Cara, which *was* in the journal, might have allowed investigators to fasten on to him earlier as the chief suspect in the Arlis Perry murder.

Having cataloged so many of Steve Crawford's untruths, I will admit that one of my first thoughts when I heard about the journal was whether he had made it all up, whether it was simply the musings of a deranged mind. After all, he had fibbed about how often he had checked the church, where he had gotten the Stanford artifacts, what his Social Security number was, how his parents had died. What were a few more lies confided to a journal? Then I realized that was the point. Crawford had no reason to lie to his journal. He did not expect the cops to read it. So he was less careful. The videos that dwelled on rape with an object were telling. A man who thinks about inserting strange objects into a woman's body cavities betrays something demented about himself.

In the end, the inner workings of that mind baffled me. I still have no firm idea of what happened early in Crawford's life that gave him such a violent hatred toward women. In the absence of anything else, I'm drawn to psychiatrist Hervey Cleckley's theories about the psychopathic personality. Steve Crawford didn't suffer the same weight of conscience as the rest of us. For more than four decades, he feigned disgust at the notion that authorities considered him a suspect in the Arlis Perry murder. His greatest lie was presenting himself to the world as a regular guy. It was only in the journal that he unlocked the truth.

CHAPTER 46

THE KILLER AND HIS VICTIM

Even with Crawford's suicide, the questions persist. What happened between the killer and his victim inside Memorial Church on that Saturday night in October 1974? What sequence led to a young woman's body being splayed behind a pew, strangled, an ice pick jammed into her brain? Was there a prequel? How did the action unfold between a security guard with a strange past and a young wife who visited the church to pray? Can the homicide be reconstructed?

The answers must be framed in intelligent speculation because the last two people in the church, Arlis Perry and Steve Crawford, are dead, one a victim, one the likely killer. As a security guard, salesman, insurance adjuster, and retiree, Crawford lived for almost forty-four years after the murder, the bulk of an adult lifetime, cloaked in suspicion but never brought to justice. Familiar with his unreliability, investigators learned to approach his statements with the forensic equivalent of Hazmat suits. But from the evidence as well as

Crawford's admissions, it's possible to trace a fuller narrative. Buried in his lies are shards of truth.

By his own words, Crawford had thought about murder in the church for at least a year and a half, and probably longer. In a general sense, the killing was premeditated, though he could not know when his chance would come. A key moment occurred in May 1973, when Crawford wrote a police report saying that he had talked repeatedly with a young man in the quad about how Memorial Church would be an "eerie" spot for murder. (See chapter eighteen, "The Crime Aficionado.")

That report revealed the germ of a lethal idea. As women visited the church late at night, he had considered several of them as potential victims. He had a type of woman in mind—blond and petite, matching the color and stature of his then-wife, Joyce. In an interview in 2016, Crawford said that he "supposed" he had seen Arlis around the grounds before that Saturday night, a change from his earlier statement that he had never seen her before. It seems likely he decided to kill Arlis within minutes of seeing her enter the church. Two things made her vulnerable. She was unaccompanied, and she had arrived near closing time. What's more, she was preoccupied with prayer. Because he had the keys, he could control the situation, a mastery that shaped how the crime unfolded. Crawford often retreated into meekness when challenged. In this situation, he was in charge, and it injected a heady excitement into his mood.

At the core of the murder lay very different understandings of the setting. Arlis saw Memorial Church as a sanctuary, the ultimate source of safety, a place where she could reveal her deepest feelings to God. The notion of danger inside a beautiful university church, even close to midnight, never would have occurred to the religious woman from Bismarck. That assurance allowed her killer to take advantage of her absorption in meditation. Crawford, meanwhile, saw murder in the church as a challenge, a chance to defy the piety of the surroundings and Stanford University itself. A lone woman in the church offered him the opportunity he yearned for.

Arlis entered Memorial Church around 11:35 or 11:40 p.m., minutes after she had turned away from Bruce near Meyer Memorial Library. As she walked up the steps and into the vestibule, she passed Crawford, who was holding his keys just outside the front entrance. Betty Banks and Stuart Cain saw her walk in as they left the church. Arlis made her way down the main aisle and took a spot on the left, about eleven or twelve pews from the front, a walk that would have taken her around thirty to forty seconds. She edged into the row and sat down about three feet from the aisle, propping her hands on the pew in front of her. It was there that she was seen praying by Brent Davis and Mark Kral, who left the church separately around 11:45 p.m. As Davis left, he saw Crawford on the steps, who told him bluntly, "It's time to go; I'm closing up." The security guard seemed impatient—and for a reason. He had decided to confront Arlis. What followed has to be conjecture, though it is based on evidence:

Shortly after he locked the outside doors, Crawford walked halfway down the main aisle, close to where Arlis was praying. Gently, he told Arlis that she could stay for a while longer. He needed time to prepare. Making sure the interior front doors were secure, he headed for the small room between the sanctuary and the Round Room, the church's office. He opened the drawer of the cabinet where the sound equipment was kept and removed the ice pick that Mark Dalyrymple used to fine-tune the sound system. An ice pick would not have been a foreign weapon to Crawford. They were widely used in Korea, a place with famously cold winters. Because he trawled through drawers and closets in his security job, he knew where to find one at Memorial Church. He stuffed the ice pick into the pocket of his jacket.

Returning to Arlis—it was now 11:50 or so—Crawford told her to walk with him to the door on the south side of the east transept, where he would let her out. Now he was more demanding, more insistent. He explained that the front doors of the church were already locked. If he found out that she was headed to Quillen House, he might have told her that the east door was closer to her destination. With a show of firmness, he escorted her from the pew and followed her toward the door. Arlis had no reason to distrust him. After all, he was a security guard in blazer and slacks, the man charged with protecting the church.

As they reached a spot near the east door, below the pulpit, Crawford grabbed her puka-shell necklace from behind and began choking her, pushing her to the floor. Arlis may have had a chance to utter a word or two, but she did not have the breath to emit much of a scream. As she fell to the floor, splitting her lips, Crawford straddled her from behind, holding her down. His fingers dug into her neck.

Arlis fought, but her air supply was cut off, and she was choked into unconsciousness, and maybe death. The bursting of tiny blood capillaries near her eyes revealed how desperate the struggle was.

Some investigators believe the attack occurred in the pew where Arlis prayed. While that underscores the element of surprise, it feels to me like too constrained a place for attack. How would a killer place himself behind Arlis or hold her down? The symmetrical bruises above her hips suggest the presence of a firm and unyielding surface, like the floor. A victim held against a pew could easily slip to one side or another. In the sheriff's reports I've seen, there is no mention of hair or saliva or blood found in the pew. From everything I know about Crawford, I'm convinced that he would have tried to talk with his victim. It was part of the challenge of the crime. A short walk would allow the prelude. Finally, the spot near the east door has an echo. Crawford told investigators he first tried to call dispatcher Charlie Papp from the area near the east door when he found the body.

When the thrashing subsided, Crawford measured her pulse. In his excitement, he could not be certain she was dead. He knew, however, that she could identify him. He had to make certain that she did not survive. Reaching into his pocket, he pulled out the ice pick with his dominant left hand. He plotted his aim on the back of her neck, concluding that his first entry point was too low. Finally, Crawford rammed the ice pick into her brain, finding the thrust easy after passing through the sheath of the skull. There wasn't much blood. For the moment, Crawford left the ice pick handle in place.

understand that he would be a suspect, he was rational enough to create a cover story. So he walked over to the inner door on the west side of the sanctuary and kicked it out. He later claimed to detectives that he had locked that door, but the evidence suggests otherwise. In his excitement, he had outthought himself. His lie about the door being locked was too easy for investigators to unravel. Leaving the church through the Round Room door, he dumped the bloody rags in the nearby dumpster.

By 3:00 a.m., Crawford was heading to his lunch break at the Jordan Quad, a few blocks away. When he got the call from dispatcher Charlie Papp asking whether he had seen the young woman that Bruce Perry reported missing, he greeted him with a joke: He had seen a bunch of people wandering around. You couldn't be certain of the gender of some of them. But someone matching the description of Arlis? No, sorry. He had locked up the church. He left Papp with the clear implication that Memorial Church wasn't worth searching. For Crawford, the crime was still too fresh. He wasn't ready for the body to be found.

What happened during the rest of the night? Crawford found a place to hunker down in the old quad, possibly in the Round Room or church basement, an out-of-the-way spot. Although he told detectives that he wanted to do homework that early Sunday morning, it's questionable that he could have assembled the wits to prepare for class. Finally, at 5:30 a.m. or so, he opened up the church. He unlocked the front doors and checked the interior door he had kicked in, making sure that the breakout looked authentic. He knew the lights were still on. He would have to explain that as an oversight, though in fact he needed them for the murder. (His fellow Stanford community service officers were right in saying that he did not like the dark.) Then he passed in front of the altar and into the east transept, where he had left Arlis. He arranged the body one more time, making sure it was ready for the detectives. Then he left the church by the front doors and got on the radio with Charlie Papp.

"Will you respond a mobile unit to the church, code two?" Crawford asked.

"Nature?" Papp responded.

Crawford's reply revealed how little he thought of his victim: "We got a stiff in here."

NOTES

CHAPTER 1—THE SECURITY GUARD

1. The mosaic behind the altar was a reproduction of Cosimo Rosselli's fresco in the Sistine Chapel in Rome. The Salviati studio, which did the work, had to obtain special permission from Pope Leo XIII to copy it.

2. Crawford talked to Deputy Nick Consolo at the church at 6:05 a.m., a quick interview that might have lasted ten or fifteen minutes. He got on the radio with Papp before 6:55 a.m., when Bruce Perry called for the second time. He did not sit down with Sgt. John Johnson at the police station until 7:30 a.m., which has led investigators to think he was gone from the scene for at least an hour.

CHAPTER 2—ARLIS

1. It was no surprise that contributions flowed into a memorial fund established in memory of Arlis. De-Kok and the congregation used the money to send

people for training in a program called "Evangelism Explosion" started by a Florida pastor seeking a more aggressive and personal way of bringing the message of Jesus worldwide.

CHAPTER 3—THE DISPATCHER

1. Papp's mistake lived on for several hours. In the first sheriff's report on the crime, the suspect was identified as "Bruce Terry."

CHAPTER 6—BRUCE

1. In May 1973, *The Bismarck Tribune* reported that Bruce set a North Dakota high school record by running the 440-yard race in 48.9 seconds. His friends say his fastest time was 48.6. For drainage reasons, the track at Bismarck High School was not banked toward the center. Had it been, Bruce's fellow runners say, he might have run it in forty-eight seconds flat.

CHAPTER 9—THE WITNESSES

1. Sheriff's investigators confirmed with the library staff that Meyer turned off its lights at midnight.

The library had also dimmed lights fifteen to twenty minutes earlier as a warning to those studying late.

CHAPTER 10—THE DEAN

1. Hamerton-Kelly's statement about writing the sermon "right on top of the murder scene" suggests he sat in the last row of the east transept as he composed his message. I haven't been able to verify that. But it does show how much he wanted to expunge the horror of the crime.

CHAPTER 14—THE MAN WHO CHANGED HIS STORY

1. Built in the mid-sixties, Jordan Quad was named for David Starr Jordan, Stanford's first president. It was constructed by Joseph Eichler, the famous builder of midcentury modern homes on the Peninsula. The quad was also home to a population of feral cats.

CHAPTER 15—THE LADY WITH A PARASOL

1. Despite her commitment to equality between the sexes, Jane decreed in 1899 that the university should never have more than five hundred women.

With larger numbers of female students, she feared Stanford could become the "Vassar of the West." The university trustees changed the restriction during the 1930s.

2. Among those married in the church was Stanford Police Officer Debbie Whittemore, who handled much of the traffic on the night of the murder. On December 7, 1974, less than two months after the killing, Whittemore was wed to Stanford fireman Nick Marinaro.

CHAPTER 17—UNUSUAL SUSPECTS

1. As strange as Jick's observation sounded, it was not totally fanciful. Only three years before, Stanford psychology professor Philip Zimbardo had organized his "Stanford prison experiment," in which some students played guards and others were inmates in a mock prison.

CHAPTER 18—CRIME AFICIONADO

1. Like all the investigators, Konar was consumed by the case. At one point, he talked to his wife, an attractive, dark-haired woman in her late twenties,

about acting as a decoy for a killer who might linger around campus. The idea never went further. Already having troubles, the couple divorced the next year.

CHAPTER 20—ODD FISH

1. The polygraph tests were performed by a state Department of Justice examiner from Sacramento, Robert Liburdy. I admit to shallowness. It struck me as an unusual name for a man who detected lies for a living. "Did you yourself cause the death of that woman in that church?" Liburdy asked. Larry answered no.

2. In the seventeenth century, a version of the Black Mass in France featured a woman splayed on the altar with a chalice balanced on her bare stomach. The host was consecrated on her body and then used in love potions.

CHAPTER 22—THE DOOR KNOCKERS

1. The sheriff's correspondence did not identify the case in Wisconsin. But at the time, the Walworth County sheriff's office was investigating the August 1974 murder of Paula Cupit, twenty-four, a maid

at a Lake Geneva resort. Assigned to clean a room, Cupit was strangled and stabbed in the heart. In late 1975, a twenty-seven-year-old Illinois man, Richard Otto Macek, was arrested in San Bernardino. Convicted of three murders and one rape, Macek earned the nickname "the Mad Biter" because he gnawed the bodies of his victims after death.

CHAPTER 26—THE DRUM MAJOR

1. Mullen grew up in the Kraft Avenue house in Studio City that later was used in the movie *Pulp Fiction* as the home of Jimmie, a minor character who helps the protagonists clean up their car. In the famous picture of top U.S. officials watching live updates from the mission that killed Osama bin Laden in 2011, Mullen stood behind President Barack Obama.

CHAPTER 27—THE PROFILER

1. A profiler was also used after the presumed murder of Jane Stanford in Hawaii in 1905. The *San Francisco Examiner* commissioned the novelist Julian Hawthorne (1846–1934), who had an interest in crime, to develop a psychological profile of a killer in an "imaginary" case. Hawthorne, the son of the

more famous writer Nathaniel Hawthorne, crafted a narrative that pointed to a subordinate who came to detest a wealthy, commanding widow who lacked a liberal education.

2. Crawford told friends that his mother once engaged in a spoof at a Macy's store in West LA. Using the "Joan Crawford" name that she sometimes employed as a dance instructor, she called Macy's and let them think she was the movie star, saying she was coming to pick up merchandise. When she arrived, a hubbub surrounded her.

CHAPTER 31—THE CIVIL LIBERTARIAN

1. The final insult was that Stanford police felt compelled to return the phony diploma to Crawford. I talked to a detective who explained that there was nothing to justify the police keeping it.

CHAPTER 32—AMATEUR DETECTIVES

1. Bundy took a Chinese language course at Stanford in the summer of 1967 and reportedly returned to the Bay Area several times afterward. Before he was executed in 1989, he told investigators he had

committed one murder in California. But they were unable to obtain specifics.

CHAPTER 34—THE BARNACLE SCRAPER

1. Just when the jeans mix-up occurred is unclear from the record. The sheriff's department did, however, repackage and relabel the evidence in 2000 so that records could be entered into the computer system.

2. Steve Crawford's house was about a mile from St. Mary's Church in Gilroy. Crawford lived there as Alanis entered his teens and went to Gilroy High School.

CHAPTER 38—THE SHOOTER

1. A few people felt the dust cover was significant. The Netflix documentary *Sons of Sam: A Descent into Darkness* explored the Arlis Perry story and ended with a picture of the seized dust cover.

CHAPTER 39—THE POLITICIAN

1. Laurie Smith was not the first woman *elected* sheriff in California. That distinction belonged to Virginia Black, a former rodeo racer who was elected Yuba County sheriff in the June 1998 primary. Smith defeated Ruben Diaz in the November general election that year. Her predecessor, Sheriff Chuck Gillingham, stepped down early, allowing Smith to be sworn in before Black on December 15, 1998.

CHAPTER 40—THE OLD MAN IN THE WHEELCHAIR

1. After the 1975 arrest, Palo Alto police forwarded Getreu's name to investigators in the Arlis Perry murder. None of the fingerprints found in the church matched Getreu's.

CHAPTER 44—CODA WRITERS

1. Hamerton-Kelly huddled in the hedgerows of arcane language. The dean emerged as an exponent of scholar Rene Girard's "mimetic theory," which

posited that all human conflict finds its root in a desire to imitate one another, a lethal keeping-up-with-the-Joneses phenomenon. As societies clash, Girard argued, the conflict is resolved through use of a "scapegoat" and the introduction of religion. Later, with Stanford graduate Peter Thiel, a cofounder of PayPal, Hamerton-Kelly established an organization called Imitato to spread word of Girard's theories.

ABOUT THE AUTHOR:

Scott Herhold spent 40 years as a reporter, editor and columnist for the San Jose Mercury News. Among other duties, he specialized in writing about unsolved crimes.

For more, see www.murderundergodseye.com.